How to FEED a TEENAGE BOY

Recipes and Strategies

GEORGIA ORCUTT

CELESTIAL ARTS
Berkeley | Toronto

Front cover photo by Adie Bush, Getty Images

Celestial Arts
Box 7123
Berkeley, California 94707
www.tenspeed.com

Distributed in Australia by Simon and Schuster Australia, in Canada by Ten Speed Press Canada, in New Zealand by Southern Publishers Group, in South Africa by Real Books, and in the United Kingdom and Europe by Publishers Group UK.

Cover and text design by Catherine Jacobes

Ken's Broccoli Cheese Dip (page 109) used by permission of Ken Haedrich; Thai Lemongrass Marinade (page 164) used by permission of Dave Dewitt, www.fiery-foods.com; Streusel Coffee Cake (page 74) used by permission of Marjorie Johnson, from *Baking for Blue Ribbons with Marjorie*.

Library of Congress Cataloging-in-Publication Data on file with publisher.

Printed in the United States

First printing, 2007

1 2 3 4 5 6 7 8 9 10 — 11 10 09 08 07

How to FEED a TEENAGE BOY

Contents

For Amos and Eli

Acknowledgments

Special thanks to Clancy Drake, my editor at Ten Speed, for her support and encouragement; Lisa Ekus, my agent, for believing in this book; dietitian Inger Hustrulid at Foundations Family Nutrition for her sound advice; Lisa Ceremsak, Catharine and Mike Fender, John Glyphis, Louise Guerin, Margie Hilton, Doris Kendall, Kalil Kendall, Mary Mallows, Debbie Mills, and Cynthia Van Hazinga for sharing ideas about food; all the boys, especially Jonathan Koh, Jamie Hayes, Matt Donelan, Eric Gustavson, Kevin McCarthy, Stefan Modzelewski, Daniel Oshima, Oliver Snider, and Douglas Wong, who sat around the table and sampled the recipes; my husband, Stephen Kendall, a teenager at heart; and my mother, Margaret Sullivan Orcutt, who loved to feed the men.

Introduction

My son Eli's first word was easy to understand—and prophetic: "More." He said this as he sat in his high chair, swallowed the last mouthful of pureed banana, and glared at the empty bowl. To meet his needs and celebrate the momentous occasion, all I had to do was produce another few spoonfuls.

But it hasn't always been so easy to feed him.

For about 12 years, even after our second son, Amos, came along, my husband, Stephen, and I managed reasonably well to have enough food in the house and to get dinner on the table. We'd figured out the major hurdles of grocery shopping, and we put a premium on family-style meals, too. Then everything changed.

Overnight it seemed (or at least soon after he became a teenager), Eli was always looking for something to eat. His school and sports schedules got much more complicated, and he and Amos were rarely hungry at the same time. Eli came home from school starving, but if he ate at four or five o'clock, he wasn't hungry for the time-honored family dinner around seven. Yet he'd be hungry again just before going to bed. And he woke up starving. Then Amos became a teenager, with his own hunger clock and his own busy schedule. It was a major challenge to keep the pantry and refrigerator stocked. And to make things even trickier, Stephen and I were busier than ever with our work lives. We'd also started to watch our waistlines, cut back on the calories we consumed, and look for ways to get more exercise into our days. Food wasn't something *we* wanted to think about all the time.

I was overwhelmed. Beyond juggling work demands and grocery store visits, I found myself wrestling with some big issues. What was my responsibility here? How much should my sons do for themselves? Although I've always enjoyed cooking, if I met this increased demand for planning meals, buying food, and preparing it, would I be spoiling them? Or was it my job, literally, to step up to the plate?

I started reading about teenage nutrition and was shocked at what I discovered about the effects of junk food and poor diet during these important years. I learned that from ages 13 to 18, during his most active years, the tremendous growth and physical development a boy normally experiences affect every organ in his body, including his brain. When he eats, he isn't just filling his stomach; he's developing his mind, his heart, and everything else. By the age of 17 his bones will have stored 90 percent of the calcium he will have for his entire life. Yet too many boys aren't getting the message about the importance of eating well. They consume an average of 34 teaspoons of sugar daily, and, according to a National Health and Nutrition Examination Survey, 76 percent of teenage boys never eat fruits or vegetables.

As a parent, I'd seen that hungry boys, like electricity, take the path of least resistance. Ten times out of ten they'll rip open a bag of cookies or chips and eat them all, rather than open the refrigerator and make themselves a turkey sandwich. During their big growing and eating years, when they present a special challenge to household food management and meal planning, it is all too easy to think that it doesn't really matter what boys eat, as long as they stop being hungry. It is also easy to think that thin boys can eat whatever they want.

Yet what happens in boys' bodies and brains when they fill up on foods high in sugar, salt, and unhealthy fat has both short-term and long-term consequences. Boys easily can become so accustomed to terrible food that they want little else. Obesity among teenagers is rising.

A study published in 2005 in *The Annals of Internal Medicine* predicts that over their lifetimes, nine out of ten men will become overweight, and a quarter of these will be obese; other studies show that even overweight boys who slim down later in life meet with shortened life expectancies. Thin boys who consume a lot of saturated fat may not put on weight, but they do not necessarily have low blood cholesterol.

Despite all these discouraging stories, healthy diets for boys are getting little attention. Parents often focus on quantity over quality of food. School lunch programs rarely offer balanced meals. It is easier and cheaper for kids to find pizza, fries, and soft drinks than fresh fruit, wraps, and healthy smoothies. And TV ads never show boys eating salads. I came to see that the only way to change things is for us parents to get involved in helping our sons learn about nutrition and form a solid connection with nourishing food. Many of them will leave home at age 18, but before they go, we have a chance to help them develop good habits for life.

I quickly decided to find more ways to put healthy food in front of my boys. I set to work figuring out what needed to happen around our house to ensure that my sons ate well and how to get everyone involved in this project and have a good time doing so. I found that it doesn't take a terrific amount of time or effort or money to set up your household to feed a teenage boy, if you keep some basic principles in mind.

First of all, understand, respect, and accept your son's hunger; don't denigrate it. These years of his life bring tremendous growth and change to his body, and it is natural and right for him to need more fuel.

Help him become more knowledgeable and autonomous around the kitchen. If he can get his hands and mouth on good food when he's hungry, it will take pressure off when you can put a meal on the table. Have things around that he can reheat or prepare for himself. Show him how to fix simple, healthy meals and snacks and talk to him about why certain food choices are better than others.

Above all, nurture him by staying positively involved with what he eats. As you shop and cook, teach him the importance of a healthy diet. Being a teenager isn't easy, but coming home to good food—and the measure of comfort, energy, and support that it brings—is vitally important. Your son won't pass this way again, and you've got a great opportunity before you to show him a path he can follow all his life.

Why Focus on Boys?

Of course, the food you'll find discussed in this book isn't just for boys. It is suitable for the whole family. All the recipes, however, have been developed to meet the tastes and nutritional needs of teenage boys and are presented with this truth in mind: when you live with a teenage boy, you also live with his frequent hunger attacks. If you want to do the best you can for him and also hang onto your sanity, you must understand and appreciate how much he needs to eat every single day and figure out how to meet his increased demand for calories.

Typically, between the ages of 13 and 19 boys have a greater growth spurt than girls, and they put on more muscle mass and size. They also develop more bone mass and need lots of calcium to support it. They become tremendous growing and eating machines, gaining as much as 50 percent of their ideal body weight. When older boys are active in sports such as basketball or cross-country, they can need 4,000 calories a day to sustain them. And they easily can be hungry every 3 hours. Therefore the solution isn't just to put huge helpings on the table at dinnertime. Instead, it means feeding them balanced meals and also having a variety of foods available for quick, easy snacks between meals. Boys need as many as six meals and snacks a day.

See How They Grow

Watching a teenage boy grow up before your very eyes is a wondrous thing. (Keep this in mind as you shop, quite often, for pants and shoes.) Some mornings, especially when he has slept in, he appears in the kitchen looking taller than he did the night before. After all, boys literally do grow in their sleep. In growth spurts that can last 2 to 4 years, they can grow 10 inches or more. For most of them, the fastest growth happens sometime between the ages of 12 and 15 in a dramatic change that starts at the outside of the body, with hands and feet being the first places to grow larger. The arms and legs lengthen next, then the spine, and lastly the chest and shoulders broaden. If your son complains about his small shoulders and narrow chest, tell him to just wait (and buy jackets that can be let out across the back). Many boys continue to broaden in the chest and shoulders until age 20.

In addition to growing in height, boys also grow stronger during their teenage years. Testosterone, which triggers growth, encourages bones to become denser and muscle fibers to increase in length and width.

As you may know or will soon see, this rapid development usually is not accompanied by periods of gracefulness. As boys grow taller, their center of gravity changes, often before their brains can calculate the adjustments needed for balance. Teenage boys can be clumsy. They spill things. They make messes. And the lovely table manners they had at age 12 often morph into terrible posture and other questionable behaviors with knife and fork. Be patient. Try to be understanding when those two left feet come into the kitchen. Just hand your boys the paper towels and teach them how to clean up spills. It is important for them to feel welcome and at ease around food.

Toe Tip

Back to those fast-growing feet for a minute: When the soccer cleats you bought for your son at the beginning of the season feel tight before the last game has been played, they probably are. Dr. David Alper, a Massachusetts podiatrist, says that growing boys can need new shoes every four months. He suggests taking teenagers to a shoe store that will measure their feet and recommend a size, rather than buying shoes off the discount rack that simply feel good. "With all the padding in athletic shoes today, it is easy for boys to wear shoes that are several sizes too small," he says. Ingrown toenails and other foot problems are the price to pay, he warns. "But," he hints, "once a professional shoe salesperson has measured his foot properly, you can always go out and buy the discounted shoes in that size."

Talk to Boys about Food

In her book *Secrets of Feeding a Healthy Family,* Ellyn Satter, an authority on child nutrition, emphasizes her golden rule, which she calls the "division of responsibility." "The parent is responsible for the what, when, and where of feeding, and the child is responsible for the how much and whether of eating." Coming to terms with this concept and accepting it will help immeasurably through the years of cooking for teenagers. Always keep in mind that you can't control what your son eats, nor should you want to. He is at a time in his life when autonomy is an exciting new idea, and it is important for him to learn to make his own decisions. You can serve him good food, be aware of nutritional issues, and share information in a positive way. Don't wait until the night your son refuses to eat your new casserole to talk about food. Work the subject into an ongoing parent-son dialogue about making choices, spending money, and values. Emphasize that good health is a complete picture that includes eating well, enjoying a wide range of foods and flavors, exercising, and respecting your body. Share tidbits you read or hear on the radio or TV about new research concerning health issues and diet. Solicit his thoughts and opinions. And above all, let him know that *his* good health and well-being are very important to you.

"I Don't Know Where He Puts It!": The Nutritional Needs of Teenage Boys

At least once during the next three hours, 15 million boys in America between the ages of 13 and 19 will think or dream about food. As their caretakers and gatekeepers, we can help put a steady stream of unhealthy, high-sugar, high-fat food loaded with artificial ingredients in their paths and move them further toward being the first generation of kids with a life span shorter than that of their parents—or we can get seriously involved in what they eat and the life-long habits they are acquiring, and do everything we can to encourage them to eat healthy food. There's a lot at stake.

Food choices today have become entwined with the special interests of the food industry and its powerful barrage of advertising. It is easy for kids to find inexpensive, salty, high-calorie foods that have been heavily promoted and that taste great to them. The extent to which kids can become manipulated by this food, and the billions of dollars the food industry spends to make it as appealing as possible, is downright scary. As Kathleen Keller, an appetite researcher at the New York Obesity Research Center, explains, many products have been developed as "feel good" foods. "The soft-drink industry has done a lot of research into this area and they know that a drink containing 10 percent sucrose is the most appealing and has the greatest effect on pleasure response in the brain," she says. And it is no coincidence that some of the most popular snack foods are high in both fat and sugar. Keller explains that foods containing both sugar and fat are developed after extensive research to have the best "mouth feel." "Humans don't like just sugar," she continued. "The addition of fat makes the sugar more palatable. The most affordable foods today are sugar/fat combinations, which are very easy to eat."

We're all seen as potential consumers, but kids are especially vulnerable. The span of years between 13 and 19 has been viewed as an important consumer group for more than 60 years. As Thomas Hine points out in *The Rise and Fall of the American Teenager,* the very word "teenager" may first have appeared in *Popular Science* magazine in 1941. "It seems to have leaked into the language from the world of advertising and marketing, where demographic information was becoming an increasingly important part of predicting which sales approaches are most effective with particular buyers," he writes.

Our current generation of teenagers has been targeted for unhealthy foods all their lives. According to a study in the *Journal of Nutrition Education,* kids see more than 100,000 TV food commercials by the time they're adolescents, and these are mainly for unhealthy high-fat, high-sugar foods. (When was the last time you saw a commercial on TV highlighting the appeal of apples or pears? When was the last time you talked with your kids about how the foods being advertised affect their bodies?)

The general message they have received since they were babies is that they deserve special foods, separate from what grown-ups eat. These foods come packaged in appealing, brightly colored boxes often featuring beloved cartoon characters, and they are supported by TV advertising that shows attractive, trim, happy kids loving each bite. One of the biggest markets today for food and other products is 6 to 11 year-olds, who exert powerful pressure on their parents. In *Food and Drink in America,* Richard Hooker points out that according to one study "in three out of four cases it was the children, not the parents, who decided where a family would eat" when they went out for dinner.

Right in keeping with the mass-marketing message, as kids reach adolescence, they (and their parents) usually consider that "teen" food is just what the kids should have: pizza, burgers, hot dogs, fries, cheesy nachos, and soft drinks, all portable, inexpensive, and oh so easy to find everywhere. Today many schools across the country serve fast-food lunches. Steven Gortmaker, a professor at the Harvard School of Public Health, notes that "on any given day, 30 percent of American children aged 4 to 19 eat fast food, and older and wealthier ones eat even more." Long considered a boon for busy parents because kids can be counted on to always eat these things, salty, sugary, high-fat food products have come under attack by health professionals as being downright bad for kids.

And don't be fooled into thinking teenagers will simply outgrow a penchant for sweet, salty, and fatty foods. Once hooked on these tastes as children, young men (and women) mostly will continue to eat the unhealthy foods that are so aggressively marketed to them.

What's a parent to do? Step up to that plate. Take a look at what your family is eating. Whenever you can, put nourishing food on the table. Find ways to talk to your teenagers about what they're eating, and why it matters. Help them recognize false advertising claims, and encourage them to think critically about messages they get through the media about food.

What Is Good Food?

One of America's largest supermarket chains has capitalized on the name Whole Foods, which refers to nutrient-packed foods that can trace their origins more to fields than to factories. An important goal in healthy eating is to get as much of the household's food as possible from sources that don't contain mysterious or artificial ingredients. Whole-grain cereals, pasta, and breads; beans and legumes; fresh or frozen fruits and vegetables; fresh, lean meats and seafood; unsweetened, low-fat dairy products; unsalted nuts; and healthy oils, such as olive and canola: these are the foods that form the backbone of a healthy diet at any age. Foods with lots of added sugars, excessive

Children and Obesity

Obesity is on the rise. According to the National Academy of Sciences Institute of Medicine, "Since the 1970s, the prevalence (or percentage) of obesity has more than doubled for preschool children aged 2–5 and adolescents ages 12–19 years, and it has more than tripled for children ages 6–11 years. At present, approximately nine million children over 6 years of age are obese." Adolescent obesity is influenced by environment, heredity, ethnic and socioeconomic factors, family dynamics, and self-image issues.

More than 25 percent of Americans under the age of 19 are overweight. Don't be fooled into thinking your son will simply outgrow those extra pounds. Research shows that most kids who are overweight or obese as teenagers will continue to be so throughout their lives, with increased risks of diabetes and a range of illnesses that will require a supplemental diet of prescription drugs and limited lifestyles. According to one recent study conducted by the USDA Human Nutrition Research Center in Boston, overweight teenage boys are twice as likely as thin adolescents to die by age 70, primarily from coronary heart disease. They are also five times more likely to develop colon cancer, even when they lose weight after their teens.

There's a lot of work ahead. "I think it will take massive cultural changes in what we eat and how we raise our kids to really see a reversal in the obesity epidemic," says Dr. Henry C. McGill Jr. at the Southwest Foundation for Biomedical Research, who has researched risk factors in childhood and adolescence. "I don't have any illusions about this happening tomorrow. It has taken 40 years to make a significant impact on smoking, and I think that's the kind of major public effort we are talking about."

With his colleagues, Dr. David Ludwig, director of the obesity program at Children's Hospital in Boston, recently looked at the dietary patterns of 6,212 American teenagers. He found that on any given day, one in three (30.3 percent) of the kids surveyed reported consuming fast food. "On fast-food days, kids took in substantially more total calories, ate more saturated fat, more added sugars, but consumed less fiber and fewer fruits and vegetables. They were getting more calories per bite, so the study suggests that fast food has an adverse affect on children's diets in many ways that could quite plausibly increase the risk for obesity."

sodium, caffeine, unhealthy fat, or artificial preservatives and other additives should be kept to a minimum in a healthy, growing boy's diet (and that of his family).

If you, as parents, aren't eating well, your kids won't either. Feeding a boy well may involve some changes in your own shopping and eating patterns; later in this chapter I'll talk more about what will have the most impact. Knowing what good food choices are, and why they are so important, can help everyone in your family get into the habit of eating well.

What Do Boys Need?

It is easy to get overwhelmed by nutritional advice. But if you understand the basics you can make informed decisions when shopping for food and planning meals. This section gives a brief look at a teenage boy's nutritional needs and explains the importance of such things as fiber, nutrients, and eating a variety of foods. (Keep in mind that there is a big difference between a 13-year-old and a 19-year-old, as well as between a boy who plays a team sport every semester and one who spends most of his time in front of a computer screen. For this reason, a range of recommendations is included.)

Calories (2,200 to 3,200 per Day)

It isn't very helpful, or practical, to constantly worry about how many calories a boy takes in every day—or to even keep track of them. We all have different rates at which our bodies burn and use fuel. If your boy is counting calories to achieve weight gain, loss, or maintenance, his calories will need to be adjusted accordingly by a doctor and/or a dietitian to meet his goals. (To find a dietitian in your community, go to www.eatright.org.) It is important, however, to separate a teenager's energy needs from your own, and to understand that boys require more calories than adults, especially if they're active in sports. If you are a parent who is trying to cut back on calories, don't cut back your son's calories as well, unless he is overweight. (If your son is overweight, talk to his pediatrician about appropriate dietary changes.) Boys who are very active in sports may need even more calories to meet their energy needs. For example, a 15-year-old boy who plays varsity basketball can burn 440 calories an hour during practices and could need 4,000 calories a day to avoid losing weight during the season.

The National Academy of Science Institute of Medicine recommends the following daily intakes, based on estimated energy requirements calculated by age and activity level. All calculations figure in the steps a boy typically takes in his day-to-day life, so a few flights of stairs don't count as activity. To understand the table, figure that sedentary refers to a boy who gets no exercise. Moderately active involves physical activity equivalent to walking about 1.5 to 3 miles per day at 3 to 4 miles per hour. This group includes boys who ride bikes, walk to friends' houses, and engage in moderate exercise. Active refers to physical activity equivalent to walking more than 3 miles a day at 3 to 4 miles per hour. This group includes boys who play team sports, such as cross-country, soccer, or basketball, that involve daily practices.

RECOMMENDED DAILY CALORIES

Activity Level	Sedentary	Moderately Active	Active
Age			
9–13	1,800	1,800–2,200	2,000–2,600
14–18	2,200	2,400–2,800	2,800–3,200
19–30	2,400	2,600–2,800	3,000

Protein (45 to 80 Grams per Day)

Although protein is what most adults think a boy needs most, he probably gets plenty of it in the course of a day. The USDA recommends a minimum of 45 to 58 grams per day, depending on a boy's age and his recommended caloric intakes. To determine your son's needs, multiply his weight by 0.36. By this calculation, a 160-pound teenager will need approximately 58 grams of protein per day. If he drinks two big glasses of milk and eats two pieces of chicken, fish, or lean beef, he'll meet the requirement. If he takes in a lot more than this, it will simply go down the toilet. An overload of protein can tax the kidneys and rob calcium from the bones.

Encourage your son to have some protein at every meal. The best choices are eggs, chicken, fish, canned beans, dairy (cheese, yogurt, and milk), and nuts. (See the list on page 14.) Remind him often that he can get all his protein needs from a balanced diet. This is especially important around age 16, when many boys long to bulk up and become fascinated by powders that sport hulking body builders on the labels. Nutrition and supplement store salesmen in malls salivate when teenage boys walk through the door. Teach your son to avoid them and the lure of instant bulk. Help him to steer clear of performance enhancers and protein pills and powders. "Kids should get their calories from real food. The protein in powders is not balanced with the other nutrients that make it possible to use it," warns Marion Nestle, chair of New York University's Department of Nutrition, Food, and Public Health. "I can't believe the labels—and the packaging! I'd advise staying away from them."

Talk with your son about fads such as binging on red meat to gain muscle or drinking several cups of coffee to remain alert in school. And warn him that skipping meals is never a good idea, even if he is trying to lose pounds.

Fat (25 Percent to 30 Percent of Daily Calories, Most from "Good Fats")

The word "fat" has become synonymous with foods to avoid, but fat is an important source of energy, and we all need some in our diets. It also plays an important role in helping the body absorb fat-soluble vitamins A, D, E, and K.

All types of fat contain 9 calories per gram, more calories than protein or carbohydrates. And since fat burns more slowly as it provides energy, it can keep us feeling full longer after we eat it.

Getting Protein into Every Meal

It's easy for boys to eat too much protein at lunch or dinner, which fills them up and doesn't leave room for fruits and vegetables. Huge burgers with cheese, steak and cheese subs, or several pieces of chicken alone don't contribute to a balanced diet. Better choices include a tuna melt, which combines smaller amounts of two protein sources (tuna and cheese), or a green salad topped with turkey or chicken, which adds protein to vegetables. "To understand how to serve a variety of foods without over-doing the protein, consider a system of 'units'" of approximately 6 to 9 grams of protein, suggests dietitian Inger Hustrulid. Dietitians recommend that most people aim for 3 units, or about 21 grams, of protein at every meal. The foods in the following list each constitute 1 unit. Refer to it as a guide to portion sizes and for ideas for including some protein in every meal, keeping in mind that boys need approximately 8 to 11 units of protein per day. It may help to visualize a 3-unit or 3-ounce portion of fish, poultry, or meat as about the same size as a deck of cards.

Poultry/Fish:	1 ounce of cooked turkey, chicken, tuna, salmon, haddock, trout, etc.
Meat:	1 ounce cooked beef, pork, lamb, etc.
Cheese:	1 ounce American, cheddar, mozzarella (a 1-inch cube) 2 ounces feta cheese 1/4 cup cottage, ricotta, or grated Parmesan
Eggs:	1 egg 2 egg whites
Dairy Products:	3/4 cup yogurt 1 cup milk
Soy Products:	3/4 cup soy milk 3 ounces soft or silken tofu 2 ounces firm tofu

2 tablespoons soy nuts

1^1/$_2$ ounces tempeh

^{1}/$_2$ cup soy beans

. . . .

Beans: ^{1}/$_2$ cup hummus

^{1}/$_2$ cup cooked beans (baked, kidney, black, lentils, lima, refried)

. . . .

Nuts: 1 ounce almonds, peanuts, pistachios, pumpkin seeds, sunflower seeds

1^1/$_2$ ounces cashews, brazil nuts, pine nuts, walnuts

3 ounces macadamia nuts, pecans

2 tablespoons peanut butter

. . . .

Source: Foundations Family Nutrition

Watching portion sizes becomes especially important in not overdoing it with fats. If your son likes nuts, give him a handful, not the entire can. If he's making a peanut butter and jelly sandwich, show him how to use 1 or 2 tablespoons of peanut butter, not 4.

The American Heart Association recommends that everyone limit fat intake to 30 percent of daily calories. A boy's 2,500 calorie-a-day diet thus allows 750 calories from fat or 83 grams of fat. But fats aren't all the same, and it is important to see that most of your family's fat calories come from healthy fat. Preparing your own food at home is a great way to watch your family's fat intake and avoid hidden fats. There are four main fat types. Health professionals consider two types to be unhealthy, two healthy.

Dairy Deliberations

We're faced with hundreds of choices at the supermarket, perhaps none more perplexing than those concerning milk and yogurt. Both are good sources of calcium, but they're also sources of fat. New dairy products seem to appear weekly. What should you buy?

Pediatricians generally agree that 1 percent milk is the best choice for a boy who is a healthy weight and who will drink milk throughout the day, since it provides fat to help him feel satiated, along with the calcium and protein. They recommend skim milk for boys who are trying to lose weight.

It's easy to think that the differences in fat content don't really matter. For a boy who only drinks one glass of milk a day this may be true. But it also depends on what else he eats throughout the day and how much fat he takes in from other sources. For a boy who drinks milk with meals and again before going to bed, the amount of saturated fat he's taking in through his milk drinking is an important consideration. If your son drinks 4 glasses of milk a day, he'll take in just over 6 grams of saturated fat with 1 percent milk, compared to 20 grams if he drinks whole milk.

If he is in the habit of having soft drinks with his meals, encourage him to switch to milk. If he doesn't like milk, buy 1 percent milk and flavor an 8-ounce glass with 2 teaspoons of chocolate syrup (not the 2 tablespoons recommended on the label). Experiment with different kinds of milk in baking. You may find that 1 percent is a better choice than skim for pancakes, cakes, and cookies. If you're trying to duplicate a taste from your childhood in puddings or sauces, you may want to use whole milk, but 1 percent will work well in many recipes.

Yogurt choices are also confusing. It's always best to read the labels of several brands to discover their differences in saturated fat content and added sugars. Brands that promise reduced fat may also be artificially sweetened or contain other artificial ingredients that you may wish to avoid. Whole-milk or low-fat yogurt will keep a boy from feeling hungry longer than nonfat. But if he eats a lot of yogurt, nonfat is probably a better choice. Although it represents convenience, fruit-flavored yogurt is high in sugar, an ingredient boys usually find in plenty of other foods. To help your budget and get your son used to a yogurt taste that isn't overly sweet, buy 32-ounce containers of plain yogurt and flavor the servings with a spoonful or two of fruit-sweetened jam.

Continued on next page

	Calories	Fat (grams)	Sat. Fat (grams)	Protein (grams)	Calcium (milligrams)
Milk (1 cup)					
Skim (fat free)	91	trace	.3	8	302
1 percent	102	3	1.6	8	300
2 percent	121	5	3	8	297
Whole	150	8	5	8	291
Yogurt (8 ounces)					
Plain nonfat	127	trace	.03	13	452
Plain lowfat	144	4	2.3	12	415
Plain whole	139	7	4.8	8	274

Source: USDA Nutritive Value of Foods

TWO UNHEALTHY FATS

As much as possible, avoid foods that are high in saturated and trans fats. They are linked to heart disease and high cholesterol.

Saturated Fat. Remaining solid at room temperature, saturated fats are found in meats; in dairy products, such as whole milk, butter, cheese, and ice cream; and in palm and coconut oil and coconut milk. Depending on their recommended caloric intake, boys should consume less than 20 to 25 grams of saturated fat per day. One tablespoon of butter contains 7.2 grams of saturated fat—more than one-third of the recommended daily amount. And a small piece of cheddar cheese, a 1-inch square cube, contains 3.6 grams of saturated fat.

Trans Fats. Made in factories, these bad fats are created when cheap soy, corn, and cottonseed oils are mixed with tiny metal particles, subjected to hydrogen gas (hydrogenation), infused with emulsifiers and starch, steam-cleaned, bleached, dyed, and flavored, so they will act like saturated fats and remain solid at room temperature. The results for the food companies are baked goods that don't get stale very fast. The promise for everyone who eats a lot of foods containing these fats is a better chance of poor health and increased risk of coronary heart disease. "Margarine's popularity represents a triumph of advertising over common sense," says nutrition writer Sally Fallon in *Consumers' Research*.

Trans fats have been shown to raise levels of bad cholesterol (LDL) and also lower good cholesterol (HDL). They're used in many packaged crackers, cookies, breads, chips, and snack foods and in most margarines and shortening; they are also a cheap source of oil for frying fast-food items, such as chicken and french fries. Check food labels and steer clear of anything that is "hydrogenated" or "partially hydrogenated." And stay tuned. A lot of people have been making a lot of noise about trans fats, and food manufacturers are now required to show on nutrition labels how much trans fat is in their products. They are, however, allowed to list as zero (0) the amount of trans fat if a product contains less than .5 grams per serving.

TWO HEALTHY FATS

Vegetables and nuts contain unsaturated fats, which are further broken down into two categories: monounsaturated and polyunsaturated. Plant oils often contain both.

Monounsaturated Fats. Found in plants, these fats stay liquid at room temperature. Researchers have found that they lower levels of bad cholesterol (LDL) and raise levels of good cholesterol (HDL). Good sources include olive, peanut, and canola oil, most nuts, and avocados. To get this good fat into your kids, use olive oil, not butter, for sautéing and seasoning vegetables, and in baking. Sprinkle nuts in salads and add them to rice and grain dishes.

Polyunsaturated Fats. The most important fats in this category are the omega-3 fatty acids and omega-6 fatty acids, which can help prevent heart disease. They can be found in soybean and corn oils, flaxseed and other seeds, whole grains, and fish. Get into the habit of cooking whole grains and serving them as side dishes, combined with vegetables. Sprinkle healthy seeds on pasta salads and add them to hot cereal.

CHOLESTEROL

One of the silliest things you'll see on food labels is a "no-cholesterol" sticker on vegetable oils, grains, vegetables, or fruit. Animals, including humans, manufacture cholesterol. In *The Family Nutrition Book,* Dr. William Sears explains its role: "Cholesterol forms an integral part of the cell membranes throughout your body, sort of like the mortar that holds a brick wall together. It is particularly important in the cellular structure of the brain and central nervous system, and is an important component of the myelin sheath that provides insulation to the nerves." Foods such as meat, poultry, eggs, cheese, and dairy products—all of which originate with animals—contain cholesterol in the form of saturated fat. When we eat them, the cholesterol they contain goes to the liver and, along with the cholesterol we make, is carried to the cells by low-density lipoproteins (LDL), which keeps any excess in the bloodstream to be deposited in the arteries. LDL is thus known as "bad cholesterol" since it is associated with a buildup that leads to heart disease. Some excess cholesterol is carried away from the cells and back to the liver by high-density lipoproteins (HDL), known as "good cholesterol." With a healthy, balanced diet, boys will take in less than 300 mg of cholesterol per day.

Since we currently focus so much attention on high-cholesterol issues among adults, it is easy to think that teenagers are too young to be affected. Dr. Henry C. McGill, Jr., warns that body weight is no indication of low cholesterol. "For more than 50 years, it has been known that atherosclerosis (a narrowing of the arteries from a buildup of plaque) begins in childhood and progresses through adolescence and young adulthood to cause coronary heart disease (CHD) in middle age and later," he says in an American Medical Association editorial. He cites a study done in 1953 that revealed a high frequency of advanced atherosclerosis in the coronary arteries of young (average age 22 years) Korean War casualties. There is some good news out there, however. "Most persons, including teenagers, respond to a fat-modified diet by lowering their blood cholesterol, particularly the LDL cholesterol," he explains.

Carbohydrates (60 to 65 Percent of Daily Calories)

Providing the most calories in a typical diet, carbs are also broken down into two camps. The heroes are the slowly digested carbohydrates that come from whole grains, whole-wheat pasta and bread, fruits, and vegetables. These need to be chewed and take a bit of time to eat. Boys rarely eat too many of them. The villains in the crowd are the easily digested, refined carbohydrates that are quickly broken down in the body and don't keep kids from being hungry for long. They lurk in many of the starchy foods most widely eaten by teenagers: white bread, bagels, soft drinks, cakes, cookies, doughnuts, sweetened cereal, candy, and snack foods. These foods, which are said to have a high glycemic index, are not the best choice for alleviating hunger, yet they're the easiest to overeat.

Among the biggest carb villains for teenagers are soft drinks, which on average contain about 40 grams or 10 teaspoons of sugar in every 12-ounce can. "Liquid candy," they deliver 150 to 160 calories but give nothing back to the body. In the May 2005 issue of *The Journal of Pediatrics,* Robert Murray, associate professor of pediatrics at Ohio State University, reported that teenagers in the United States consume, on average, about two 12-ounce cans of soda or sweetened fruit drinks a day, the equivalent of 20 teaspoons of refined sugar. And one-fourth of all teens down as many as four cans of soda (40 teaspoons of sugar) per day—600 calories, or the equivalent of a meal. There's good reason to believe all that sugar affects how much food teenagers eat as well. Contrary to what you might think, it doesn't spoil their appetites. Dr. David Ludwig of Children's Hospital Boston says that kids who drink soft drinks tend to eat much more than kids who avoid them, since the sugary drinks cause a rapid rise in insulin, which makes adolescents hungry. According to David Levitsky, professor of nutritional sciences and psychology at Cornell, children who every day drink more than 12 ounces of soda, bottled iced tea, fruit punch, or drinks made from flavored powders gained significantly more weight than kids who limited their intake of these drinks to less than 6 ounces a day.

And Dr. David L. Katz, professor of public health and medicine at Yale University and author of *The Way to Eat,* points out that kids who drink two or three 12-ounce sodas or one supersized 44-ounce sweetened drink a day take in enough liquid calories to gain one pound a week.

According to the Center for Science in the Public Interest, one-third of the weight in some popular breakfast cereals is sugar, making them more like candy than cereal. Be especially cautions about "less-sugar" banners on cereal packages. The best choices contain less than 9 grams of sugar, no artificial sweeteners, and more than 4 grams of fiber per serving.

If all that sugar weren't worrisome enough, many health professionals warn about the effects of high-fructose corn syrup (HFCS), used today to sweeten soft drinks as well as juice drinks, candy, baked goods, syrup, many brands of yogurt, soup, cereals, and pasta sauces. (According to the USDA, the average American consumes over 55 pounds of it per year.) Developed in the 1970s as an inexpensive and versatile liquid sweetener that could be transported easily, it is processed from hydrolyzed corn starch and has come under attack for slowing down the body's fat burning ability; lowering levels of leptin, which trigger the feeling of being full; and affecting a rise in the hormone ghrelin, which triggers hunger. In other words, foods high in HFCS don't necessarily take away hunger, and they can set up cravings for more. Check package labels and try to avoid foods that contain it.

Check labels as well for sources of sugars and syrups that are added to foods during processing or preparation—as opposed to those that occur naturally in milk or fruit. These added sugars include corn sweetener, corn syrup, dextrose, fructose, fruit juice concentrates, glucose, lactose, maltose, malt syrup, sucrose, and syrup.

Some treats now and then are fine, so don't toss out grandma's sugar cookie recipe. Help kids develop a sense of how much sugar they're taking in. The USDA recommends limiting added sugars (not counting the natural sugars in fruit or milk) to 40 grams (10 teaspoons) for a 2,000-calorie diet, 56 grams (14 teaspoons) for a 2,400-calorie diet, and 72 grams (18 teaspoons) for a 2,800-calorie diet.

Fiber (30 to 38 Grams per Day)

Dietary fiber, a form of carbohydrate, helps slow down digestion and is important in a boy's diet since it can keep him from feeling hungry for at least a few hours. There are two kinds of dietary fiber. Soluble fiber, which dissolves in water and forms a gel in the intestines, is found in barley, oatmeal, kidney beans, and some fruits and vegetables. Insoluble fiber, found in wheat bran, whole grains, many vegetables, and skins of fruit, passes through the digestive system almost intact, creating bulk, acting as a sponge in absorbing water, and preventing constipation. Both kinds of fiber are important for proper bowel function. They also reduce the risk of diabetes and heart disease. Good sources include whole grains, such as oatmeal and other hot cereals, granola, whole-wheat bread, and brown rice. The Whole Grains Council recommends that boys between the ages of 14 and 18 should have 3.5 to 7 servings (each about 16 grams) of whole grains daily. Foods that supply one serving include one slice of whole grain bread; $1/2$ whole grain English muffin; $1/2$ cup cooked whole wheat pasta; $1/2$ cup cooked brown rice, bulgur, barley, or other cooked grain; or 2 cups of popped popcorn.

Fruits and vegetables are also important sources of fiber. To boost consumption, push oranges rather than orange juice, apples rather than apple juice, and eating the skin and membranes of cleaned fruits and vegetables. And find ways to work canned beans into a number of meals each week. Boys need about 16 grams of fiber for every 1,000 calories they eat. As they increase fiber consumption, they should drink more water.

GOOD SOURCES OF FIBER

Food	Measure	Fiber (g insoluble)	Fiber (g soluble)
Barley	$1/2$ cup dry	16	3
Bran cereal 100 percent	$1/2$ cup	12.6	—
Navy beans	$1/2$ cup cooked	9.5	2.8
Kidney beans	$1/2$ cup cooked	8.2	3.4
Flaxmeal	$1/4$ cup	8	—
Raisin Bran cereal	1 cup	7	—
Whole-wheat pasta	1 cup cooked	6	.84
Chickpeas	$1/2$ cup canned	5	—
Pear, with skin	1	5	1
Bulgur	$1/2$ cup cooked	4	.7
Raspberries, fresh	$1/2$ cup	4	—
Steel cut oats	$1/4$ cup dry	4	2
Blackberries, fresh	$1/2$ cup	3.8	—
Baked potato, with skin	1	3.8	.95
Brown rice	1 cup cooked	3.5	.4
Apple	1	3.3	.33
Banana	1	3.1	—
Orange	1	3.1	.56
Broccoli	1 cup	2.7	—

Source: Foundations Family Nutrition

Iron (12 Mg per Day)

Teenagers who aren't getting enough iron can feel tired all the time, since iron helps supply oxygen to red-blood cells. Calves' liver is an excellent source, but few boys will go there. Those who eat red meat, chicken, and eggs usually have enough iron in their diets. Vegetarians can get enough iron from canned beans, wheat germ, seeds and nuts, and tofu. Another good source is potato skin; don't peel potatoes when you make oven fries and get everyone to eat the skin of a baked potato. Eating foods rich in vitamin C helps the body absorb iron. Serve broccoli, cabbage, cantaloupe, green peppers, oranges, strawberries, and tomatoes with iron-rich foods.

GOOD SOURCES OF IRON

Food	Serving Size	Iron (milligrams)
Fortified cereals	1 cup	5–18
Prune juice	1 cup	7–8
Chicken or beef liver	3 ounces	7
Pumpkin seed kernels	2 ounces	4
Sunflower seed kernels	2 ounces	4
Prunes	10	3
Peanuts	1/2 cup	3
Raisins or dates	1/2 cup	3
Wheat germ	1 ounce	3
Beef or pork	3 ounces	2–3
Sesame seeds	2 ounces	2
Leafy greens (spinach, Swiss chard, mustard greens)	1/2 cup	2
Molasses (blackstrap)	1 tablespoon	2
Tofu	1/2 cup	2
Chicken or lamb	3 ounces	.3
Egg	1	1
Bread, enriched	1 slice	1
Broccoli	1/2 cup	1
Green beans	1/2 cup	1
Green peas	1/2 cup	1

Source: Foundations Family Nutrition

Sodium (Less than 2,300 Mg per Day)

Sodium helps regulate water in the body. An excess of it can cause water retention and has been linked to hypertension and high blood pressure. Most Americans consume about 2 teaspoons of salt a day, or 4,000 milligrams. Salt is the hidden additive in most processed foods. Just look at the amount of sodium in one serving of canned soup (800 mg or more) or in 1 tablespoon of soy sauce (900 mg or more). A single entree in a Chinese restaurant can have more than 3,000 mg of sodium. And teen food is salty stuff. Chips, snack foods, and dried onion soup, prized as a dip ingredient, are all very high in sodium. As much as possible, encourage kids not to have more than one food a day that contains more than 480 mg of sodium per serving. Buy low-sodium or sodium-free seasoning blends and use them in cooking instead of salt. Use reduced-sodium soy sauce. And add chopped fresh or dried herbs to increase flavor in soups, stews, and vegetable dishes.

FOODS HIGH IN SODIUM

Food	Serving Size	Sodium (milligrams)
Cheese curls	8 ounces	2,640
Onion soup mix	1 packet	2,440
Beef jerky	4 ounces	2,400
Sour cream and onion chips	8 ounces	1,680
Frozen pizza	for 1	1,190
Pretzels	18	1,120
Fried chicken	4 ounces	990
Beef stew canned	1 cup	970
Chicken noodle soup	1/2 cup	890
Hot dog	1	570
Teriyaki marinade	1 tablespoon	420

Source: supermarket labels

Calcium (1,200 to 1,500 Mg per Day)

A recent survey conducted by the National Institutes of Health's Institute of Arthritis and Musculoskeletal Diseases shows that seven out of ten boys aren't getting enough calcium. This is troubling news. By the age of 17, boys have already stored in their bones 90 percent of all the calcium they will have as adults. A diet high in soft drinks and low in milk and dairy products actually sabotages the skeleton. Boys often grow the fastest between the ages of 12 and 15 and can put on as many as 4 inches a year. They need from 1,200 to 1,500 mg of calcium during this time to support their rapid increase in bone mass and help prevent osteoporosis later in life. (It is not just women who are affected by this disease.) Encourage your son to drink 1 percent milk (resort to 1 percent chocolate milk if he won't drink plain milk) and to eat canned beans, fish, tofu, and dark green vegetables.

And as you think about ways to help your son build strong bones through his diet, encourage him to be active, too. "Among children and young adults, vigorous physical activity sketches the blueprint for the growing skeleton," says Dr. Walter Willet in his national bestseller, *Eat, Drink, and Be Healthy.* "The more activity and healthy stress on bones, the more bone is built and the larger the bone reservoir upon which to draw during adulthood and old age."

GOOD SOURCES OF CALCIUM

Food	Serving Size	Calcium (milligrams)
Milk	8 ounces	300
Yogurt (low-fat)	8 ounces	270
Swiss cheese	1 ounce	270
Tofu (calcium fortified)	4 ounces	260
Provolone	1 ounce	215
Cheddar cheese	1 ounce	205
Mozzarella cheese (part-skim)	1 ounce	185
Spinach (cooked)	1/2 cup	120
Kale (cooked)	1/2 cup	90
Cottage cheese (low-fat)	1/2 cup	70
Broccoli (cooked)	1/2 cup	50

Source: Foundations Family Nutrition

Potassium

Increasingly making the nutritional news, potassium is an important mineral that can prevent bone loss, lower blood pressure, and keep the body healthy in a number of other ways. In February 2004, a National Academy of Sciences Institute of Medicine panel set the adequate potassium intake for everyone over age 14 at 4,600 milligrams. Impossible to achieve with a diet high in junk food, this target presents a challenge, but it is worth considering how to meet it. The table below presents some possibilities.

GOOD SOURCES OF POTASSIUM

Food	Serving Size	Potassium (milligrams)
Sweet potato, baked	1	694
Tomato paste	1/4 cup	664
Beet greens, cooked	1/2 cup	655
Potato, baked, flesh	1	610
White beans, canned	1/2 cup	595
Yogurt, plain, non-fat	8 ounces	579
Clams, canned	3 ounces	534
Yogurt, plain, low-fat	8 ounces	531
Prune juice	3/4 cup	530
Carrot juice	3/4 cup	517
Blackstrap molasses	1 tablespoon	498
Halibut, cooked	3 ounces	490
Soybeans, green, cooked	1/2 cup	485
Tuna, yellowfin, cooked	3 ounces	484
Lima beans, cooked	1/2 cup	484
Winter squash, cooked	1/2 cup	448
Cod, Pacific, cooked	3 ounces	439
Bananas	1 medium	422
Spinach, cooked	1/2 cup	419
Tomato juice	3/4 cup	417
Tomato sauce	1/2 cup	405
Prunes, stewed	1/2 cup	398
Milk, nonfat	1 cup	382

Food	Serving Size	Potassium (milligrams)
Pork chop, center loin, cooked	3 ounces	382
Apricots, dried, uncooked	1/4 cup	378
Rainbow trout, farmed, cooked	3 ounces	375
Buttermilk, cultured, low-fat	1 cup	370
Cantaloupe	1/4 medium	368
1% or 2% milk	1 cup	366
Lentils, cooked	1/2 cup	365
Kidney beans, cooked	1/2 cup	358
Orange juice	3/4 cup	355

Source: USDA Nutrient Database for Standard Reference

Cracking the Label Codes

For an easy-to-understand guide to nearly every inch of that confusing label, visit www.fda.gov/opacom/backgrounders/foodlabel/newlabel.html. (Note that as of this writing, this tool does not include information about trans fats, which are a new addition to FDA-mandated food labeling.) To access a free food database that contains nutritional information on more than 40,000 generic and brand name foods, including fast-food chain fare, visit www.calorieking.com.

Perplexed by the meaning of terms such as whole grain, multigrain, stone-ground, and enriched? Go to www.foodsubs.com and click on "grains" for a detailed explanation of grains along with helpful color photos.

Smart Food Basics

When you shop for food, concentrate on choosing whole-grain products, fruits, and vegetables and buy a variety of them. Everyone—whether old, young, male, female, underweight, overweight, just right—is best served by eating a diet rich in these foods. They are also important for teenage boys because they keep them feeling full the longest.

Wean kids off sugar and unhealthy types of fat by cutting back on how much of each you use at home and getting your family's palates accustomed to the taste of foods that aren't fatty or sugary. Steam, bake, or stir-fry foods, don't deep-fat fry them. Sauté in canola or olive oil instead of butter, and top vegetables with a bit of olive oil and chopped garlic rather than butter. Instead of soft drinks, buy bottled water, flavored seltzer, fruit spritzers, and 1 percent milk. Avoid caffeinated energy drinks, which boys may learn about from teammates. Check out the drinks chapter in this book for more ideas.

As much as possible, avoid buying packaged and processed foods and anything with a label that reads like a chemistry experiment. Pay special attention to the labels on store-bought baked goods; because they need a long shelf life and an appealing taste, these products are usually loaded with trans fats, added sugars, and artificial colors, flavors, and preservatives.

Limit saturated fat intake from consumption of foods such as bacon, sausages, fatty ground beef, doughnuts, french fries, and pizza-parlor pizza. Buy turkey bacon or sausage and lean ground beef; make baked potato sticks instead of french fries, and teach your boy to make a healthier pizza at home (see page 183).

Go for balance and a wide selection of foods. If you eat beef one night, have chicken the next and fish the night after that. Watch out for routines that keep you going back to unhealthy food.

Make it easy for boys to eat as many of their meals as possible at home. When they eat away from home with their friends, they'll most likely fill up on fatty, salty, sugary foods that sabotage a healthy diet.

When the family goes out for dinner, avoid fast food, buffets, and places famous for serving oversized portions. Instead, seek out restaurants where everyone can sample tidbits and mini-meal helpings of foods that are different from what you might cook at home: Chinese dim sum offers a selection of small dishes including vegetable rolls, steamed dumplings, and lean meats; Spanish tapas feature little plates of grilled vegetables, meats, and seafood; Japanese bento includes a variety of foods served in a lacquered box. At a traditional restaurant, share one or two main-course items. Order soup, shrimp cocktail, salads, and vegetable dishes, and share a dessert.

Guide boys in balancing caloric intake with energy expenditure. Encourage them to be physically active by walking or riding a bike to destinations in the neighborhood, joining sports teams at school, finding club teams outside of school, or becoming members of the YMCA or a local gym. (Active parents are great role models.)

Vegetarian Diets

If your family hasn't been following a vegetarian diet, it can come as a shock when your son announces that he is no longer eating meat. Support his convictions. Studies show that people who consider themselves vegetarian, semivegetarian, or vegan are less likely than red-meat eaters to be overweight or obese. And eating less red meat and more vegetables and grains is kinder to the earth. Be sure vegetarian boys find replacement foods for the protein and iron supplied by meats (see pages 14 and 23). Good combinations for them include beans and brown rice; tofu and brown rice; peanut butter and whole-grain bread. You and your son might find it helpful to meet with a registered dietitian to ensure that proper nutrition is being attained.

A Typical Day?

Keeping the recommended daily dietary intakes in mind, let's look at a typical day of eating for two different teenagers, Lennie and Charles. How would your son's diet compare to these?

Lennie (see table below)

If this boy is sedentary, he's probably seriously overweight or heading in that direction. He's taking in enough calories for two boys. He's also

	Food	Calories	Fat (grams)	Sat. Fat (grams)	
Breakfast	Chocolate glazed donut	252.0	12.0	3.0	
	Orange drink (1 cup)	220.0	1.0	—	
Lunch	Hot dog with bun	280.0	17.0	6.0	
	Mac and cheese (1 cup)	353.0	13.0	4.0	
	2 jumbo chocolate chip cookies	560.0	26.0	16.0	
	1 can of soda	162.0	—	—	
Snack	M&Ms kingsize	434.0	18.5	11.0	
	1 can of soda	162.0	—	—	
Dinner	Large chocolate shake (19.5 ounces)	760.0	17.5	10.5	
	Double quarter-pound burger with cheese	732.0	40.0	19.0	
	Large french fries (6 ounces)	525.0	25.0	4.6	
Late Snack	Sour cream & onion chips (7 ounces)	1,051.0	67.0	17.0	
	1 can of soda	162.0	—	—	
Total		5,653.0	237.0	91.1	

putting himself at serious risk for heart disease, since he's getting almost three times the recommended fat, almost five times the recommended saturated fat, and more than three times too much sodium. He's also getting too much cholesterol and sugar. He is getting enough calcium. These figures, however, don't begin to show the serious imbalance in his diet. In an entire day this boy hasn't eaten a single fruit, and his only vegetable has been in the form of fries or chips. In this he represents the seven out of ten teenage boys who say they never eat fruits or vegetables.

Cholesterol (milligrams)	Sodium (milligrams)	Carbs (milligrams)	Fiber (grams)	Sugars (grams)	Protein (grams)	Calcium (milligrams)
5.0	100.0	33.0	1.0	21.0	3.0	
—	10.0	54.0	1.0	54.0	1.0	20.0
35.0	710.0	22.0	1.0	4.0	11.0	40.0
19.0	651.0	48.0	2.0	10.0	12.0	170.0
80.0	360.0	76.0	—	36.0	6.0	40.0
—	50.0	40.5	—	40.5	—	—
9.0	56.0	63.0	1.9	57.5	3.7	
—	50.0	40.5	—	40.5	—	—
70.0	333.0	133.0	—	110.3	17.5	612.0
160.0	1,330.0	46.0	3.0	9.0	47.0	300.0
—	324.0	69.0	7.0	—	4.6	46.2
14.0	1,238.0	102.0	10.3	—	16.0	142.6
—	50.0	40.5	—	40.5	—	—
392.0	5,262.0	767.5	27.2	423.3	121.8	1,370.8

Charles (see table below)

If this boy is very active and between 14 and 18 years old, he could take in another 500 or so calories and still be within his recommended energy range. He's well within the guidelines for fat, saturated fat, and cholesterol. He's getting twice the recommended amount of sodium

	Food	Calories	Fat (grams)	Sat. Fat (grams)
Breakfast	1 orange	85.0	0.2	—
	2 slices whole grain bread	140.0	4.0	—
	2 tbsp peanut butter	190.0	16.5	2.5
	1% milk (1 cup)	103.0	2.4	1.4
Lunch	Hamburger (3.7 ounces)	388.0	9.5	4.0
	Green salad (2 cups)	70.0	—	—
	2 tbsp light dressing	53.0	4.5	0.4
	1% milk (1 cup)	103.0	2.4	1.4
	1 medium apple	92.0	0.6	—
Snack	Corn chips (20)	150.0	6.0	1.0
	Hummus (1/2 cup)	194.0	9.6	1.4
	1 carrot	30.0	0.2	—
	Glass of water			
Dinner	1 chicken breast	231.0	5.0	1.4
	Pasta (1 cup)	192.0	0.8	—
	Green beans (1/2 cup)	21.0	0.1	—
	Green salad (1 cup)	70.0	—	—
	2 tbsp light dressing	53.0	4.5	0.4
	Whole wheat dinner roll	70.0	1.0	—
	1% milk (2 cups)	206.0	4.8	2.8
Late Snack	Blackberry smoothie	185.0	1.8	—
Total		2,626.0	73.9	16.7

and more protein and calcium than his basic requirement. He's getting plenty of dietary fiber from a variety of whole grains, fruits, and vegetables; this will fill him up and keep him going throughout the day. His sugar intake is moderate, and most of it is from fruit and dairy, not added sugar.

Cholesterol (milligrams)	Sodium (milligrams)	Carbs (milligrams)	Fiber (grams)	Sugars (grams)	Protein (grams)	Calcium (milligrams)
—	—	21.2	4.3	16.8	1.7	72.0
—	320.0	30.0	6.0	1.0	8.0	60.0
—	—	6.0	2.0	1.0	8.0	20.0
10.0	125.0	12.0	—	12.7	8.4	307.0
30.0	771.0	22.0	2.0	7.0	16.0	210.0
—	66.0	16.0	12.0	6.0	4.0	56.0
—	228.0	2.5	0.4	1.5	0.3	
10.0	125.0	12.0	—	12.7	8.4	307.0
—	—	24.0	4.2	19.6	0.3	10.9
—	75.0	21.0	2.0	—	2.0	40.0
—	277.0	23.0	5.7		4.0	57.0
—	50.0	6.9	2.0	3.3	0.7	23.8
119.0	104.0	—	—	—	43.4	
—	1.0	40.0	2.0		7.0	9.8
—	3.0	4.1	1.9		1.0	21.1
—	66.0	16.0	12.0	6.0	4.0	54.0
—	228.0	2.5	0.4	1.5	0.3	
—	160.0	15.0	3.0	1.0	4.0	30.0
20.0	250.0	24.0	—	25.4	16.8	614.0
—	2.0	38.0	6.4	20.0	5.9	90.0
189.0	2,851.0	336.2	66.3	135.5	144.2	1,984.6

Is Your Son Overweight?

Use a calculation called the Body Mass Index (BMI), created for adults, as a guideline: multiply his weight in pounds by 703. Divide that answer by his height in inches. Divide that answer again by his height in inches. A BMI of 26 to 29.9 is considered overweight for an adult; 30 or more is obese for an adult. Ask a doctor or registered dietitian to plot your son's weight on a growth chart to determine if he is overweight or at risk for becoming so.

Doctors report that eating habits developed early in life are very hard to change and usually lead to lifelong eating patterns that maintain obesity. If your son is overweight or obese, ask your doctor for help. Treatment consists of a referral to a registered dietitian who can review your family's diet and eating habits and make recommendations for losing weight, along with individual counseling, behavior modification, individual or group therapy, and the very important support and encouragement for making changes and following recommended treatment. (In many cases, such a program will be covered by your health insurance.)

Guide to a Good Day's Eating

It is easy to get overwhelmed when considering the number of servings per day recommended by dietitians and the USDA. Don't become obsessed with portion sizes or let too much measuring take the pleasure out of feeding your family. Use these calculations to review what goes into a balanced diet. Since each serving is actually small by many people's standards, it is quite easy to provide your son with a good variety of foods and stay within a reasonable budget. See page 35 for tips on visualizing a recommended serving size.

Vegetables (3 to 5 Servings)

1 serving	=	1 cup raw leafy vegetables (salad)
	=	$1/2$ cup cooked vegetable
	=	1 cup chopped raw vegetables
	=	$3/4$ cup vegetable juice

How Much Is a Serving?

One of the biggest mistakes we make in feeding our kids and ourselves is creating oversized portions. Keep in mind that just $1/2$ cup is the amount the USDA recommends as one serving size for most fruits and vegetables. If you adhere to controlled portion sizes, you can eat a variety of foods at every meal without overeating. And small portions of a several different foods make for a more interesting meal. Here are some easy guidelines for visualizing the USDA's recommended serving sizes.

$1/2$ cup cooked cereal, pasta, rice	half a baseball
1 medium apple, orange, or peach	tennis ball
$1/4$ cup dried fruit	golf ball
$1/2$ cup fruit or vegetable	half a baseball
1 cup broccoli	light bulb
1 medium potato	computer mouse
1 cup leafy greens	baseball
3 ounces cooked meat, fish, or poultry	average deck of cards
1 ounce hard cheese	2 dominoes or 4 dice
2 tablespoons peanut butter	ping-pong ball
$1/3$ cup nuts	one handful

Since it is often difficult for boys to find vegetables at school lunches, plan to have three or four servings, with dips, for them to eat at home. Buy precut vegetables if you don't have time for chopping. Add vegetables to salads, stuff them into wraps and sandwiches, and serve them with pasta and rice.

Milk, Yogurt, Cheese (2 to 3 Servings)

1 serving	=	1 cup milk or yogurt
	=	$1^{1}/_{2}$ ounces (3 tablespoons) natural cheese (not processed cheese)
	=	1 ounce low-fat cheese

Skim or 1 percent milk is an excellent drink for boys. Encourage them to drink a glass with every meal and develop a routine for buying it so there's always some on hand. Plain nonfat or low-fat yogurt flavored with a spoonful of fruit-sweetened jam is more economical than fruit-flavored yogurt, which is also high in sugar. Mix in $1/4$ cup nuts or granola or fresh or frozen fruit to create a nutritious snack or dessert.

Bread, Cereal, Rice, Pasta (6 to 10 Servings)

1 serving	=	1 slice bread
	=	1 ounce (1 cup) cold cereal
	=	$1/2$ cup cooked cereal, rice, or pasta

Choose whole-grain breads, crackers, and cereals over products made with refined white flour to boost the nutritional advantages of these easy-to-serve foods. Make oatmeal a morning staple, or encourage your son to eat a bowl of healthy, high-fiber (more than 4 grams), unsweetened or lightly sweetened cereal in the morning and again at night if he's hungry at bedtime. (Forgo the bedtime cereal if your son is overweight.) Cook brown rice and a variety of whole grains, such as barley and bulgur rather than white rice, and buy whole-wheat, spinach, or vegetable pasta, which is available in a wide range of shapes and sizes.

Fruit (2 to 4 Servings)

1 serving	=	1 medium apple, pear, orange, etc.
	=	$1/2$ cup chopped, cooked fruit
	=	$3/4$ cup fruit juice

Keep fresh fruit on hand and encourage your son to reach for it, rather than juice, to quickly satiate his hunger. Well-washed apples and pears, with their skins, make great high-fiber snacks, as do whole, peeled oranges, clementines, and grapefruits. Serve fresh fruit for breakfast or dessert, topped with yogurt, and add a sliced apple or a bunch of grapes to a dinner plate to boost the number of daily servings.

Meat, Poultry, Fish, Beans, Eggs, and Nuts (3 Servings, for a Total of 7 Ounces)

1 serving	=	3 ounces cooked lean meat, poultry, or fish
	=	$1/2$ cup cooked canned beans
	=	1 egg or 2 egg whites
	=	2 tablespoons peanut butter

For this important protein component, favor lean meats such as chicken and pork over fatty ribs and steaks. When you think about making a favorite recipe that calls for ground beef, try ground turkey or ground light or dark chicken instead. Include vegetable proteins, such as tofu and peanuts, in your weekly meals by adding them to stir-fries. Rely on canned beans to add extra protein to soups and stews, and serve them with rice or other grains for a complete meal. Find ways to use eggs beyond breakfast, in omelets and frittatas and hard-cooked for snacks and sandwiches.

How to Feed a Teenage Boy

Anyone who has lived with a teenage boy will tell you that these years are filled with challenges. It isn't easy for parents to know how and where the effects of social turbulence, academic pressure, and athletic competition on boys will spill over into family dynamics. But it isn't fair to jam your son into a stereotype. He's a creature who is full of surprises and his journey from age 13 to 20 covers a lot of territory indeed. The media has long focused on the problems of teenage girls who suffer from anorexia, bulimia, and other eating disorders that can be triggered by low self-esteem. Boys are not spared, although their appetites rarely suffer. Instead, they often worry silently. They want to be good looking, have terrific muscles, star on sports teams, get a leading role in the school play, win the essay contest, play great music, and know that everyone will laugh at their jokes during lunch. But in truth, they spend a lot of time looking in the mirror, too, fearing that their ears are too big, their noses too long, their freckles too numerous, their chests too small.

As boys begin to figure out who they are and, in the process, seek their independence, they can seem moody and distant at times. They often take a step or two forward and several back, a developmental dance that can try parents' patience. Who is this kid who gives single-word answers one day and talks incessantly the next? Who has all the bravado of a bull-fighter on Monday but can't decide what to wear to a party on Friday? Who has lots of time to hang out with friends and find out which store sells the latest CD, but never has time to get a trash can to the curb or return a library book? Yet, in the scheme of things, this phase is quickly passing. Having a ringside seat as a teenager morphs into a man presents an astonishing and emotionally rich spectacle. Being at the center of it to feed him can give you a strong point of connection to him at a time when not many other doors are open. In addition to getting enough good food into him when he's hungry, your role during this time involves helping shape his attitudes about eating and teaching him how to make good food choices for himself. Here are some strategies for getting the most out of the experience.

Stay Positive

Ask the parent of a teenager about his or her son's eating habits, and you'll most likely hear exasperation, shock, and awe. All the clichés come tumbling out: "I don't know where he puts it." "He eats us out of house and home." "I can't fill him up." "He's a bottomless pit." "He inhales his supper." "I spend all my time at the grocery store." Instead of complaining about a boy's good appetite and being critical about his longing for food during this important stage of growth and development, learn about his nutritional needs and help him eat right. Complaints or snide remarks directed at his hunger (even if you are half-joking) never do anything to help a boy feel good about himself, or foster an interest in healthy eating.

Cut Yourself Some Slack

Silence the nagging voice that says you should be spending a lot more time in the kitchen, or that makes you feel inadequate when you go food shopping, or that worries about the occasional greasy fast-food meal. As parents we're all busy people and guilt trips over dinner preparation don't help make mealtimes pleasant. Do what you can and ask for help.

Be Flexible about Mealtimes

It is great for families to eat together as often as possible. Sitting together around a table is an important ritual for maintaining communication. But for everyone's sanity and good health, allow mealtimes to vary when there are teenagers in the house and the world of after-school sports, play practices, clubs, music lessons, and a host of other commitments comes roaring along. Dr. Leann Birch, head of the Department of Human Development and Family Studies at Penn State, has focused on children's eating habits for two decades and concludes that what is available in the house probably has a greater impact on healthy food intake than sitting around the table. Keep meals simple and make things that can be reheated easily, so you need never complain that your dinner is ruined when a boy comes home later than expected.

Count on More than Three Meals a Day

Teenage boys wake up hungry and are often hungry at bedtime. But an enormous quantity of food at one meal isn't the answer. Most teenage boys do better when they eat something every 3 or 4 hours. Instead of planning big dinners, adjust your focus to find ways to keep a variety of foods on hand that can be combined for spontaneous, smaller meals or hearty, healthy snacks.

Keep the Big Picture in Mind

Try to remember that your job in feeding a boy is one of caregiver. Don't take it personally if he isn't hungry when you want to feed him, or if you make a meal and he picks at it. Focus your energy on preparing food that can be eaten another day.

Recognize the Things You Can't Control

You won't know what your teenager eats at school or at friends' houses, or what he buys on the way home from school or at the movies. Let it be when he shows interest in foods you may have kept out of his diet when he was a little kid. Give him the space to make his own decisions away from home, and keep your cool when you find a few candy bar wrappers in his room. (If you find heaps of wrappers use the discovery as an opportunity to talk calmly about making better choices.) Jadine Kairns, a nutritionist at the BC Children's Hospital in Vancouver, warns about the "forbidden fruit" issue: "I even advocate chips and candy once in a while. I believe junk food does have a place in our diet, because the more you say no to yourself or have someone say no to you, the more you can really value that." So let some things go under your radar.

Buy the Freshest Food You Can

The fresher the food and the less that's done to it between the time it leaves the supplier to when it appears on your table, the better. "A serving of broccoli is naturally rich in vitamins A and B, and has more vitamin C than citrus fruit. But raised in an industrial farm monoculture, shipped over a long distance and stored before and after being delivered to your supermarket, it loses up to 80 percent of its vitamin C and 95 percent of its calcium, iron, and potassium," says New York chef and local produce advocate Dan Barber in *The New York Times.* Move beyond chain stores to support your local food producers and farmers markets. Buy fresh organic produce as much as possible. According to the magazine *Cooking Light,* "A research review of 41 studies conducted by the University of California at Davis found that, on average, organic produce contains as much as 27 percent more vitamin C, 21 percent more iron, and 29 percent more magnesium compared to traditionally grown foods."

Choose Wisely

If you don't want your kids to guzzle soft drinks, gorge on candy, fill up on cookies, or devour bags of chips, don't bring any of it into the house, and don't eat it yourself. Period. Plenty of this stuff will cross their paths when they're away from home. If you keep junk out of the house and calmly explain your reasons for not buying it, you can quickly establish a boundary kids will learn to accept and respect. This is a lot easier than you may think when boys are involved, because they really do get very hungry and will eat good food if there's no junk around. If you are not in the habit of doing this already, the strategy is simple: Just quietly start to bring a healthy selection of foods into the house. Buy whole-grain bread, not potato chips. Buy nuts, apples, and oranges, not candy and cookies. Buy 1 percent milk and bottled water, not soft drinks.

Cook When It Isn't Dinner Time

CSI can wait. If you are away from the kitchen during the day, spend 1 hour after dinner twice a week preparing food for upcoming meals. Cook rice, bulgur, or oatmeal to keep in the refrigerator. Grind bread crumbs, chop vegetables, make dips and dressings. Cook turkey breasts, chicken, and roast meats for dinners and sandwiches; make lasagnas and other dishes that can be reheated. Make marinades and soak chicken, beef, or tofu for the next day's meal.

Provide Pregame Snacks

Encourage athletic boys to eat well 2 to 3 hours before a game and have a snack 1 to 2 hours before, so they'll have enough energy to do their best. If your high school athlete goes directly from classes to practices and games, suggest he tuck a durable snack from home into his backpack. Good choices include whole-grain bread with peanut butter or an energy bar with a 2 to 1 carb to protein ratio.

Get Your Kids Involved with Food

When asked in surveys why they prefer fast food to what they can prepare for themselves, most boys say they don't know how to cook. All kitchen knowledge, however simple, needs to be learned, and it is your role to help your boy start to get comfortable cooking for himself. Don't assume that he knows how to do anything. Show him how to peel carrots, chop onions, open a can of tuna fish and drain it, crack eggs, and grate cheese. Teach him to make simple meals for himself: how to cook pasta, know when it is done, and drain it; how to scramble eggs; how to prepare a simple stir-fry.

Talk about Food and Nutrition

Teenagers hate lectures, but it is important to share facts about food with them. You may want to appeal to a boy's vanity and his curiosity about his changing body, which is easy to do. Tell him if he wants to look good, have a fit body, have good-looking skin and hair, he needs to eat right. Help him understand that certain foods will give him more energy, while others will make him feel tired. Invest some time in showing him how to read labels and telling him what certain foods can do for him. Although he may not hang on to every word, talk with him about the foods you've bought, what stores you frequent, and why you favor certain cooking methods. As if by osmosis, a good bit of this information will make its way into his brain and undoubtedly influence his decisions in the future.

Speak Out

Find ways to get involved in community groups and national organizations that share an interest in kids and nutrition. Many school districts have recently banned the sale of soft drinks and candy through the efforts of concerned parents. (Vending machines that dispense bottled water, flavored water, and juice make just as much money for the school as soft drinks.) Thanks to pressure from the Alliance for a Healthier Generation, created by the American Heart Association and

the William J. Clinton Foundation, in May of 2006 the soft drink industry agreed to withdraw sweetened soft drinks and sweetened juices
from schools, putting new standards in place by 2009. Active school
boards across the country are developing more nutritious and organic
lunch programs for kids of all ages. The Center for Science in the
Public Interest (CSPI) has published a "School Foods Tool Kit" with
advice on working with school officials. Go to www.cspinet.org/school-
food.

Celebrate!

Last but not least, turn to food as a way to mark milestones and have
fun around the table. Plan birthday feasts. Make a splendid birthday
cake. Indulge in ice cream sundaes on the first night of a new month.
Insist that the extended family come to your house for a holiday meal.
Invite friends and neighbors to a buffet meal or organize a potluck
party. Find ways to share meals with other people in your home as
much as possible so your son experiences the enjoyment and importance of sharing food.

CHAPTER 2

Getting Organized to Keep Healthy Food within Easy Reach

On weekdays around five o'clock, supermarkets are filled with busy parents scrambling to find something for dinner, constantly looking at their watches as they wait in the long checkout lines. We've all been there, and it isn't much fun. It also doesn't inspire you to think about tomorrow's dinner, which your son will be looking for in less than 24 hours, or breakfast, or weekend lunches, or the basketball team dinner you promised to host on Saturday, or the salads you've decided to take to work for lunch. Unless you focus on quick and healthy food your family can eat for a week at a time and vow to get organized, you'll find yourself grabbing packaged or prepared foods or turning to unhealthy pizza and fast food, and spending more money than you want.

Find out when the stores you like are open and arrange a time other than dinner hour to go there. Early mornings and evenings generally will be the best. (Call the managers of your local stores and ask about the quietest times to shop.) Consider a trip to the store your main mission, not one stop in a long list of errands, so you remain focused and give yourself enough time to make good choices. Spend most of your time selecting foods from the perimeter of the market where fresh vegetables, fruits, seafood, meat, and dairy products are sold. Don't wander in the snack food, soft drink, and cookie aisles.

Do take some time now and then to look in the frozen food cases and the produce section for new items to share with your family. It is easy to get into a rut and buy the same things over and over again, because you know they're an easy sell at your table. But bringing home something new—as simple as a different variety of pear—gives you another opportunity to talk with your son about food and share with him ideas about making choices. Supermarkets, natural foods stores, and gourmet markets are constantly introducing new products, many of them designed for shoppers who are looking for organic foods and healthy alternatives to old standbys, such as canned soup. Read the labels carefully, keeping in mind the guidelines outlined in Chapter 1. Choose foods that contain "healthy" fats over those that scream "low-fat." Try golden beets, purple barley, dinosaur kale, salad mixes, arugula, new apple varieties, whole wheat and spinach pastas, different cheeses.

Pay special attention to where and how groceries are stored in your house. Never underestimate how blind boys can be. Make it easy for them to navigate. Set up your refrigerator, freezer, pantry, kitchen cupboards, and countertop to make it easy to find a healthy snack or the makings of a good, quick meal and so you can easily take stock of what's on hand and what needs to be replenished. Maintain the kitchen as a clean and tidy space that's all about food and that has inviting spaces to work. Clear away clutter. Don't store unread newspapers or stacks of mail on the counters. If need be, put a cardboard box on the kitchen floor and fill it with gadgets and small appliances you don't use. Take it to the basement or the thrift shop. Discard any opened packaged foods that have been sitting in the cupboard.

Organize what's in the refrigerator. Toss out any open bottles or packages that you haven't used for weeks. Make sure the vegetable bins are clean and contain only fresh produce. Store leftovers in clear glass or plastic containers or clear plastic bags so they're easy to see. Establish a "sandwich bin" (a rectangular plastic box made to hold leftovers is ideal) for cold cuts, sliced cheese, washed lettuce or other greens, and various spreads and dips as well so a boy can pull the whole business out onto the counter and make his own sandwich. (See page 88 for more suggestions.) Whenever possible label cold cuts with the date you bring them home. Use them within 3 or 4 days. Police the leftovers and toss out anything past its prime.

Keep a plastic box without a lid full of apples in the refrigerator, where they're easy to see and where they stay crisp for several weeks. Cut ripe melons into chunks and store in a clear container. Wash baby carrots and combine them in another clear container with celery cut into sticks, so these snacks are ready to eat. Also keep eggs, granola, freshly ground peanut butter, fruit-sweetened jam or jelly, low-fat milk and yogurt, bottled water, lettuce, olives, and feta cheese.

Stock your pantry or cupboards with staples, such as extra virgin olive oil and canola oil for sautéing vegetables; peanut oil for stir-fries; canned tuna and salmon; whole-wheat, spinach, veggie pastas; boxed mac and cheese; canned noodle soups (free of MSG and trans fats); canned black, pinto, and cannellini beans and garbanzos; rice, bulgur, barley, and other whole grains; whole-grain crackers, rice cakes, corn chips, oatmeal, and cold cereal (containing less than 8 grams of sugar per serving). Keep whole-grain pancake mixes on hand so you can make great batter in seconds.

Put several wooden hinged clothespins in a kitchen drawer and teach your son to use them to reseal packages of crackers or cereal so they don't get stale. Designate a drawer or a bin for storing plastic bags and storage containers with covers, show it to your son, and require that he put leftovers away.

Use the freezer—a lot. Don't turn your nose up at frozen foods, which are both convenient and nutritious. In today's global marketplace, where the average fresh food item travels 1,500 miles to reach your kitchen, frozen fish, meats, vegetables, and fruits, processed on site immediately after harvesting, may well contain more nutrients than fresh foods that have been sitting around for several days. Fresh spinach, for example, can lose half of its health-enhancing vitamins if it sits in the refrigerator for 4 days. Keep blocks of frozen spinach on hand to add unthawed to soups and stews, or thaw to use in egg and rice dishes. Toss frozen blueberries into muffins or pancakes, use frozen fruit mixtures to make smoothies, or heat frozen green beans, corn kernels, or baby peas in boiling water for 2 minutes to make a side dish most boys will eat.

Don't keep your freezer stocked with giant vats of ice cream, frozen cakes, snack foods, or prepared desserts. They're impossible to resist and send to your son the message that the freezer is a place to look for something sweet. Better choices that turn it into a source of healthier foods include plenty of ice and fruit for smoothies and other drinks; whole turkey breasts, which create plenty of leftovers for sandwiches or pot pies; chicken tenderloin pieces that can be baked in 20 minutes; pork tenderloins, which cook quickly; chicken or turkey sausages, good simmered and served whole or sliced in pasta or rice dishes; lean ground beef for tacos or burgers; shrimp and scallops, which cook in minutes; and ravioli and tortellini for meatless dinners. For extra-quick meals, include chicken nuggets; reduced-fat hot dogs, chicken dogs, or tofu dogs; burritos; and spinach pies.

Delegate!

Step back a minute and consider that feeding a family requires at least six jobs:

Meal planning/list making

Food shopping

Carrying food into the house

Putting food away in cupboards, pantry, refrigerator, and freezer

Preparation, cooking, and serving

Cleanup

Don't take it all on by yourself. Get every family member, including your son, involved, as a way to help him become familiar with food as part of daily home life. When you have groceries in the car, ask him to help carry them into the house and put them away, so he handles the items you buy and understands where they go. Once he has his driver's license, send him on errands to pick up milk and eggs, fruits and vegetables, so he learns his way around a grocery store. Teach him how to peel carrots, chop onions, wash salad greens, and grate cheese as well as how to set the table and pack and unpack the dishwasher.

What's in Your Kitchen?

Take a look at the following list of foods. How often are these available in your house?

Apples

Avocados

Blueberries

Broccoli

Brown rice

Butternut squash

Canned beans

Fish and seafood, including canned salmon and tuna

Fruit (fresh and frozen)

Kiwifruit

Nuts (preferably unsalted)

Oats and oatmeal (preferably steel-cut)

Olives and olive oil

Onions

Peanut butter (unsweetened)

Soy foods

Spinach and other leafy greens

Strawberries

Sweet potatoes

Tomatoes

Vegetables (fresh and frozen)

Whole-grain breakfast cereals (preferably those containing more than 4 grams of fiber and less than 8 grams of sugar per serving)

Whole-grain bread (preferably 100 percent whole wheat)

Yogurt (preferably plain)

Dietitians list all of the above foods as among the most important in a healthy diet for providing essential vitamins, minerals, macronutrients, and fiber. They also add variety to mealtimes.

Be careful about getting too caught up in the hoarding mentality. When you see a good deal at the store, it is wise to take advantage of it and buy extra to freeze. But when you are feeding boys and always planning to have food in the house, don't forget about what you have on hand. Every weekend, or at least once a week, thaw and cook something that's in the freezer. Put dates on whatever you freeze. Assuming your freezer is 0°F, vegetables, beef, poultry, uncooked shrimp, and lean fish, such as cod and flounder, have a freezer life of 6 months; pork, ground meats, lamb, and fatty fish, such as bluefish or salmon, should be used within 3 months.

Keep healthy snacks out on the kitchen counter. Put bananas, plums, pears, oranges, clementines, or other easy-to-eat fruit in a bowl. Keep a bowl of unsalted peanuts in their shells out on the counter, for occasional grazing, if no one in your family is overweight. (An old-fashioned side-by-side vegetable dish is the perfect bowl; fill one side with peanuts and leave the other for shells.)

As you look through the recipes in this book, you'll discover that milk, yogurt, cheese, sour cream, cream cheese, mayonnaise, soy sauce, and coconut milk are listed without adjectives such as light, low-fat, nonfat, reduced fat, or reduced sodium. As fat is removed from some products, manufacturers add sugars, preservatives, and artificial ingredients that you may wish to avoid. And while it's generally advisable to choose low-sodium soy sauce and light coconut milk to further reduce the sodium and saturated fat in your family's diet, it is important to pay attention to the quantities of these ingredients you use, no matter what is written on the label. The words "low" or "light" don't mean you can forget about portion control. Please read Chapter 1, which outlines many dietitians' current thinking about what boys need—and don't need—in a healthy, balanced diet. Then read labels and look at ingredient lists as you consider what to buy. Use all this information, and your knowledge of your own family's situation, to help you balance meals in your household.

Equipping the Kitchen

You don't need an arsenal of gadgets, pots, pans, or appliances to cook for your family. Here's a quick review of some basics for making the recipes in this book, and a few luxuries that will help you prepare meals quickly and efficiently.

Baking sheet. The very best are made of stainless steel. Use for heating tortillas, toasting bread, roasting vegetables, and making cookies.

Blender. Keep one out on the counter for smoothies and drinks. Put your son in charge and encourage him to be creative.

Dutch oven. Use for soups, stews, chicken, and roasts. Spring for one that holds 6 to 8 quarts and is made of heavy-duty enameled steel, and you'll find that you use it constantly.

Food processor. This is a must for shredding vegetables and cheese; pureeing soups; grinding bread crumbs and nuts; and making dips, pie crust, and puddings.

Frying pans. Keep several sizes for a variety of jobs. A small, 8-inch stainless steel pan is ideal for scrambling eggs, making omelets, sautéing one onion or a few vegetables, or cooking crepes. Use a large 12- or 13-inch stainless steel pan to cook chicken, prepare stir-fries, make curries, or simmer other stovetop main dishes for four to six people. A 10-inch cast-iron frying pan is also useful for making oven pancakes, baking desserts, and starting egg dishes or steaks on the stovetop and finishing them off in the oven. Get hold of Grandma's cast-iron pan if you can. It will be perfectly seasoned (food wouldn't dare stick to it), making it an ideal pancake griddle and the perfect pan for home fries and hash.

Instant-read thermometer. Slick and compact, this is an essential tool for judging doneness in roasted meat and poultry. It also prevents having to slice into barbecued foods to see if they're cooked.

Knives. A chef's knife, a paring knife, and a bread knife will let you do just about any job. Buy good ones and keep them sharp. A bread knife has a serrated blade and should be used only for bread. It makes short work of whole-wheat and whole-grain loaves, and slices focaccia and calzones without tearing them.

Panini maker. This is a hinged grill with two nonstick plates. A luxury, but useful for making hot sandwiches and bruschetta with perfect grill marks. It can also be used to cook bacon, burgers, chicken, or steak. Look for models with removable plates for easy cleanup.

Popcorn popper. The newest air-popping models use only 2 teaspoons of oil and make great presents for boys.

Ramekins. Ovenproof ramekins in both $1/2$- and 1-cup sizes have many uses and go a long way toward helping control portion sizes. The smaller ones are ideal for serving puddings and nuts and holding dips and salsa; the larger sizes are ideal for rice, pasta, popcorn, and ice cream. They're also helpful for serving small bits of a variety of foods. (Kids love to eat things served in them.)

Ricer. Buy a hand-held, stainless steel model. It makes fabulous mashed potatoes and eliminates the need for peeling potatoes before cooking them. (Simply cut the potatoes in half, boil until soft, and squeeze cut side down.)

Roasting pan. Buy a large one in stainless steel for cooking a whole turkey, a chicken, a pork roast, a party lasagna, and other slow-baked dishes.

Salad spinner. Use to wash lettuce, spinach, and other greens in seconds.

Saucepans. Have at least three good-quality stainless steel pans with lids, one small (1 quart), one medium (2 quarts), and one large (4 quarts), for a wide range of stovetop uses: making hot chocolate and hard-cooked eggs; cooking grains, pasta, and potatoes; reheating or making soup. A large saucepan with a steamer insert is useful for cooking vegetables.

Soapstone griddle. Best used over a gas flame, this special gadget for a family of pancake enthusiasts requires very little butter or oil, provides even heat, and produces perfect pancakes. It is also useful for baking pizzas or calzones in the oven.

Slow-cooker. This is a great time-saver for making many meals, including soups, stews, fillings for hot sandwiches, chicken stock, spaghetti sauce, and hot cider. Buy the 4-quart size, which is helpful when feeding 6 to 12 people.

Stir-fry pan. It needn't be a wok, which is often too large for cooking a simple family meal. Buy one made of stainless steel with a base of about 12 inches and gently sloping sides, so you can also use it for sautéing. There are lots of new designs.

Strainer. Keep a stainless steel or plastic one on hand for draining pasta and grains, removing the moisture from frozen spinach, and making yogurt cheese. The most useful are colanders, with a base that keeps them stable on a flat surface.

Stockpot. When you're making chicken stock or cooking for a gang, an 8- to 12-quart stainless steel stockpot with steep sides and a lid comes in handy. Use it for poaching chicken, steaming lobster, cooking pasta, soup, chili, or stew.

Plan for a Week of Healthy Eating

Turn what seems like a never-ending chore into a challenge you can meet. Sit down with an 8½ by 11-inch piece of paper or open a new document on the computer and along the left-hand side, draw up a menu for the week, listing breakfast, lunch, dinner, and healthy snacks. Keep it simple. No five-course meals. Come up with a good balance of seafood, chicken, turkey, lean meat, tofu, eggs, and canned beans and other legumes in starring dinner roles. Match them with quick-cooking side dishes, such as pasta, rice, bulgur, couscous, potatoes, or whole-grain bread. List vegetables and fruits to serve cooked and raw along with each dinner.

Plan to always have a selection of fresh and frozen fruit and vegetables on hand so your family never breaks the healthy habit of including these foods in daily meals. Shop two or three times a week for fresh produce. Think about ways to stretch at least two of the week's meals by serving leftovers in wraps, stews, or curries. (Look through the recipes in this book for quick and easy dinner ideas.) Not so hard, is it?

Ask your son and all family members to help plan the menu and use their deliberations to get them involved in thinking about healthy food. The first time you try this, ask them to list three of their favorite fruits and vegetables. Be open to special requests (chocolate milk, sparkling cider, fresh raspberries) and add occasional treats, such as cookies from a local bakery. Be patient. Your son may not give you more than a few sentences the first time you create a weekly menu, but he will soon realize that it is in his own best interest to participate. Use the menu-making as another opportunity to talk about food.

With the menu pinned down, figure out what you have on hand and what you need to buy. Create a shopping list on the right-hand side of the page. Include some foods to freeze for later in the week. And jot down reminders of portion sizes to help you buy the right amount when you are faced with the weights listed on packages (see page 35). For example, when buying lean meat, chicken, or fish, allow about 3 ounces, or a piece the size of a deck of cards, per person.

CHAPTER 3

Good Quick Breakfasts (and a Few Slower Ones)

Although a teenage boy can find it especially difficult to open his eyes on school mornings, help him wake up and get going in time to eat breakfast every day. It is an essential routine for him to establish, and it is critical that you do whatever you can to inspire your son to always eat breakfast, even if now and then he grabs something on his way out the door: a container of yogurt, a piece of fruit, or a small bag of dry cereal. When he skips a morning meal, he goes 14 or more hours without food, which hardly guarantees stamina to get through the school day.

Health professionals stress the importance of a good breakfast to boost energy levels, stimulate the metabolism, help with weight control, and prevent overeating at lunchtime. Studies show that kids who consistently eat breakfast perform better in school, have a better attendance record, and are less likely to be overweight than kids who don't eat in the morning.

The best meal is a high-fiber, low-fat blend of carbohydrates for energy and protein to keep your son going for 3 or 4 hours, with brainpower to pay attention to calculus, economics, French, and art history. And because he comes to the table tired, you have a great opportunity to get fruits, dairy products, and whole grains into him. (Chances are he will devour anything you provide.) Good choices include whole-wheat bread or cereal with milk and a piece of fruit; a toasted whole-wheat English muffin with peanut butter or hummus; yogurt with a sprinkling of granola and chopped apple; oatmeal with fruit; eggs and Canadian bacon or turkey bacon; and yogurt-based smoothies (see page 225). Encourage eating fresh fruit over drinking juice, and pair whole wheat toast or muffins with a glass of milk.

Help your son become accustomed to breakfast tastes that aren't sweet. Skip the store-bought doughnuts, frosting-laced coffee cakes,

World's Fastest Breakfasts

Don't let your son skip breakfast! Instead, make him one of these protein- and fiber-loaded meals in seconds. Wrap in foil for traveling. They won't leave any crumbs in the car.

Peanut Butter–Banana Roll-Up   Serves 1

  1 (8-inch) whole-wheat tortilla
  2 tablespoons peanut butter
  1 whole small banana, peeled

Lay the tortilla out on a cutting board or counter and spread with the peanut butter. Lay the banana horizontally about 3 inches from the bottom and roll up.

Morning Pita   Serves 1

  1 whole-wheat pita bread
  $1/4$ cup small-curd cottage cheese
  1 medium apple, thinly sliced

Cut the pita in half. Cut one half into two pieces, open each piece, and use it to line the other pita half, creating a double layer of bread. Stuff with the cottage cheese and apple slices.

giant muffins, and toaster pastries, which qualify as desserts. As a treat on weekends when the family is together, indulge in French toast or waffles topped with a small amount of maple syrup or berries, or bake your own muffins or quick bread to serve with fresh fruit and eggs. Teach your son to make pancakes using a multigrain packaged mix and give him the job of feeding the family now and then.

Keep the pantry stocked with a variety of cold cereals, but be cereal savvy. When buying cold cereals and breads, pay attention to the words used on the labels to find genuine whole-grain products. (Visit www.wholegrainscouncil.org for the latest guidelines.) If it says "100% whole grain," it doesn't contain refined flour. "Made with whole grain" doesn't say how much, and could mean the food contains a lot of refined flour. "Multigrain" could also contain significant amounts of refined flour. The amount of fiber can be a clue to whole grains. Choose cereals that contain 4 or 5 grams of fiber per serving.

Morning Wrap   Serves 1

When there's time to do a little cooking but you'd still like a portable breakfast, prepare eggs as you would for an omelet and then roll them up in a wrap. Turkey bacon, which is much lower in fat than pork bacon, cooks in just a few minutes in a skillet. Make it ahead of time so all you have to do is scatter it over the eggs.

Turn to this recipe for a quick lunch, too.

> **1 teaspoon olive oil**
>
> **2 eggs**
>
> **1 whole-wheat tortilla (about 8 inches) or 1 whole-wheat flat bread**
>
> **1 tablespoon salsa or ketchup (optional)**
>
> **2 strips turkey bacon, cooked and crumbled**

Heat the oil in a small skillet over medium heat. Beat the eggs in a small bowl and pour into the pan. Cook for 2 minutes without stirring. Using a spatula, gently lift up the edge in several places and tilt the pan to allow any uncooked egg on the top to run into the bottom of the pan. Cook for another minute and flip to the other side. Cook for 1 minute longer. Lay the tortilla out on a flat surface and slide the egg pancake on top of it. Spread with salsa, if using. Sprinkle with bacon and roll up.

- Scramble the eggs.

- Sprinkle 2 tablespoons shredded cheese on top of the eggs.

- Line the wrap with baby spinach leaves before adding the egg pancake.

Granola-to-Go   Serves 1

Invest in some sturdy, 12-ounce cups with lids and some plastic spoons. Making use of whatever fresh fruit you have on hand, build this layered, one-dish meal, cover it tightly, and hand it to your son as he rushes out the door.

> $1/2$ cup sliced strawberries, blueberries, or diced apple
>
> 1 cup yogurt, plain or any flavor
>
> $1/2$ cup granola
>
> 1 tablespoon flaxmeal

Put a layer of fruit in the bottom of a cup. Top with the yogurt. (Blend it first with a spoon if it has fruit on the bottom.) Top with the granola and flaxmeal and seal with the lid.

VARIATIONS:

- Add $1/4$ cup chopped walnuts, almonds, or pecans.

- Substitute cottage cheese for the yogurt.

- To make a hot breakfast, use just-cooked or microwave-heated oatmeal in place of the granola.

- Substitute whole-grain cereal for the granola.

Cinnamon Toast   Serves 1

Steer clear of toaster pastries with dozens of scary-sounding ingredients and give your kids the benefit of a breakfast that will sustain them longer than an overload of sugar. This toast contains just a hint of sweetness. Keep a shaker of sugar-cinnamon on hand so you can make it in seconds. Serve with a glass of milk and a bowl of strawberries.

> 2 slices whole-wheat bread
>
> 2 teaspoons butter, softened
>
> $1/2$ teaspoon Cinnamon Sugar (recipe follows)

Preheat the broiler. Lightly spread each piece of bread with butter. Sprinkle the cinnamon sugar on each piece. Broil for about 1 minute, just until the cinnamon sugar melts. (The bread will still be very soft, not toasted through.) Slice on the diagonal and serve the pieces arranged in a single row, slightly overlapping.

Cinnamon Sugar   Makes 4 teaspoons

1 tablespoon sugar

1 teaspoon ground cinnamon

Combine the sugar and cinnamon in a small dish and stir with a spoon until well blended. Store in an airtight container.

Cinnamon-Apple English Muffin   Serves 1

Help your son become accustomed to eating an English muffin rather than a bagel in the morning. (English muffins contain about 8 percent of the daily value for carbohydrates, while a 5-ounce bagel can contain 25 to 30 percent or more, and is the equivalent of eating thirteen slices of bread.) Keep a package or two in the freezer and find ways, such as this, to dress them up. Serve with a glass of milk.

1 whole-wheat English muffin

1 tablespoon cream cheese or ricotta cheese

1 small apple, thinly sliced

Cinnamon sugar (above)

Preheat the broiler. Using a fork, separate the English muffin into two halves. Broil for 1 minute, or until just barely toasted. Spread both halves lightly with cream cheese. Top each half with apple slices and sprinkle lightly with cinnamon sugar. Broil for about 1 minute longer, until the cinnamon sugar is lightly browned.

VARIATION: Substitute peanut butter for the cream cheese.

Poppy Seed–Buttermilk Pancakes

Makes 12 (3-inch) pancakes; serves 3 to 4

Buttermilk gives a tangy flavor to these nutritious pancakes, which also have a special crunch from the poppy seeds. Keep a container of powdered buttermilk in the pantry so you don't need a special trip to the store for this morning treat.

> 2 cups whole-wheat flour
>
> ^{1}/$_2$ teaspoon baking soda
>
> ^{1}/$_4$ teaspoon salt
>
> 1 tablespoon light brown sugar
>
> 1 tablespoon poppy seeds
>
> 1 egg
>
> 1 cup buttermilk
>
> 1 cup milk
>
> Maple syrup or yogurt, to serve

Heat a soapstone griddle or large frying pan over medium heat until a few drops of cold water sizzle and dance on the surface. (Heat an electric griddle to 375°F.) Lightly grease the cooking surface with a paper towel dipped in canola oil. Combine the flour, baking soda, salt, brown sugar, and poppy seeds in a mixing bowl and blend with a whisk. Add the egg, buttermilk, and milk and blend with the whisk just until smooth. Using a spoon that holds about 2 tablespoons, drop the batter onto the griddle and cook until bubbles form on the surface and the edges are firm, about 1 minute. Flip the pancakes and brown on the other side for about 30 seconds. Serve immediately with maple syrup or yogurt.

Oven Pancake
Serves 1

Teach your son to make this very easy popover-type pancake on a weekend or vacation day morning. It goes into the oven as a pool of batter and comes out golden and puffy, a thing of impressive beauty in which any cook can take pride. Serve it plain or lightly dusted with confectioners' sugar, with a bowl of berries or sliced fruit and a glass of milk.

> **2 eggs**
>
> **$1/2$ cup milk**
>
> **$1/2$ cup all-purpose flour**
>
> **2 tablespoons butter**

Preheat the oven to 400°F. Combine the eggs and milk in a bowl and whisk until smooth. Add the flour and whisk again to form a smooth batter. Put the butter in a 10-inch cast-iron frying pan or ovenproof baking dish and melt in the oven, taking care that it doesn't burn. (If your son is helping, stress the importance of using an oven mitt to handle the pan.) Tilt the pan to evenly coat the bottom with the butter. Pour the batter into the pan and bake for 20 minutes. Serve immediately.

French Toast Two Ways

If your son isn't wild about eggs, serve them to him in this economical favorite, a great way to make use of whole-wheat or whole-grain bread that's slightly past its prime. Keep bread and eggs on hand so you can make this any time. It is terrific comfort food—appealing to boys who are sick or needing a pick-me-up after a week of final exams. This protein-rich breakfast dish can be made two ways: on the stovetop or baked in the oven. The former is faster, the latter takes a bit more planning but means you don't have to stand watch at the stove. Serve with maple syrup, confectioners' sugar, fruit-sweetened jam, or sliced fresh fruit.

Whichever method you prefer, save time in the future by making a few more slices than you need. When cool, stack them with pieces of wax paper between the slices to prevent sticking, wrap in aluminum foil, and freeze. Unwrap and reheat in the toaster, or on a baking sheet in a 325°F oven for 10 minutes.

Stovetop French Toast   Serves 1 to 2

> 2 eggs
>
> 3 tablespoons low-fat milk or water
>
> 1 tablespoon butter or canola oil
>
> 2 slices firm whole-grain bread

Combine the eggs and milk in a shallow bowl large enough to accommodate the bread and beat with a fork or whisk until smooth. Melt the butter in a frying pan large enough to accommodate both pieces of bread over medium heat. Watching that the butter doesn't burn, put one piece of bread into the egg mixture and press it gently down so the bottom side is completely submerged in the liquid. Using tongs or a fork, immediately turn it over, submerge the other side, and then, letting any excess liquid drip back into the bowl, put it into the skillet. Repeat with the remaining slice. Cook for 3 minutes, or until the bottom is lightly browned. Turn and cook on the other side for 3 minutes longer, or until browned. Serve hot.

Oven-Baked French Toast
Serves 2 to 4

4 eggs

$1/2$ cup milk or water

4 slices whole-grain bread or $1/2$ French baguette, sliced

Combine the eggs and milk in a 7 by 11-inch baking dish and beat with a whisk until smooth. Place the bread on top of the egg mixture and let it sit for several minutes. Using tongs or a fork, turn the bread over. Let it sit for 10 minutes. (Or, cover the pan with plastic wrap and chill overnight.)

In the morning, preheat the oven to 350°F. Bake, uncovered, for 20 minutes or until the top is lightly browned and all of the liquid has solidified. Serve hot.

Classic Oatmeal
Serves 4 to 6

Oatmeal provides amazing ballast—enough energy, for example, to allow a boy to sit through 4 hours of SAT exams without thinking once about food. If it is a hard sell to kids who are used to crunchy cereals, combine it with granola or dress it up with fresh or dried fruit and nuts to provide some texture. Add a spoonful of brown sugar or maple syrup, if need be.

4 cups water

1 cup steel-cut oats

2 cups fresh or frozen blueberries

$1/2$ cup chopped pecans or walnuts

Yogurt or milk

Bring the water to a boil in a medium saucepan over medium-high heat. Stir in the oats, turn the heat down to medium-low, and simmer, stirring occasionally, until the oats have softened and formed a thick porridge, about 20 to 30 minutes. Spoon into bowls, add portions of the blueberries, pecans, and yogurt, stir gently, and serve.

TIMELY TIP: Don't try to cook oatmeal on a busy school morning. Instead, make it ahead when you have time to stir it and get the consistency just right. Then store it tightly covered in the refrigerator for up to 4 days. To serve, spoon frozen berries into the bottom of a cereal bowl, top with cold cooked oatmeal, microwave for 2 minutes, and spoon yogurt on top.

NUTRITIONAL NOTE: Packages of instant oatmeal from a supermarket are better than eating no breakfast at all, but many of them are high in sugar (as much as 15 grams) and laced with hydrogenated oil to give them a creamy texture. They also contain numerous additives and artificial flavorings. Read the labels and look for brands that are high in fiber (at least 4 grams) and low in sugar (no more than 8 grams). A better choice than instant oatmeal is rolled oats, sometimes called "old-fashioned" oats, which cook in about 15 minutes The best choice is steel-cut oats, which take as long as 30 minutes to cook, but contain 4 grams of fiber and 6 grams of protein per serving.

Morning Fruit

Fruit is a great source of fiber, vitamins, and natural compounds that help the body fight disease. Keep several kinds of fresh and frozen fruit on hand but don't go overboard and buy more than your family can eat before it spoils: Remember that 1 cup or one small fruit is enough for one serving (out of four fruit servings a boy needs each day). It isn't enough to have a bowl of fruit on the kitchen counter. Sleepy boys won't even see it. To help them learn to make fresh fruit part of their morning meal, prepare it for them, and it will disappear. Put a long-handled fondue fork on the table along with a serving of fruit; boys will enjoy the stabbing action and eat every bite. Serve just one kind of fruit, or combine several and top with yogurt. Add a sprinkling of wheat germ or flaxmeal for an added boost of fiber.

Apples. High in soluble fiber and pectin, which are linked to lowering cholesterol. A better choice than apple juice. Cut unpeeled into slices or leave whole for your son to tuck into his backpack on a day when he might otherwise miss breakfast.

Bananas. A good source of potassium and magnesium. Peel or cut into chunks, allowing about half a banana per serving.

Blackberries. Contain bioflavonoids, which may help prevent heart disease and cancer. Serve in combination with other fruits to minimize their seedy character, or add to smoothies where the seeds aren't an issue.

Blueberries. An excellent source of antioxidants and vitamin C. Wild blueberries are high in anthocyanin, a natural compound linked to reducing eyestrain and improving night vision. Serve fresh seasonal berries in a bowl. Or put about $1/2$ cup frozen berries in a bowl, microwave for 1 minute to thaw, and top with plain or vanilla yogurt.

Cantaloupe. Rich in vitamins A and C and beta carotene. Cut into chunks or slices, or scoop out the seeds and serve quarters with a spoon. Sprinkle lightly with lemon or lime juice to bring out the flavor.

Kiwifruit. Provides more vitamin C than an orange, along with vitamins E and A. Peel, slice, and serve on a plate with eggs or toast, or combine in a bowl with bananas and raspberries and top with yogurt or cottage cheese.

Mangoes. High in vitamins A and C, potassium, and beta carotene. Peel and slice into chunks.

Oranges. Great source of vitamin C and potassium. Favor oranges over juice for the benefits of added fiber. Cut into thin slices, and then cut each slice in half and arrange the semicircles in a row on a small plate.

Papaya. High in calcium, folic acid, vitamin C, and enzymes that aid digestion. Cut in half, scoop out the seeds, peel, and slice.

Pears. If unpeeled, a good source of vitamin C and fiber. Holding the pear upright, slice into four sections. Discard the core and stem.

Pineapple. High in manganese and digestive enzymes. Cut crosswise into round slices, slice off the rind, and cut into chunks or triangles, leaving the core behind.

Raspberries. Rich in vitamins A, C, and E. Since fresh raspberries tend to be pricey, combine with cantaloupe and blueberries to stretch a serving. Or buy frozen in bags and microwave for 30 seconds. Top with yogurt and a sprinkling of granola.

Strawberries. Prized for vitamins C and K and manganese, plus antioxidants linked to prevention of heart disease and cancer. Remove the hulls and slice in half or serve whole, with yogurt on the side for dipping.

Watermelon. A good source of water for hydration as well as the antioxidant lycopene, especially important to boys for its link to preventing prostate cancer. Cut into chunks or slices or puree in smoothies.

Two Dressings for Fresh Fruit

While fresh fruit tastes wonderful all by itself, adding a dressing and a handful of nuts can make it a special treat. Serve these two dressings with any mixture of fruits. Spoon them on individual servings just before eating. The dressing gets watery if fruit sits in it for more than 20 minutes. Both dressings will keep for 5 days in the refrigerator. Stir to blend before using.

Yogurt Dressing   Makes 1¼ cups

1 cup plain, strawberry, or raspberry yogurt

1 banana

Combine the yogurt and banana in a blender or food processor and blend until smooth.

Pineapple Dressing   Makes 1 cup

¹/₃ cup plain yogurt

1 cup chopped fresh pineapple

¹/₄ cup buttermilk

¹/₄ cup chopped dates (optional)

1 teaspoon orange juice concentrate

Combine all ingredients in a blender or food processor and blend for about 1 minute, until very smooth.

Any Day Muffins   Makes 12 muffins

Supermarkets and wholesale chain stores sell gigantic, softball-sized muffins packaged by the dozen in a range of flavors. Don't buy them. They're more like pieces of cake, loaded with unhealthy fat, sugar, and artificial ingredients, and they won't provide enough staying power to get a boy through his first class. Whenever you can find the time, make your own muffins. You can add all sorts of nutritious ingredients to the batter, and you'll know for sure what they contain.

2 cups all-purpose or whole-wheat flour

2 teaspoons baking powder

¹/₄ teaspoon salt

2 tablespoons canola oil or melted butter

1 egg

$1/3$ cup white or brown sugar, honey, or maple syrup

1 cup milk, fresh orange juice, or buttermilk

$1/2$ teaspoon baking soda (optional; add if using buttermilk)

**$1/2$ to 1 cup chopped nuts, chopped or grated apple, applesauce,
mashed very ripe banana, canned pumpkin, raisins, chopped
dried fruit, grated carrot, and/or grated zucchini (optional)**

Preheat the oven to 400°F. Grease a 12-cup muffin pan.

Combine the flour, baking powder, and salt in a mixing bowl and stir with a whisk until blended. Add the oil, egg, sugar, milk, and baking soda, if using, and blend with the whisk just until smooth. Add any optional ingredients and gently stir in with a spoon. Fill the muffin cups $2/3$ full with the batter.

Bake for 20 minutes or until the tops are lightly browned and a toothpick inserted in the center of one of the muffins comes out clean. Set the muffin pan on a rack to cool for 5 minutes before removing the muffins.

VARIATIONS:

• Substitute up to 1 cup old-fashioned rolled oats, cornmeal, oat bran, or crushed dry cereal for 1 cup of the flour.

• Substitute $1/2$ cup flaxmeal or toasted wheat germ for $1/2$ cup of the flour.

TIMELY TIPS: At night before you go to bed, measure the dry ingredients into a bowl, cover with a dinner plate, and leave out on the counter. In the morning, toss in the wet ingredients and the optional ingredients, mix, and bake. Serve the muffins hot. Cool leftovers and store in a tightly sealed in a plastic bag for up to 3 days. Split, spread with a thin layer of fruit-sweetened jam, and reheat for a few minutes under the broiler.

Zucchini-Cranberry Muffins
Makes 12 muffins

Zucchini is the secret ingredient in these tasty muffins, but since it gets absorbed into the batter, no one can tell. They're surprisingly good with a bit of peanut butter. Tightly covered, they'll keep for several days at room temperature.

1 cup whole-wheat flour

1 cup all-purpose flour

$2^1/2$ teaspoons baking powder

$^1/_2$ teaspoon salt

$^1/_2$ teaspoon ground cinnamon

$^1/_4$ cup canola oil

1 egg

$^1/_4$ cup firmly packed brown sugar

1 cup milk

1 medium zucchini, grated (about 1 cup)

$^1/_2$ cup dried cranberries, currants, or raisins

Preheat the oven to 400°F. Grease a 12-cup muffin pan.

Combine the flour, baking powder, salt, and cinnamon in a mixing bowl and stir with a whisk until the cinnamon is evenly distributed. Add the oil, egg, brown sugar, and milk, and blend with the whisk just until smooth. Stir in the zucchini and cranberries. Fill the muffin cups $^2/_3$ full with the batter.

Bake for 20 minutes, or until the tops are lightly browned and a toothpick inserted in the center of one of the muffins comes out clean. Set the muffin pan on a rack to cool for 5 minutes before removing the muffins.

VARIATION: Substitute grated carrot for the zucchini. This is a good way to use up what's left of an opened bag of peeled baby carrot.

Refrigerator Muffins

Makes 18 muffins (3 batches of 6 muffins)

An entire batch of this batter will make 18 muffins, more than most families need for one breakfast. Think of it as making three batches of 6 muffins each. It keeps in the refrigerator for up to two weeks. On a busy morning, having it waiting there, all ready to bake, is like holding an ace. Although muffins generally taste best hot from the oven, these actually develop more character as they cool, and they keep well for 3 days, tightly sealed in a plastic bag.

3 cups raisin bran or bran flakes cereal

2 cups buttermilk

$^1/_3$ cup canola oil

2 eggs, beaten

$^1/_4$ cup firmly packed light brown sugar

$^1/_4$ cup white sugar

2$^1/_2$ teaspoons baking soda

1 teaspoon salt

1 cup all-purpose flour

1¹/₂ cups whole-wheat flour

Combine all ingredients in a large plastic or glass container with a tight-fitting lid, and stir until evenly moistened. Let the batter sit overnight.

The next day, preheat the oven to 400°F. Grease a 6-cup muffin tin. Scoop some of the batter into the muffin cups, filling them about ²/₃ full. Refrigerate the remaining batter.

Bake for 15 to 20 minutes, until the muffins are lightly browned and firm on top.

Banana Bread Makes 1 loaf

With the added fiber from oats, one or two pieces of this not-too-sweet bread make a good breakfast treat, as well as an afternoon or bedtime snack. Bake it at night, let it cool completely, wrap it tightly in foil, and all you have to do is slice it in the morning. It will stay fresh for up to 5 days at room temperature. Spread it with peanut butter or fruit-sweetened jam.

1 cup whole-wheat flour

³/₄ cup all-purpose flour

1¹/₂ teaspoons baking powder

¹/₂ teaspoon baking soda

¹/₄ teaspoon salt

¹/₄ cup butter, at room temperature

¹/₂ cup firmly packed light or dark brown sugar

2 eggs

1 teaspoon vanilla extract

2 very ripe bananas

¹/₄ cup buttermilk

1 cup old-fashioned rolled oats

Preheat the oven to 350°F. Grease a 5 by 7-inch loaf pan.

Combine the flours, baking powder, baking soda, and salt in a medium bowl and stir with a whisk until blended. Set aside. Combine the butter and brown sugar in a mixing bowl and beat for about 1 minute. Add the eggs and vanilla and beat until smooth. Put the bananas on a plate and mash them with a fork. Scrape them into the batter, add the buttermilk, and beat until smooth. Add the oats and the flour mixture and beat just until moistened. Pour the batter into the prepared pan.

Bake for 40 to 45 minutes, or until the bread is just starting to pull away from the edges of the pan and the top is browned. Let it cool on a rack for 10 minutes. Run a knife around the edges of the pan, turn the bread out onto the rack, and let it cool for another 5 minutes before slicing.

Currant-Nut Bread   Serves 10 to 12

This recipe, adapted from Julia Child's *The Way to Cook*, is good for breakfast and makes a great after-school snack, spread with peanut butter. Unlike typical quick breads, it uses very little oil. Let the bread sit for 24 hours before tasting it; fresh from the oven it will seem a little too wet, but as it cools, it becomes firmer. Store it at room temperature, wrapped in foil. It will keep for a week.

1 cup currants

1^1/$_2$ cups whole-wheat flour

1 tablespoon baking powder

^{1}/$_2$ cup firmly packed light brown sugar

1 teaspoon ground cloves

1 teaspoon ground cinnamon

1 teaspoon unsweetened cocoa powder

^{1}/$_4$ teaspoon salt

^{1}/$_4$ cup canola oil

1 cup applesauce

1 cup chopped pecans or walnuts

Preheat the oven to 300°F. Grease a 5 by 7-inch loaf pan, line the bottom with wax paper, and lightly grease the wax paper.

Combine the currants, flour, baking powder, brown sugar, cloves, cinnamon, cocoa, and salt in a mixing bowl and toss with a fork until well blended. Add the canola oil and applesauce and stir gently until all the dry ingredients are moistened. Add the nuts and stir. The batter will be very thick. Spoon the batter into the prepared pan.

Bake for 1^1/$_2$ hours, or until the top is firm. Transfer to a rack and let cool for 15 minutes. Unmold the loaf and let it cool completely. Wrap tightly in aluminum foil and let sit for 24 hours. Cut into thin slices.

Overnight Apricot Bread Pudding   Serves 8

Tasty in the morning as well as for dessert, this old favorite takes on nutritional stature when made with a hearty whole-grain bread. Leave the crusts on and cut the bread into ^{1}/$_2$-inch cubes. The nuts add a nice texture.

- **8 cups whole-grain bread cubes**
- **^{1}/$_2$ cup chopped walnuts or pecans**
- **^{1}/$_2$ cup diced dried apricots**
- **3 cups milk**
- **2 eggs**
- **3 tablespoons maple syrup or light brown sugar**
- **2 teaspoons vanilla extract**

Arrange half of the bread cubes in a layer in a greased 8-inch square baking dish. Scatter the nuts and apricots on top and add the remaining bread cubes to form an even layer. Combine the milk, eggs, maple syrup, and vanilla in a medium bowl and blend with a whisk until smooth. Pour the milk mixture evenly over the bread cubes. Let stand for 10 minutes. Gently press down on the cubes with a spatula until the bread on top begins to absorb some of the liquid. Cover the pan with plastic wrap and refrigerate overnight.

Preheat the oven to 350°F.

Bake, uncovered, for 30 to 45 minutes, until the top of the pudding is toasted and a knife inserted in the center comes out clean. Let the pudding cool for 10 minutes before serving.

VARIATION: Substitute any other dried fruit such as currants, raisins, cranberries, blueberries, or pineapple for the apricots.

Egg and Potato Pie   Serves 8 to 10

Allow an hour to assemble and bake this one-dish meal, which is recommended for a morning when the sleepover has been at your house. It is also a great recipe for planning ahead: If you bake it at night, you can serve slices quickly reheated in the microwave for breakfast the next day. Put a slice between two pieces of whole-wheat bread for a hearty breakfast your son can eat on the way to school. Leftovers also make good after-school snacks. If you are only feeding a few people, cut the recipe in half and bake it in an 8-inch square pan. Serve with fresh fruit and hot chocolate.

1 pound frozen shredded potatoes

6 slices chopped cooked turkey bacon

1 cup shredded cheddar cheese or a mixture
    of cheddar and Monterey Jack cheese

6 eggs

1 cup milk

1 cup small-curd cottage cheese

Salt and freshly ground black pepper

$1/2$ cup freshly grated Parmesan cheese

Preheat the oven to 425°F. Lightly grease a 9 by 12-inch baking dish.

Put the frozen potatoes in the bottom of the baking dish, making an even layer. Bake for 20 minutes, or until the potatoes are soft and heated through. Remove the dish from the oven. Scatter the bacon on top of the potatoes. Scatter the cheddar cheese on top of the bacon. Combine the eggs, milk, cottage cheese, salt, and pepper in a medium mixing bowl and blend with a whisk until smooth. Pour the egg and cheese mixture into the pan in an even layer. Sprinkle the Parmesan cheese on top.

Bake for 30 minutes, or until the pie is firm to the touch and just starting to brown at the edges. Let cool for 5 minutes. Cut into squares and serve hot.

VARIATION: To use freshly peeled and grated potatoes, salt them lightly and place in a strainer over a bowl. Let sit for 20 minutes. Squeeze well to remove as much moisture as possible before proceeding with the recipe.

Country Granola   Makes 6 pounds or 24 ($1/2$-cup) servings

Making your own granola guarantees a fresh taste and a great price. This recipe, which costs less than $3 per pound, is a variation of the granola developed in the 1970s by David Hatch, whose parents Ira and Mildred started a natural foods store in the early 1950s in St. Johnsbury, Vermont. If you can't find all the ingredients, increase the quantity of the oats to make up the difference. Don't add the dried fruit until after the granola is baked, or it will stick and burn.

^{1}/$_2$ cup sesame seeds

1^1/$_4$ cups rye flakes

7 cups old-fashioned rolled oats (not instant)

^{1}/$_2$ cup soy nuts

2 cups shredded unsweetened coconut

1 cup unsalted sunflower seeds

1 cup slivered almonds

1 cup safflower or canola oil

1 cup honey

2 cups diced dried apples

1 cup raisins

1 cup dried cranberries or blueberries

Preheat the oven to 325°F. Grease two 11 by 14-inch baking pans.

Combine the sesame seeds, rye flakes, oats, soy nuts, coconut, sunflower seeds, and almonds in a large bowl and stir with a spoon until mixed. Combine the oil and honey in a medium bowl and blend with a whisk until smooth. Pour the oil and honey mixture over the dry ingredients and gently mix with a large spoon. Spread the mixture in the prepared baking pans. The mixture should be about 1 inch deep for even baking.

Position the pans on the lower and middle oven racks and bake, stirring approximately every 6 minutes, for about 30 minutes, until you can smell the almonds. About halfway through the baking time, switch the pan positions.

Remove the pans from the oven and let cool for about 5 minutes. Return the mixture in the pans to the large bowl, add the dried fruit, and mix gently with a large spoon. Let the mixture cool completely. Store what your family will eat in about 2 weeks in large glass jars with tight-fitting lids in the refrigerator. Pack the rest into heavy-duty plastic bags and freeze until needed.

A Sweet Indulgence

Streusel Coffee Cake   Makes two coffee cakes, each serving 6 to 8

For a special occasion or leisurely morning, make this delicious coffee cake. It smells wonderful as it bakes and will be a welcome surprise for a Sunday breakfast or brunch. The recipe was developed by Marjorie Johnson, a Minnesota baker who has won more than 2,000 ribbons at state fair competitions. She always uses sour cream for the recipe; but you can also use yogurt, which cuts down on the saturated fat. It makes two coffee cakes, one for your family and one to give as a present. Cut the recipe in half to make one.

BATTER

$3/4$ cup ($1^1/2$ sticks) butter, at room temperature

$1^1/2$ cups white sugar

1 teaspoon vanilla extract

4 eggs

3 cups all-purpose flour

$1^1/2$ teaspoons baking powder

$1^1/2$ teaspoons baking soda

$1/2$ teaspoon salt

$1^1/2$ cups sour cream or plain yogurt

STREUSEL

2 tablespoons melted butter

$1/2$ cup firmly packed light brown sugar

2 tablespoons all-purpose flour

$1/4$ cup shredded unsweetened coconut

$1/2$ cup sliced almonds or chopped nuts

GLAZE

$1/2$ cup confectioners' sugar

$1/4$ teaspoon almond or vanilla extract

1 to 3 teaspoons milk

Preheat the oven to 350°F. Grease and flour two 8 or 9-inch cake pans.

To make the batter, combine the butter, sugar, and vanilla in a mixing bowl and cream with an electric mixer at medium speed until smooth. Add the eggs, one at a time, beating well after each addition. Combine the flour, baking powder, baking soda, and salt in a mixing bowl and blend with a whisk until smooth. On low speed or by hand, beat the flour mixture into the creamed ingredients alternately with the sour cream, beginning and ending with the flour mixture, until the batter is evenly mixed. Spoon one-quarter of the batter into each pan and smooth it into an even layer.

To make the streusel, combine all the streusel ingredients in a small bowl and mix with a fork. Sprinkle one-quarter of the mixture over the top of each portion of batter in the pan. Spoon the remaining batter equally into the two pans and gently smooth it to cover the streusel. Sprinkle the top of each with an equal amount of the remaining streusel.

Bake for 30 to 35 minutes, until a toothpick inserted in the center comes out clean and the tops of the cakes feel firm to the touch. Remove the cakes from the oven and let them rest for 10 minutes. Remove from the pans and let cool on wire racks.

To make the glaze, combine the glaze ingredients in a small bowl and stir with a spoon until smooth. Drizzle over the tops of the cakes.

CHAPTER 4

Healthy Sandwiches and Mini-Meals for Any Hour

A growing boy easily can become hungry every three hours, which means he will be looking for food the minute he leaves school in the afternoon and again before he goes to bed, with dinner in between. These are two times of the day that present the greatest danger he'll gorge on junk—pizza, soft drinks, fries, and chips with friends on the way home, and ice cream, cake, and cookies at night.

Make your home a place where your son can count on finding nutritious foods that can provide immediate energy and satisfy hunger, and that he can assemble for himself. Keep the refrigerator stocked with the makings of sandwiches, and always have fresh fruit on hand. Encourage him to come home to eat rather than spend his money on fast food.

Break the habit of relying on packaged foods currently marketed as "snacks." Don't keep potato chips in the pantry. They're loaded with saturated fat and sodium, and as everyone knows, it's impossible to eat just a few once the bag is open. Snack bars, cookies, and candy are high in unhealthy fat and sugar, making them poor choices for filling up that hollow leg. Along with soft drinks, they can actually make a boy feel hungrier.

The Snack Factory

Remember how you once packed school lunches for your son? Muster some of those organizational skills and take a few minutes every day to oversee the makings for mini-meals arranged so a boy can easily find them. (Never underestimate how difficult it is for boys to see anything when they open the refrigerator door!)

If you don't use a bread box, put whole-wheat bread or sandwich rolls in a basket on the counter, along with whole-grain crackers, rice cakes, melba toasts, whole-wheat pretzels, or breadsticks. Buy a clear rectangular storage box (about 12 by 18 inches) with a tight-fitting lid; fill it with everything he needs to make his own snack, sandwich, or wrap; and store it in the refrigerator, so he can simply put the whole business on the counter, remove the lid, and get to work. Buy a few small containers as well for holding spreads and dips (see pages 96–99) and cut-up vegetables and fruit to go in the box, too.

Good choices for the snack factory include hummus; mayonnaise; mustard; unsweetened peanut butter; fruit-sweetened jam; lunch meats, such as turkey, turkey salami, and chicken; sliced or grated cheese; and a small bag of washed lettuce. Include a small container of carrots, celery sticks, raw sliced broccoli, or sliced cucumbers for nibbling, along with a small jar of dressing; olives; several apples or small containers of cut-up melon or pineapple chunks or grapes; and one or two cartons of yogurt. Tuck in a can of tuna (after teaching him how to open the can and drain it) and a small bag of nuts. Add containers of leftovers, too, so he sees them: a piece of quiche, a helping of chili, leftover pasta, a rice salad.

As a guideline, dietitians at the Mayo Clinic recommend foods with daily values close to 5 percent for healthy fat, sugar, or sodium and suggest avoiding those with 20 percent or more. They say that the best snacks are foods with at least 2 grams of dietary fiber per serving.

One of the keys to meeting a boy's increased demand for calories is teaching him to think not about a "snack" but about a balanced "mini-meal" that includes protein or a healthy fat to increase satiety. Good choices that provide fullness include a sliced apple with peanut butter for dipping, an English muffin with a slice of cheese, a peanut butter and jelly sandwich, or fresh veggies with hummus or a light salad dressing for dipping. Cold cereal with 1 percent milk also provides a good mini-meal. Choose whole-grain cereals that contain at least 4 grams of fiber per serving.

Sandwiches made with whole-grain bread can be a great source of healthy calories and are easy for boys to make for themselves. Turkey, chicken, tuna, and egg salad deliver a good mix of protein and carbs. Wraps, tacos, and crepes and the multitude of possible fillings can also provide a teenager with a fast, nutritious mini-meal.

Curried Chicken Sandwiches   Serves 6

Chicken and curry are meant for each other, and they make a great sandwich filling. Spread the bread with chutney for further adventure. Or serve a scoop of this tasty mixture on top of a plate of lettuce. Leftover chicken salad, tightly covered, will keep for up to 3 days in the refrigerator.

- 1 tablespoon plain yogurt
- 1 tablespoon sour cream or mayonnaise
- 1 teaspoon curry powder, or more to taste
- 2 stalks celery, finely chopped

1 medium apple, finely chopped

1/2 cup chopped pecans or walnuts

3 cups chopped cooked chicken

12 slices whole-grain bread

Dijon-style mustard

Baby spinach leaves

Combine the yogurt and sour cream in a small bowl. Add the curry powder and stir until smooth. Combine the celery, apple, pecans, and chicken in a medium bowl, add the yogurt-curry mixture, and toss gently until all the ingredients are well coated.

Spread two pieces of whole-grain bread with mustard, top each with a few spinach leaves, and fill with the curried chicken. Repeat to make a total of six sandwiches.

Hot Chicken Teriyaki Sandwiches   Serves 4

A sandwich doesn't have to be a spur-of-the-moment choice. And when it is made with something hot, it becomes a more serious meal. Using frozen chicken, which is easy to keep on hand, this one is ready in 30 minutes. Serve with red or green grapes and sliced cucumbers.

1/2 cup Orange-Teriyaki Marinade (recipe follows)

10 to 12 frozen chicken breast tenderloins

1 baguette

Mustard

Lettuce

Preheat the oven to 350°F. Pour the marinade into an 8 by 10-inch ovenproof baking dish. Arrange the chicken on top. Let sit for 5 minutes, turn the chicken over, and let it sit for 5 minutes longer.

Bake the chicken for 10 minutes. Turn and bake for 10 minutes longer.

Cut the bread into four pieces and cut each piece in half horizontally. Spread the bread with mustard and fill with chicken and lettuce.

VARIATION: For an even faster meal, use fresh chicken or turkey tenderloins and bake at 375°F for 15 minutes. Keep a bag of chicken breast tenderloins in the freezer. They're individually frozen, so it is easy to take out just the amount of chicken you need.

Orange-Teriyaki Marinade Makes ¹/₂ cup

3 tablespoons soy sauce

1 tablespoon olive oil

¹/₄ cup fresh orange juice

2 cloves garlic, minced

Combine all the ingredients in a shallow bowl and blend with a whisk until smooth.

TIMELY TIP: Buy bottled teriyaki sauce to cut down on preparation time. Compare the amounts of sodium in commercial sauces, and favor those with the lowest amount.

Hot Turkey Sandwich Serves 1

Cold cuts don't have to be served cold. Heating the turkey for this sandwich gives it a different character.

2 teaspoons olive oil

3 to 4 slices deli turkey, chopped

Mustard

2 slices whole-grain bread or ¹/₄ baguette, cut in half horizontally

Thinly sliced tomato or cucumber

Lettuce

Heat the olive oil in a small skillet over medium heat. Add the turkey and cook, stirring several times, for 2 minutes, to heat it through. Spread the mustard on two slices of bread, and add the turkey, tomato, and lettuce.

Turkey Quesadillas Serves 2

By heating the tortillas in the oven, you can make these quick sandwiches in minutes. Cut them into quarters to turn them into finger food. This is a great recipe to teach your son to make, especially since it allows for lots of creativity.

4 (8-inch) flour tortillas

¹/₂ cup mixed shredded cheddar and Monterey jack cheese mix

4 slices deli turkey

Preheat the oven to 400°F.

Arrange two tortillas on a baking sheet. Top each with half the cheese. Bake for 2 minutes, until the cheese is just starting to melt. Remove from the oven, put two slices of turkey on each tortilla, covering the cheese as much as possible, and put one of the remaining tortillas on top of each. Bake for 4 to 5 minutes, until the cheese is completely melted. Cut each quesadilla in half and serve immediately.

VARIATIONS:

• Put 2 to 3 tablespoons chopped tomatoes on top of the cheese before adding the turkey.

• For a spicier blend, add a chopped jalapeño.

• Substitute smoked salmon for the turkey.

Flank Steak Sandwiches   Serves 6

Flank steak is a very thin, flat, and relatively lean cut of beef that costs between $6 and $8 per pound and cooks quickly, making it a good choice for a week-night meal. Keep a piece or two in the freezer and let it thaw overnight, refrigerated, in the marinade. Leftovers keep for several days in the refrigerator and can be used for tacos or wraps, or chopped for Fried Rice (page 189). Skip the marinade if you don't have time.

> Juice of 1 lime
>
> 3 tablespoons soy sauce
>
> 1 flank steak, about 1^1/$_2$ pounds
>
> Mayonnaise
>
> 6 sandwich rolls or 12 slices whole-grain bread
>
> 2 ripe tomatoes, thinly sliced
>
> 2 cucumbers, peeled and thinly sliced
>
> Dijon-style mustard
>
> 1 head romaine lettuce, sliced into thin ribbons

Combine the lime juice and soy sauce in a shallow baking dish. Add the flank steak, turn, and marinate for at least 30 minutes. Preheat the broiler.

Remove the steak from the marinade, place it on a broiler pan, and broil it about 6 inches from the heat for 4 minutes. Turn and broil for 4 minutes longer. Transfer to a cutting board and let rest for 5 minutes. Slice thinly.

Spread the mayonnaise lightly inside the rolls. Line them with tomato and cucumber slices. Spread a thin layer of mustard on top. Add a layer of steak and a layer of lettuce.

TIMELY TIP: Buy several pieces of flank steak when you find it on sale, and keep them in the freezer.

Bean Burgers   Serves 8

You can find lots of different veggie burgers in the frozen foods section at your local supermarket, but making your own at home is economical and allows for adjusting the ingredients as you wish. This version uses both bread crumbs and rice. Make it ahead, allowing time to chill the mixture for at least four hours, and ideally overnight, before you shape the patties. Otherwise they will be very sticky. Serve plain or in buns.

> 2 tablespoons olive oil
>
> 1 onion, chopped
>
> 1 carrot, chopped
>
> 2 cloves garlic, or more to taste, chopped
>
> 1 egg
>
> 1 (15-ounce) can pinto beans, drained and rinsed,
>   or 2 cups cooked beans
>
> $1/2$ cup chopped walnuts
>
> 1 cup whole-grain bread crumbs
>
> 1 cup cooked brown rice

Heat 1 tablespoon of the oil in a large frying pan over medium heat. Add the onion and carrot and cook, stirring occasionally, for about 15 minutes, until the onion is very soft and just starting to brown. Add the garlic and cook for 2 minutes longer. Transfer the mixture to a food processor. Add the egg and blend until smooth. Add the beans and walnuts and blend well. Using a rubber spatula, scrape the mixture into a mixing bowl. Add the bread crumbs and rice and stir by hand until the mixture is smooth. Cover with plastic wrap and chill for 4 to 12 hours.

Remove the burger mixture from the refrigerator and form it into eight 4-inch patties. Heat the remaining 1 tablespoon of oil in the frying pan over medium-high heat. Cook the patties, in batches, for 6 to 8 minutes on each side, until they are browned. Serve hot.

Boys and Burgers

It is easy to think these two words are practically inseparable. But is a big, juicy hamburger the right kind of meal for a hungry teenager? As doctors and health professionals recommend that everyone cut back on the consumption of red meat to as little as once or twice a week, and watch portion sizes when they do eat meat, the oversized hamburger doesn't stand up as a smart choice.

Ground beef contains about 20 grams of protein in a 3-ounce serving, which is equivalent to the dimensions of a deck of cards. If you buy extra-lean beef and cook this size burger at home, you can control the portion and what else goes along with it. Add a multigrain bun, a green salad, some fruit, and a glass of milk, and you've got a good meal for a teenager now and then. But if he fills up at the typical fast-food burger chain restaurant, what he gets is a whole lot more than he needs: The biggest burger with cheese, large fries, and a large shake delivers more than 70 grams of fat, 27 grams of saturated fat, and more than 1,600 calories *in just one meal!* (One chain offers a burger that alone contains 1,400 calories. And a pub in Clearfield, Pennsylvania, is famous for its 6-pound burger, which comes with the promise of a prize to any customer who can eat it in under three hours.)

Help your son understand that as the amount of beef goes up, so do the calories and the amount of saturated fat. Find alternatives to beef hamburgers. (Boys love to eat things in buns.) Although more expensive than beef, quick-cooking buffalo meat provides about 13 grams of fat, 5 grams of saturated fat, and 22 grams of protein in a 3-ounce serving. Buy alternatives to beef such as salmon burgers and veggie burgers, available in a variety of flavors. Both can be cooked frozen. Look for buns made with whole-grain flours and topped with sesame seeds.

Oven Grilled Cheese   Serves 2

Cheese is high in saturated fat; 1 ounce, about the size of a slice that will cover a standard piece of bread, contains 4 to 6 grams of saturated fat. So don't load it on. Buy natural cheese in blocks and slice it thinly (a cheese slicer is a useful tool) or buy bags of shredded cheese blends that make it possible to use just a sprinkling. Avoid processed cheese and cheese food, which have taken a very long journey from the cow.

4 slices whole-grain bread

Mustard (optional)

4 to 8 thin slices cheddar or Swiss cheese

Preheat the broiler.

Arrange the bread on a baking sheet and spread lightly with mustard. Add enough cheese to cover the top of each piece of bread in a single layer.

Broil for about 2 minutes, until the cheese is melted and bubbly. Put the bread together to make two sandwiches and cut on the diagonal.

VARIATIONS:

- After assembling the sandwiches, lightly toast on both sides before cutting in half.

- After the cheese has melted, top two pieces of bread with very thin slices of fresh tomato and/or 2 or 3 fresh basil leaves.

Slow-Cooker Spicy Beef Brisket Sandwiches   Serves 8 to 10

Here's *the* lunch or dinner to make a day ahead when you're expecting a gang of hungry boys. They can be counted on to devour these sandwiches, which are very easy to make in a slow-cooker. As the fat melts away from the meat, the tough tissues soften, and the meat literally falls apart. While 4 pounds of brisket looks like enough for an army, it shrinks a lot during cooking. The meat and sauce will keep for 3 days in the refrigerator, making this another good recipe to have on hand, ready for reheating. Serve with cole slaw on the side, or layer it on top of the meat in the sandwiches.

BARBECUE SAUCE

4 cups water

2 cups ketchup

$1/2$ cup cider vinegar

$1/3$ cup Worcestershire sauce

$1/4$ cup light brown sugar

$1/4$ cup Dijon-style mustard

1 tablespoon crushed red pepper flakes

SANDWICHES

1 beef brisket, about 4 pounds

4 onions, sliced

8 to 10 whole-grain hamburger buns

To make the sauce, combine 3 cups of the water, the ketchup, vinegar, Worcestershire sauce, brown sugar, mustard, and red pepper flakes in a stainless steel saucepan and stir with a whisk to mix. Bring to a boil over medium-high heat, turn the heat down to low, and simmer, stirring occasionally, for 30 minutes, until the sauce begins to thicken slightly. Remove from the heat. (You should have 4 cups.) Pour 2 cups of sauce into a measuring cup and set aside.

Place the brisket on a cutting board. With a sharp knife, remove as much fat as possible and discard it. Slice the brisket into two pieces. Put half of the onions in the bottom of the slow-cooker. Add the two pieces of brisket, one on top of the other, and cover with the remaining onions. Add the remaining 1 cup water to the remaining barbecue sauce in the pan, stir until smooth, and pour over the meat and onions in the slow-cooker.

Cook for 8 hours on low or 4 hours on high, or until the meat is very easy to pull apart.

Transfer the meat to a cutting board, let cool, and cut or shred into thin pieces. Discard the liquid in the slow-cooker. Return the meat to the slow-cooker along with the reserved 2 cups of barbecue sauce. Heat on high for about 30 minutes, until hot. Spoon the meat into the buns and serve immediately.

VARIATIONS:

- If you don't have time for the brisket to reheat in the slow-cooker, combine the meat and the sauce in a large saucepan and reheat on the stovetop over medium-low heat, stirring occasionally and watching that it doesn't burn.

- Substitute a 4-pound pork roast for the brisket. When the meat is done, let it cool and then pull it apart with your fingers.

- If you don't have a slow-cooker, use a Dutch oven. Bake at 300°F for approximately 4 hours, checking every half hour to be sure there are at least 3 inches of liquid in the pan. Reheat the meat and sauce on the stovetop over low heat for about 30 minutes.

Slow-Cooker Sloppy Joes

Serves 8

Is there any boy who doesn't love these tasty, hot, drippy sandwiches? They're a good solution to supper on a night when the whole family wants to watch your son play in a baseball or basketball game, and you'll all come home hungry. This recipe sneaks in some vegetables, too, which soften into the mixture as it cooks. To cut down on how much meat your family eats, reduce the beef to $1/2$ pound and double the quantity of vegetables. Serve with cole slaw.

> 1 pound lean ground beef
>
> 1 tablespoon olive oil
>
> 1 onion, diced
>
> 2 stalks celery, diced
>
> 1 large red bell pepper, diced
>
> 2 tablespoons taco seasoning, or to taste
>
> 1 cup tomato sauce
>
> Salt and freshly ground black pepper
>
> 8 whole-wheat hamburger buns

Cook the ground beef in a large frying pan over medium-high heat for about 5 minutes, breaking it up with a spoon, until no pink is showing. Using a slotted spoon, transfer the meat from the frying pan to the slow-cooker. Pour off any fat in the pan. Add the olive oil to the pan and sauté the onion, celery, and bell pepper for 4 minutes, or until soft. Add the taco seasoning and cook, stirring, for 2 minutes. Transfer the mixture to the slow-cooker and add the tomato sauce. Cover and cook on low for 2 to 6 hours, until the vegetables are soft and the mixture is hot and thickened. Season with salt and pepper. Spoon the meat into the buns and serve.

VARIATIONS:

- To stretch this meal into as many as 16 servings, separate the buns and arrange the halves on a baking sheet. Top each half with a spoonful of the meat mixture and sprinkle with grated Parmesan or cheddar cheese. Broil about 8 inches from the heat for several minutes, until the cheese melts and the edges of the buns are toasted.

- Omit the beef and add one (15-ounce) can rinsed and drained pinto or black beans.

The All-Important Sandwich

Never apologize for serving a sandwich as a main meal. It's a very clever way to get a teenager to eat good food, since you can tuck all sorts of great things inside. And you'll soon discover, if you haven't already, that a hungry boy often unquestioningly devours what he can't see. He may also be adventuresome in creating his own sandwich layers. Encourage him heartily to make use of leftovers and to try his own combinations.

Teach your son that what's in a sandwich is more important than how large it is. Buy 3 or 4-inch whole-grain rolls or whole-wheat hot dog buns instead of 8-inch enriched-bread sub rolls. Use the best bread you can, ideally made from whole wheat or whole grain, which is slowly digested and will keep your son feeling full for several hours. Quickly digested, cheap supermarket white bread, pumped fill of air and loaded with chemical additives, provides half the calories, half the protein, and about one-quarter of the fiber of whole-grain breads, while delivering unhealthy hydrogenated oil and artificial ingredients. Read the labels. A good sandwich bread for growing boys won't contain "enriched flour"; it will have at least 4 grams of protein and 2 grams of fiber per slice. Search locally for artisan bakeries where good bread and sandwich rolls cost a bit more but are worth every bite.

If you can find time to make your own mayonnaise—a favorite in just about any sandwich—do so, and enjoy its wonderful, fresh taste. When shopping for bottled mayonnaise at the supermarket, pay close attention to the labels. Canola mayonnaise averages 1 gram of saturated fat per tablespoon. "Light" mayonnaise has half as much saturated fat as regular mayonnaise and "reduced fat" mayonnaise has only a trace, but these products use high-fructose corn syrup, preservatives, and artificial ingredients not found in regular mayonnaise. Use any mayonnaise sparingly, and experiment with hummus, bean dips, or other healthy spreads in its place. See suggestions for wraps on page 94.

Get into the habit of thinking about the possibilities for sandwiches when you go shopping, and buy ingredients such as avocados, sprouts, prewashed greens, hummus, fancy mustard, and pickles for building masterpieces that are low in unhealthy fat and high in fiber, protein, and other nutrients.

Stock the freezer with possibilities for sandwich fillings that can be cooked frozen: turkey meatballs, turkey and chicken breast tenderloins, fish fillets. Teach your son how to prepare them.

Grate and save scraps of cheese in a container in the freezer, and use about 1/4 cup for grilled cheese and open-faced sandwiches.

Don't use bagels or croissants for sandwiches. A bagel is very high in carbohydrates, and a croissant contains about 18 grams of saturated fat, compared to about 2 grams in 2 slices of whole-wheat bread.

Quick Chicken Tacos
Serves 4 to 6

On a busy night when everyone is starving, this quick, easy, and versatile recipe comes to the rescue. It contains many of the ingredients that are easy to sell to boys—chicken, ketchup, and rice—and it is a hold-in-your-hand meal, fun and relaxing. Look in Middle Eastern markets for pomegranate molasses, which has a haunting sweet-sour taste.

1 pound boneless, skinless chicken breasts

1 tablespoon olive oil

1 onion, chopped

2 cloves garlic, minced

1/2 cup ketchup

1 tablespoon soy sauce

1 tablespoon pomegranate molasses or light brown sugar

1 cup water

4 (8-inch) flour tortillas

1 cup shredded cheddar or Mexican blend cheese

1 cup cooked white or brown rice

Slice the chicken into 1/4-inch thick strips and cut each strip in half.

Heat the oil in a large frying pan over medium heat. Add the onion and garlic and sauté, stirring occasionally, for about 4 minutes, until the onion is soft. Add the ketchup, soy sauce, pomegranate molasses, and water and stir until smooth. Add the chicken, cover the pan, turn the heat down to medium-low, and cook for 10 minutes, or until the chicken is thoroughly cooked and shows no pink.

While the chicken is cooking, preheat the broiler.

Arrange the tortillas on a baking sheet and sprinkle each one with about $1/4$ cup of cheese. Broil about 8 inches from the heat for 1 to 2 minutes, just until the cheese is melted. Remove from the oven. Spoon some of the chicken into the center of each tortilla, sprinkle about $1/4$ cup of rice on top of the chicken, roll up, and serve immediately.

VARIATIONS:

• Substitute 1 pork tenderloin (about 1 pound) for the chicken.

• Add 1 cup frozen peas during the last 5 minutes of cooking time.

• For a vegetarian version, substitute 1 cup frozen corn kernels and 1 cup cooked black or kidney beans for the chicken and cook for 5 minutes in the sauce, or until heated through.

• If you don't have leftover rice on hand, make some bulgur, which only takes a few minutes (page 132).

Tuesday Night Pork Sandwiches   Serves 4

Here's an easy way to pull supper together, combining an economical cut of pork and nutritious green peppers, and using the broiler for quick cooking. Put your son in charge of the cooking, which only takes a few minutes and includes the fun of using a basting brush.

2 tablespoons olive oil

1 tablespoon balsamic vinegar

1 teaspoon anise seeds

1$1/2$ pounds pork sirloin cutlets or 6 pork chops

3 green bell peppers, seeded and sliced

1 large red onion, sliced

4 whole-grain rolls

Dijon-style mustard

1 cup shredded mozzarella cheese

Preheat the broiler.

Combine the oil, vinegar, and anise seeds in a small bowl and blend with a fork. Arrange the pork, peppers, and onion in a single layer on a baking sheet. Brush the pork with the oil and vinegar mixture. Broil about 8 inches from the heat for 4 minutes. Turn the pork over, brush the other side with the oil and vinegar mixture, and broil for 4 minutes longer, or until the pork is lightly browned and sizzling and the peppers and onion are soft and just starting to brown. Remove from the oven and cover with foil to keep warm.

Split the rolls, keeping them "hinged," and spread lightly with mustard. Top each half with a sprinkling of cheese. Arrange the rolls on a baking sheet and broil for about 2 minutes, just until the cheese melts and the rolls are warmed. Slice the pork and place strips in each sandwich, along with some peppers and onions. Serve hot.

Tuna Melts

Serves 2

With a can of tuna in the cupboard and grated cheese in the freezer, you can easily turn to this protein-rich old favorite for a quick lunch or dinner. If you don't have English muffins, use slices of whole-grain bread, or improvise with tortillas or pita bread. Serve with a green salad and a small bunch of grapes.

1 (6-ounce) can tuna, drained

2 tablespoons mayonnaise

2 whole-wheat English muffins, split

4 to 8 slices cheddar or Swiss cheese

Preheat the broiler.

Put the tuna in a small bowl and flake it with a fork. Add the mayonnaise and blend until smooth.

Broil the four muffin halves about 4 inches from the heat for 2 minutes, until the tops are lightly toasted. Spread the tuna on them and top with one or two slices of cheese, using just enough to cover the tuna in a single layer. Broil for 2 or 3 minutes, until the cheese melts and is just starting to bubble. Serve hot.

VARIATION: Dice 1 stalk celery and add to the tuna.

Spiedies

Broome County, New York, is the home of this sandwich treat, celebrated at Binghamton's annual Spiedie Cooking Contest. The name, pronounced "speedy," comes from the Italian word for kabobs, but many local cooks don't skewer the meat. Be sure to keep the pieces large enough so they don't fall through the grill grate. Put your teenager in charge of the grill. A plastic squeeze bottle with a pointed tip helps you easily squirt just a bit of dressing on the sandwiches. Use just a few cubes of meat per sandwich and save leftovers to enjoy cold the next day.

Chicken or Turkey Spiedies   Serves 4 to 6

- **2 pounds boneless, skinless chicken or turkey breast**
- **$1/4$ cup olive oil**
- **2 tablespoons white wine vinegar**
- **1 teaspoon Dijon-style mustard**
- **2 cloves garlic, minced**
- **$1/2$ teaspoon dried oregano**
- **$1/2$ teaspoon dried tarragon**
- **4 to 6 sandwich rolls**
- **Italian dressing**

Cut the chicken into 2-inch cubes. Combine the oil, vinegar, mustard, garlic, oregano, and tarragon in a glass or ceramic bowl and blend with a whisk. Add the chicken, toss to coat evenly with the mixture, cover, and marinate in the refrigerator for 24 to 48 hours.

Beef Spiedies   Serves 4 to 6

- **2 pounds beef tri-tip or chuck**
- **$1/4$ cup olive oil**
- **2 tablespoons red wine vinegar**
- **2 tablespoons Worcestershire sauce**
- **4 cloves garlic, minced**
- **$1/2$ teaspoon dried thyme**
- **4 to 6 sandwich rolls**
- **Italian dressing**

Cut the meat into 2-inch cubes. Combine the oil, vinegar, Worcestershire sauce, garlic, and thyme in a glass or ceramic bowl and blend with a whisk. Add the meat, toss to coat evenly with the mixture, cover, and marinate in the refrigerator for 24 to 48 hours.

Lamb Spiedies

Serves 4 to 6

2 pounds lamb

1/4 cup olive oil

2 tablespoons fresh lemon juice

1 tablespoon white balsamic vinegar

3 cloves garlic, minced

1 teaspoon dried mint

4 to 6 sandwich rolls

Italian dressing

Cut the lamb into 2-inch cubes. Combine the oil, lemon juice, vinegar, garlic, and mint in a glass or ceramic bowl and blend with a whisk. Add the meat, toss to coat evenly with the mixture, cover, and marinate in the refrigerator for 24 to 48 hours.

To cook the spiedies, rub the grill grate with olive oil. Make a medium fire in a charcoal grill or heat a gas grill to 350°F.

Using tongs, remove the meat from the marinade and place on the grill. Cook in batches, turning the meat every 3 or 4 minutes with tongs so all sides are cooked, for a total cooking time of about 10 minutes. (Cut into one now and then to sample it. Be careful not to overcook them or they'll be dry.) Fill a roll with cooked cubes, drizzle with Italian dressing, and serve hot.

Variations:

• Thread the spiedies onto six skewers and grill. When done, place the entire skewer inside the roll, fold the bread over the meat, press down, and pull out the skewer.

• Cook spiedies under the oven broiler about 6 inches from the heat, turning every 3 or 4 minutes for a total cooking time of 10 to 12 minutes.

• Serve the spiedies on a bed of lettuce instead of in rolls.

Wraps and Pockets

A great foundation for sandwich architecture, wraps make it possible to use relatively small pieces of food that would tumble out of a conventional two-piece-of-bread sandwich. They offer nutritional advantages, too, since they are lower in carbohydrates than many other breads, and you can pack them with high-protein foods. Look for them near the deli counter. They go by various names (flatbread, lavash, wrap bread) and come in a variety of flavors at supermarkets and food clubs. Compare the different labels to find breads that don't contain hydrogenated oils, but that are high in fiber and protein. (Look for brands that provide 12 to 14 grams of fiber and about 10 grams of protein in one 3-ounce piece.) Most packages will keep for at least a week, or can be frozen for up to a month. Let frozen bread sit at room temperature for about 30 minutes before using. You can also fill split pitas or tortillas with wrap fillings. Avoid packaged pocket sandwiches sold frozen at the supermarket; they're loaded with fats and artificial ingredients and taste nothing like what you can make at home.

To make a wrap, lay a piece of flatbread out on a cutting board or counter, the short edge parallel to the edge of the work surface. Spread mayonnaise or another sandwich spread evenly but very lightly over most of the surface. Arrange a layer of sliced meat and or/cheese over about two-thirds of the surface, leaving about 3 to 4 inches at the very top uncovered. Top the meat layer with shredded lettuce, cole slaw mix, fresh baby spinach or sprouts, and roasted or thinly sliced fresh vegetables. Roll up tightly. If the filling seems especially juicy, fold one long end in over the filling before rolling, burrito-style. Serve immediately, or wrap in aluminum foil and chill for up to 4 hours. Cut in half to serve as a sandwich, or cut the wrap into 1-inch pinwheels and arrange on a platter with fresh fruit.

Wrap Combos

Reach for the leftovers when making wraps, and experiment with what's on hand. Artichoke hearts, canned beans, pickles, various salad dressings, cooked vegetables, and leftover cooked whole grains make great fillings. To save preparation time, buy packages of chopped lettuce, cole slaw mix, or broccoli slaw.

1. Spread the bread with goat cheese. Add thinly sliced tomatoes, chopped olives, croutons, fresh spinach, and fresh basil. Drizzle with balsamic vinegar and olive oil.

2. Spread the bread with pesto. Add roasted mushrooms, peppers, and zucchini; Swiss cheese; and mesclun mix.

3. Spread the bread with hummus. Add crumbled feta cheese, kalamata olives, sliced cucumbers, and spinach.

4. Spread the bread with Black Bean Spread (page 97) or Guacamole (page 99). Add chopped tomatoes, cooked rice, cooked corn kernels, Monterey jack cheese, shredded lettuce, and a few spoonfuls of salsa.

5. Spread the bread with light mayonnaise. Add flaked, drained tuna, grated carrot, raisins, slivered almonds, thinly sliced apples, and shredded lettuce. Drizzle lightly with honey-mustard vinaigrette before rolling.

6. Spread the bread with mustard. Add sliced teriyaki chicken, avocado, crumbled turkey bacon, chopped tomatoes, and mesclun mix.

7. Spread with bread with whipped cream cheese (or use cottage cheese blended in a food processor). Add thinly sliced roast beef, sliced cucumbers, sliced red onion, and cole slaw.

8. Spread the bread with pesto. Add $1/2$ (7.5-ounce) can of drained, flaked salmon, a layer of Oven-Dried Tomatoes (page 99), and a layer of baby spinach or mesclun mix.

9. Spread the bread with cranberry relish. Add sliced turkey breast and cole slaw, and top with honey-mustard dressing.

10. Leave the bread plain. Combine chopped, cooked chicken with leftover rice and leftover cooked green beans or broccoli. Add a tablespoon of teriyaki sauce and toss to blend. Scatter on the bread and top with a layer of baby spinach.

Mixed Mayonnaise

Makes 2 cups

Regular mayonnaise can contain as much as 12 grams of fat and 1 gram of saturated fat per tablespoon. Try this special blend to cut back on the fat and add flavor; adapt as you wish.

1 cup mayonnaise

1 cup nonfat plain yogurt

1 to 2 tablespoons Dijon-style mustard

1 tablespoon chopped fresh basil, tarragon, or chives

Combine all the ingredients in a small bowl and stir until well mixed. Spoon into a jar. It will keep for 2 weeks in the refrigerator.

Pesto

Makes 1 1/2 cups

If you have even a postage stamp of ground in a sunny location, grow your own basil for this hauntingly wonderful sauce, which can be used on sandwiches in place of or mixed in with mayonnaise, to top vegetables, in dressings, and to transform cooked pasta. Buy a quantity of fresh basil whenever you can and make several batches of pesto—one for right now and several for the freezer. It will keep frozen, stored in tightly sealed plastic bags, for months.

4 cups fresh basil leaves

$^1/_4$ cup grated Parmesan cheese

$^1/_4$ cup pine nuts, chopped walnuts, or chopped pecans

3 to 4 cloves garlic, minced

$^1/_2$ cup olive oil

Salt and freshly ground black pepper

Put the basil in a food processor and add the cheese, nuts, and garlic. Turn the machine on and with the motor running, add the oil in the thin stream. Season to taste with salt and pepper. If necessary, scrape down the sides of the bowl and pulse once or twice until smooth.

Spinach Spread

Makes 2$^1/_2$ cups

Another alternative to mayonnaise, this makes a nutritious spread for sandwiches and wraps. Just $^1/_2$ cup of cottage cheese contains 13 grams of protein, and the spinach is rich in iron and calcium, so a mixture of the two delivers a lot more nutrition than mayonnaise. The addition of basil gives it a lovely pestolike flavor.

2 cups cottage cheese

1 cup chopped fresh spinach

1 cup chopped fresh basil

Combine all ingredients in a food processor and blend until smooth. Store tightly covered in the refrigerator, where it will keep for up to 1 week.

Black Bean Spread

Makes 3 cups

Here's an easy way to get protein-rich beans into a boy, even if he claims not to like them. Use in place of mayonnaise as a spread for sandwiches and wraps or serve as a dip with raw vegetables. Store tightly covered in the refrigerator, where it will keep for up to 1 week.

1 tablespoon olive oil

3 onions, sliced

2 cups cooked black beans or 1 (15-ounce) can, drained and rinsed

1 cup coarsely chopped walnuts

Heat the oil in a large frying pan over medium heat. Add the onions and cook for 10 minutes, stirring occasionally, until they are very soft but not brown. Transfer the onions to a food processor, along with the beans and walnuts. Blend for several minutes until smooth.

VARIATION: Substitute pinto beans, garbanzos, or lentils for the black beans.

Olive Spread
Makes 1 cup

Use a thin layer of this tangy spread instead of mayonnaise when making chicken, turkey, or ham sandwiches. Include sliced tomatoes and a bit of feta cheese. The spread will keep for a week, covered, in the refrigerator. Save a little money and buy olives with pits. To remove them, line up a row of olives on a cutting board and press down on each one with the flat blade of a chef's knife. Once the olive has split open, flick out the pit.

> $1^{1}/_{3}$ **cups pitted kalamata or green olives**
>
> **1 tablespoon drained capers**
>
> **1 teaspoon Dijon-style mustard**
>
> **1 clove garlic, minced**
>
> **1 to 2 teaspoons anchovy paste**
>
> $^{1}/_{4}$ **cup olive oil**
>
> **Salt and freshly ground black pepper**

Combine the olives, capers, mustard, garlic, and anchovy paste in a food processor. With the motor running, slowly add the olive oil and blend until smooth. Season with salt and pepper.

VARIATION: Stir a tablespoon or two of olive spread into 1 cup of softened cream cheese or Yogurt Cheese (page 108) and spread on crackers or melba toasts.

Smoked Salmon Spread
Makes 1 cup

With about 5 grams of protein per ounce, salmon makes a substantial snack and delivers great flavor. This spread is delicious on whole-wheat bread or crackers. Use as a sandwich filling, or thin with 2 or 3 more tablespoons of milk and serve as a dip with crackers or corn chips. Look for smoked salmon pieces sold in economical 4-ounce packages. You can also substitute a less expensive smoked fish, such as whiting.

2 ounces smoked salmon pieces

1 (8-ounce) package cream cheese

2 teaspoons Dijon-style mustard

2 tablespoons milk

Freshly ground black pepper

Combine all the ingredients in a food processor and blend until smooth.

Guacamole

Makes $^2/_3$ cup

Avocados are rich in magnesium, which helps build strong bones. Instead of serving this classic mixture as a dip, use it instead of mayonnaise when making sandwiches or wraps. Keep leftover guacamole tightly covered in the refrigerator. It will keep for 2 days.

1 ripe avocado

1 tablespoon fresh lemon juice

$^1/_4$ teaspoon salt

2 scallions, minced

4 cherry tomatoes, finely chopped

Cut the avocado in half, remove the pit, and scoop the flesh into a shallow bowl. Add the lemon juice, salt, scallions, and tomatoes and mash with a fork until well blended.

Oven-Dried Tomatoes

Makes 24 halves

This alternative to pricey sun-dried tomatoes yields a great sandwich ingredient, one that even boys who don't like tomatoes usually gobble up. Make them at any time of the year (and even overnight), since the slow-oven cooking method helps even the dullest, middle-of-winter supermarket plum tomatoes taste great. Use in sandwiches and salads, or simply pass them around the table on a tray garnished with a bit of lettuce.

12 plum tomatoes

$^1/_4$ cup olive oil

Coarse or kosher salt, for sprinkling

Preheat the oven to 200°F.

Cut the tomatoes in half lengthwise and arrange cut sides up in a shallow glass or stainless steel roasting pan. Brush the tomatoes with oil and sprinkle each with a pinch of salt.

Bake for 8 hours, or until the tomatoes are shriveled, quite dry, and flattened. Serve warm, or let cool and refrigerate for up to a week in a tightly sealed container.

Roasted Red Peppers   Makes 4 cups

Supermarkets sell roasted red peppers packed in oil, but the flavor doesn't come close to what you can make in your home oven. Any color of bell pepper will work. A mixture of green, red, yellow, orange, and purple is lovely to play with. Add them to sandwiches, wraps, and salads, or top with a slice of mozzarella cheese and serve them on whole-grain crackers or multiseeded flatbread as a snack.

6 bell peppers

2 tablespoons olive oil

Preheat the oven to 450°F. Lightly oil a large baking dish.

Stand the peppers upright on a cutting board and slice from top to bottom, creating four large, flat pieces from each pepper, and leaving the seeds behind. Toss the peppers with oil. Arrange in a single layer, skin side up, on the baking dish.

Bake for 20 to 30 minutes, until the skins are just starting to darken and the peppers are very soft. Remove from the oven and let cool for 10 minutes. Using a knife, strip the skins from the peppers. Serve warm, or let cool and refrigerate for up to a week in a tightly sealed container.

Roasted Vegetable Medley   Makes about 5 cups

When vegetables are cooked at high temperatures, they become sweeter as well as softer. Hot, cold, or at room temperature, they make great sandwich and salad ingredients. A wrap can accommodate as much as $1/2$ cup. Leftovers will keep for 3 days in the refrigerator.

2 medium red onions, thinly sliced

2 carrots, cut into 2-inch slices, or 10 to 12 baby carrots, cut in half lengthwise

1 fennel bulb, thinly sliced

3 tablespoons olive oil

1 medium zucchini, thinly sliced

$^1/_2$ pound mushrooms, cut lengthwise into thin slices

Preheat the oven to 450°F. Lightly oil an ovenproof baking dish.

Combine the onions, carrots, and fennel in the prepared baking dish, drizzle with oil, and toss gently to mix.

Bake for 15 minutes. Add the zucchini and mushrooms, toss, and bake for 10 minutes longer, or until all the vegetables are soft and just starting to darken around the edges. Serve warm, or let cool and refrigerate for up to three days in a tightly sealed container.

Marinated Tofu
Serves 4 to 8

Fuss around with tofu a little bit, and it can acquire terrific flavor and become a versatile sandwich ingredient. Made from soy, it is high in protein and a good substitute for meat and dairy. Store shelves are stocked with lots of possibilities for adding a little zip to tofu, including barbecue sauces, curry sauces, and marinades. Choose a sauce that doesn't contain high-fructose corn syrup or more than 400 mg of sodium per 2 tablespoons. Use one or two slices in a sandwich along with lettuce, sprouts, and roasted vegetables.

1 pound extra-firm tofu

$^1/_2$ cup barbecue sauce or Orange-Teriyaki Marinade (see page 81)

Cut the tofu in half lengthwise. Then cut each half lengthwise again, and repeat one more time to make eight slices, each about $^1/_4$ inch thick. Line a $7^1/_2$ by 11-inch baking dish with paper towels, arrange the tofu slices in a single layer on top of the towels, and cover with a second layer of towels. Press down gently on the slices to remove excess moisture and let them sit for 10 minutes. Press down again and remove the towels. Pour the sauce into the baking dish and turn the slices so they are well covered. Cover the dish and refrigerate for 1 hour or overnight.

Preheat the broiler.

Broil the tofu slices in the marinade about 8 inches from the heat for about 5 minutes per side, until they are lightly browned. Serve warm, or let cool and refrigerate for up to a week in a tightly sealed container.

Railroad Sandwiches

Makes 2 sandwiches

In *With Bold Knife and Fork,* M. F. K. Fisher refers to an unusual treat—one of her all-time family favorites—a sandwich that takes on special character when someone purposely sits on it. Introduce the idea to your teenage son, and he will most likely want to try it immediately. For the best results buy the best French bread you can find, the kind with the firm outer crust that cracks when weight is put on it. These sandwiches are ideal for long car rides and, of course, a journey by train.

1 baguette

2 tablespoons butter or mayonnaise

6 slices deli ham

Dijon-style mustard

Cut the bread in half and slice each half open, sandwich style. Using your fingers, gently scrape out some of the inner crumbs to hollow it out a bit, leaving the crust and a good layer of bread intact. Spread each sandwich half with butter, add half of the ham, and spread with mustard. Put the halves back together, wrap each sandwich tightly in foil, and then wrap each sandwich again in a clean towel. Ask two teenage boys to sit on them for 20 minutes or longer.

Spinach Crepes

Serves 6 to 8

Crepes are easy to make and wonderfully versatile, and boys who like pancakes will love them. Kids who aren't crazy about spinach will often devour these.

2 tablespoons butter

2 tablespoons all-purpose flour

1¹/₂ cups milk, warmed to about 110°F

¹/₂ cup grated cheddar or Swiss cheese

1 (10-ounce) package frozen spinach, thawed and squeezed dry

10 to 12 crepes (recipe follows)

Preheat the oven to 200°F.

Melt the butter over low heat in a heavy saucepan. Add the flour and cook, stirring constantly with a whisk, for about 2 minutes, until the mixture bubbles and turns golden. Add the milk, turn the heat up to medium, and cook, stirring constantly, for about 4 minutes, until the sauce thickens. Add the cheese and cook, stirring, for about 2 minutes longer, until the cheese melts. Add the spinach and cook for 3 minutes more.

Place a cooked crepe on a work surface and top with several tablespoons of the spinach sauce. Roll up, place on a platter, and keep warm in the oven. Repeat until all the spinach is used, and serve the crepes immediately.

VARIATION: Add a slice of deli ham to each crepe before adding the filling.

Crepes

Makes 10 to 12

Allow time to let the batter chill after you make it. Stack any cooled, leftover, unfilled crepes on a plate and refrigerate, tightly covered with plastic wrap. They'll keep for 4 days. To use leftover crepes, melt 1 teaspoon of butter in a small skillet and heat a crepe over medium heat for about 2 minutes. Sprinkle with Cinnamon Sugar (page 59) and serve hot, for breakfast.

- **1 cup water**
- **1 cup milk**
- **4 eggs**
- **1 cup all-purpose flour**
- **1 cup whole-wheat flour**
- **$1/4$ teaspoon salt**
- **$1/4$ cup butter, melted**

Combine all the ingredients in a blender and blend until smooth, stopping several times to scrape down any dry ingredients that stick to the sides of the blender jar. Pour the batter into a bowl, cover with plastic wrap, and chill overnight, or for at least two hours.

Preheat the oven to 200°F.

Heat a heavy 8-inch frying pan over medium-high heat and rub it with a paper towel dipped in olive oil. Put the bowl of batter near the stovetop. Using a $1/4$-cup measure, scoop out some batter, pour it into the middle of the hot pan, and immediately tilt the pan so the batter evenly coats the bottom. Set the pan over the heat and cook for about a minute. Shake the pan slightly to loosen the crepe, lift it with a spatula or your fingers, flip, and cook for about 30 seconds longer, until the underside is lightly browned. Put the crepe on a plate and move to the oven to keep warm. Repeat, stacking the crepes in the oven, until all the batter has been cooked. The crepes are now ready to be filled.

Spinach Noggins with Dipping Sauce

Here's a perfect way to get a boy to eat spinach. Baked into little cakes, it becomes finger food, and when served with a dip, a plate of these snacks disappears in seconds. And they're versatile, since you can make them ahead of time, freeze them in the pan, and then store them in a plastic bag, and bake frozen, as you want them, for a vegetable serving at suppertime. Show your son how to heat them up for himself in the toaster oven.

DIPPING SAUCE

1/2 cup sour cream or plain yogurt

1 teaspoon Dijon-style mustard

1 teaspoon apricot jam (or any other kind)

NOGGINS

2 (10-ounce) packages frozen chopped spinach, thawed

1 cup crumbled feta cheese

4 eggs

2 cups fine fresh whole-wheat bread crumbs

4 tablespoons (1/2 stick) butter, melted

Salt and freshly ground black pepper

To make the dipping sauce, combine the sour cream, mustard, and jam in a small bowl and blend with a whisk until smooth.

To make the noggins, squeeze the spinach with your hands to remove as much water as possible. Combine the spinach, cheese, eggs, and bread crumbs in a food processor and blend until smooth. With the motor running, add the butter in a thin stream and blend for 1 minute more, or until the mixture is very smooth. Season with salt and pepper.

Preheat the oven to 350°F.

Use a tablespoon to spoon the mixture into a 24-cup nonstick mini-muffin pan, or form them into 1-tablespoon-size patties and arrange on a lightly greased baking sheet.

Bake for 10 minutes, or until they are lightly browned and firm to the touch. Let cool for 5 minutes. Serve warm, with the dipping sauce.

TIMELY TIP: To keep a supply of these snacks in the freezer, fill the mini-muffin pan or arrange the patties on a baking sheet and freeze. When solid, unmold and store frozen in a plastic bag or a plastic container with a tight-fitting lid. Take out just a few, place on a baking sheet, and bake in a preheated 350°F oven for 15 to 20 minutes.

Deviled Eggs   Makes 12

Inexpensive and protein-rich, hard-cooked eggs are easy to keep on hand. Cookbook author Marie Simmons recommends this method of cooking the eggs gently in a hot-water bath. It keeps the yolks tender and prevents the unpleasant grayish-green fuzz on the yolk. Store deviled eggs tightly covered in the refrigerator for up to 3 days.

6 large or extra-large eggs

3 tablespoons mayonnaise

3 tablespoons plain yogurt

1 tablespoon Dijon-style mustard

Paprika for dusting (optional)

Place the eggs in a large saucepan and add room temperature (not cold) water to cover them by 1 inch. Bring the water just to a boil over medium-high heat, watching for the first few big bubbles to come to the surface. Remove the pan from the heat, cover, and let stand 11 minutes for large eggs, 15 minutes for extra large. Pour most of the water out of the pan, keeping the eggs in the bottom, and immediately fill the pan with cold water. Soak the eggs in cold water for 30 minutes, refreshing the cold water several times to get the eggs well chilled. (If you skip this step the shells may be impossible to remove from the whites.) Gently crack the shells all over with a spoon and peel the eggs.

Set the whole eggs on their sides on a cutting board and slice them lengthwise into halves. Carefully hold each half over a plate and use a pointed spoon or small knife to coax out the yolks. Add the mayonnaise, yogurt, and mustard to the yolks and mash all the ingredients together with a fork until blended. Using a pointed teaspoon, gently stuff the yolk mixture into the whites, mounding the filling. Dust with paprika. Serve at room temperature.

VARIATIONS:

• Chop leftover deviled eggs and use as a sandwich filling.

• Combine hard-cooked egg with 1 cup cottage cheese and blend in the food processor. Use as a spread for crackers or a filling for a pita pocket.

Hummus

Makes 1 1/2 cups

This high-protein Middle Eastern garbanzo (chickpea) dip is traditionally made with tahini, a sesame-seed paste, but if you don't have any, use unsweetened peanut butter. Set out a bowl of hummus, dressed up with a dash of paprika, for a gang to use as a dip with raw vegetables or chips. It will disappear quickly. Use in place of mayonnaise in sandwiches and wraps or to stuff celery.

1 (15-ounce) can garbanzos, rinsed and drained,
or 1 1/2 cups cooked garbanzos

1/3 cup tahini or unsweetened peanut butter

Juice of 1 lemon

2 tablespoons olive oil

2 cloves garlic, minced

Water (optional)

Combine the garbanzos, tahini, lemon juice, oil, and garlic in a food processor and blend until smooth. Spoon into a serving bowl, cover, and chill for at least 1 hour to let the flavors mix. If the dip seems a little thick, add a few tablespoons of water.

SHOPPING TIP: Look for hummus at the supermarket, where it is often available in different flavors, such as red pepper, herb, or olive.

Yogurt-Feta Dip

Makes 2 cups

Here's a healthy low-fat alternative to dips made with sour cream. Bulgarian feta, which is soft, creamy, and tangy, makes a very smooth dip. Look for it in Middle Eastern markets. You can use a drier feta, which will give the dip a slightly grainy but not unpleasant consistency. Serve it with corn chips or a veggie assortment: baby carrots, sliced cucumbers, sliced red peppers, cherry or grape tomatoes, celery sticks, and snow peas.

1 cup plain yogurt

1 cup feta cheese or cottage cheese

1 tablespoon chopped fresh chives, scallions, or basil (optional)

Combine the yogurt and feta in a food processor and blend until smooth. Stir in the chives, if using.

Quick Raw Veggie Snacks

Boys may not have the patience to prepare vegetable snacks for themselves, but they'll usually devour any they find in their paths that require nothing more than eating. Here are several good ways to serve vegetables for lunch or dinner. Add one or two to a plate containing a sandwich or a main dish.

Carrot swords. An antidote to baby carrot overload. Find the longest carrots you can. Peel and slice in two lengthwise.

Carrot tongues. Peel several medium carrots. Using a cheese slicer, cut them lengthwise into very thin slices.

Fennel chunks. Slice a fennel bulb into quarters and arrange on a plate with a favorite dip.

Fresh peas. Buy a big bag of garden fresh, unshelled peas. Set them out on the table in a bowl for grazing and provide a second bowl for the pods.

Pepper boats. Take two different colored bell peppers (red, green, yellow, orange, or purple), stand them up on a cutting board, and slice them into four pieces—the boats. Stuff with dip, a small slice of mozzarella, a bit of cottage cheese, or a dollop of pesto.

Stuffed celery. Cut stalks into 4-inch pieces and stuff with hummus, peanut butter, cream cheese, or a healthy dip.

Curry Dip
Makes 1 cup

The sharp bite of yogurt, the complexity of chutney, and the spiciness of curry powder come together to create a dip that goes well with corn chips or raw veggies. You need to plan ahead at least 4 hours to transform yogurt into "cheese," but the result is well worth the extra time since it produces a great low-fat alternative to sour cream.

> 1 cup Yogurt Cheese (page 108)
>
> $1/4$ cup mango chutney
>
> 2 teaspoons curry powder

Combine all the ingredients in a food processor and blend until smooth.

Yogurt Cheese

Line a strainer (or small colander) with cheesecloth or a coffee filter, cut to fit as necessary. Set the strainer over a bowl. Spoon 1 large (32-ounce) container of plain nonfat yogurt into the lined strainer. Let it sit on the counter for 4 hours or refrigerate overnight. Use the resulting "cheese" as a substitute for sour cream in your favorite dips and in baking. Tightly covered, it will keep for 1 week in the refrigerator.

Potato-Olive Dip

This tangy dip is a good way to use leftover mashed potatoes. The flavor will be at its best if you make this 1 day ahead, though it will keep for up to a week in the refrigerator. Spread it on crackers or bread to buy a little time before dinner, or serve it with raw vegetables or corn chips. If your family loves garlic, use 3 or 4 cloves.

2 cups fresh whole-wheat bread crumbs

2 cloves garlic, coarsely chopped

$1/2$ cup green salad olives, with pimentos

Juice of 1 lemon

$1/4$ cup pine nuts or chopped walnuts

$1/3$ cup olive oil

1 cup mashed potatoes

Water (optional)

Put the bread crumbs in a medium bowl, cover with cold water, and let sit for 5 minutes. Drain in a strainer. Press down on them with a large kitchen spoon to squeeze out most of the water.

Combine the wet crumbs and the garlic in a food processor and blend for 1 minute to form a thick paste. Add the olives, lemon juice, and pine nuts and blend for several seconds until smooth. With the motor running, slowly add the oil and blend for several seconds more. Transfer the mixture to a medium bowl and stir in the mashed potato. (The mixture will become unpleasantly gluey if you put the potato in the food processor.)

Refrigerate for several hours, ideally overnight, before serving. If the dip is too thick after chilling, thin it with several tablespoons of water.

Ken's Broccoli-Cheese Dip

Makes 2 cups

This tasty puree is an excellent way to get boys to eat broccoli. It is great on crackers, in sandwiches, as a dip with corn chips, or even tossed with hot pasta. Food writer Ken Haedrich, who developed the recipe, remembers his son, Sam, as a teenager, eating the whole batch at one sitting.

1 head broccoli

2 tablespoons olive oil

1 onion, chopped

1 clove garlic, minced

$^1/_2$ cup freshly grated Parmesan cheese

2 tablespoons cottage cheese, cream cheese, or mayonnaise

Juice of $^1/_2$ lemon

1 tablespoon chopped fresh basil, or 1 teaspoon dried

Salt and freshly ground black pepper

Cut the broccoli into florets and chop the stalks coarsely. You should have about 4 cups. Steam until tender, about 6 to 7 minutes, or cook in a large pan of boiling water for about 4 minutes, and drain well. Transfer to a plate and cool.

Heat the oil in a small frying pan over medium heat. Add the onion and sauté for about 6 minutes, until translucent. Stir in the garlic and sauté for 30 seconds. Remove from the heat.

Put the cooked broccoli, sautéed onion, Parmesan, cottage cheese, lemon juice, basil, and salt and pepper in a food processor. Process to a smooth but still slightly textured puree. Transfer to a bowl. Cover and refrigerate until serving.

Focaccia Pizza

Serves 4 to 6

Make this fast snack in less than 10 minutes, using a round flatbread as the base. Look for flavors such as caramelized onion, rosemary, and cheese. For a recipe and instructions on making your own pizza dough, see page 184.

1 (9-inch) focaccia

$^1/_2$ cup freshly grated Parmesan cheese

1 cup tomato sauce

$^1/_2$ cup shredded mozzarella, cheddar, or Monterey
   jack cheese

$^1/_4$ cup chopped fresh basil

Preheat the oven to 400°F.

Slice the focaccia in half through the center to create two "crusts." Place cut sides up on a baking sheet. Sprinkle each piece with $^1/_4$ cup of Parmesan cheese. Spread each with half of the tomato sauce and half of the mozzarella. Bake for 5 minutes, or until the mozzarella is bubbly. Sprinkle each pizza with half of the basil and serve hot.

VARIATIONS:

• Top the tomato sauce with some roasted vegetables (see page 100) before adding the cheese.

• Use six whole-wheat English muffins in place of the focaccia and toast them lightly before proceeding.

The Problem with Pizza

Your son will encounter plenty of pizza during his teenage years—at school lunches, after school, at parties, after sports events. He probably likes it, as do all his friends, and he may get into the habit of stopping to eat several slices on his way home from school. It is inexpensive, too, and you may have a few frozen pizzas tucked away to heat up for supper now and then. Unfortunately, several slices of pizza isn't a healthy mini-meal or lunch or dinner. The cheese and crust alone in three slices of a typical 12-inch cheese pizza provide more than 84 grams of carbohydrates—the same number your son would get from eating 21 teaspoons of sugar. Instead of buying a 12- or 14-inch pizza, look for smaller, 8-inch pizzas. Or, make them at home (see page 184) from scratch, so you can work some whole-wheat flour into the crust, control the portion size, and top it with vegetables and protein, such as chicken or a small amount of cheese, so it becomes a healthier meal.

Fried Ravioli Serves 4 to 6

Vegetarian cookbook author Jeanne Lemlin created this fabulous food as a quick dinner for her son, Daniel, who, she says, could probably eat them every day of the week. The outsides of the ravioli turn crunchy while the insides remain very soft. Since they cook quickly, and there are just a few simple steps required to get them ready, fried ravioli is a good candidate to teach boys to make for themselves as an after-school snack. The crumbs stick easily to fresh ravioli, which are made with a wide range of fillings. And you can buy a pound or two, take out and cook six pieces, and freeze the rest in six-piece batches, to help with portion control. Keep a package of cheese ravioli in the freezer, too, so you can make this snack any day. Let it thaw in the refrigerator; it is okay if the ravioli are slightly frozen when you start cooking them.

24 fresh or frozen, slightly thawed cheese raviolis

1 cup milk

2 cups fine dry bread crumbs

2 tablespoons olive oil, plus more as needed for frying

$1/2$ cup marinara sauce

Preheat the oven to 200°F.

Put the ravioli on a platter. Line a second platter with paper towels. Pour the milk into a small bowl. Put the bread crumbs into a second shallow bowl. Dip the ravioli into the milk, then into the bread crumbs, turning so both sides are coated with crumbs. Return them to the platter.

Heat the oil in a large frying pan over medium-high heat. Add a single layer of ravioli and fry for 2 to 3 minutes per side, until they are golden. Using tongs, transfer the cooked ravioli to the paper towel–lined platter and keep warm in the oven. Repeat until all the ravioli are fried, adding more olive oil as necessary. Pour the marinara sauce into a small serving bowl. Serve hot, with the marinara sauce on the side, for dipping.

PANTRY TIPS: You can find lots of different kinds of dry bread crumbs at the supermarket. Most come from breads that contain partially hydrogenated oils, sugar, and lots of artificial ingredients. Look for panko, dry crumbs made from Japanese bread. It makes a very nice, crispy coating.

To make your own bread crumbs, toast several slices oven for 10 minutes or until very crisp, and then grind in a

Booster Bars

These aren't cookies, but rather energy bars, designed to deliver ballast to a hungry boy after school or before sports. Adjust the recipe as you wish to include a variety of nuts, seeds, or dried fruit. (Allow a total of $3^1/2$ cups of dried fruit and nuts.) After cooling and cutting, wrap the bars individually in aluminum foil and store in the freezer, where they stay soft and can be eaten immediately. They travel well in backpacks and gym bags.

1 (12-ounce) package frozen cooked winter squash, thawed

$^1/_2$ cup honey

2 cups old-fashioned rolled oats

1 cup chopped, pitted prunes

1 cup shredded unsweetened coconut

1 cup powdered nonfat dry milk

1 cup toasted wheat germ

1 cup chocolate chips

$^1/_2$ cup chopped dried apples

$^1/_2$ cup raisins

$^1/_2$ cup unsalted sunflower seeds

$^1/_2$ cup chopped walnuts

$^1/_2$ cup chopped pecans

2 teaspoons ground cinnamon

1 teaspoon ground ginger

Preheat the oven to 350°F.

Combine the squash and honey in a mixing bowl and beat with an electric mixer on medium speed for 1 minute. Add the oats, prunes, coconut, powdered milk, wheat germ, chocolate chips, dried apples, raisins, sunflower seeds, walnuts, pecans, cinnamon, and ginger. Beat on low speed for 2 minutes or stir by hand to mix well. Spread into an ungreased 10 by 15-inch baking pan and smooth the top with a spatula.

Bake for 20 minutes, or until the edges are just starting to brown and the top feels firm. Cool in the pan for 15 minutes. Cut into 2 by 3-inch bars. Store tightly covered at room temperature for 1 week, or freeze for up to 6 months.

• Substitute 2 mashed bananas or 1 (15-ounce) can pumpkin for the squash.

• Add 1 cup unsweetened peanut butter along with the squash and honey.

• Omit the coconut and wheat germ and add 2 cups oat bran.

Seeded Flatbread

Making this delicious snack is a 2-day event, since the dough needs about 24 hours to rise, but there's nothing difficult about it. In fact, your son might have fun helping to roll out the dough. Serve with hummus, goat cheese, or a dip.

1 teaspoon active dry yeast

1¹/₄ cups water

3¹/₂ cups all-purpose flour

¹/₄ cup whole-wheat flour

¹/₄ cup rye flour

2 teaspoons table salt

1 tablespoon sesame seeds

1 tablespoon fennel seeds

1 tablespoon poppy seeds

3 tablespoons olive oil, plus more for brushing on the dough

¹/₄ cup white wine

Coarse salt

In a small bowl dissolve the yeast in ¹/₄ cup of the water. Add a few pinches of the flour. Combine the remaining all-purpose flour, whole-wheat flour, rye flour, table salt, sesame seeds, fennel seeds, and poppy seeds in a medium mixing bowl. Using a fork, stir in the remaining 1 cup water, oil, wine, and the dissolved yeast mixture. Turn the dough out on the counter and knead for 10 minutes. The dough will be very stiff. Place it in a lightly greased bowl, cover with plastic wrap, and let rise in the refrigerator overnight.

The next day, preheat the oven to 400°F. Oil a baking sheet.

Keeping the dough as cold as possible as you work with it, form it into a log about 12 inches long and cut it into 6 roughly equal pieces. Roll each piece out with a rolling pin to about ¹/₈-inch thickness. Lay two sheets of dough on the baking sheet, brush lightly with olive oil, and season with coarse salt.

Bake for 15 to 17 minutes, until nicely browned and crisp. Keep whole or break into pieces to serve.

VARIATIONS:

- Experiment with different kinds of seeds, including caraway and dill.
- Roll the dough through a pasta machine to get it very thin. It will bake into more of a cracker than a flatbread.

CHAPTER 5

Nourishing Soups, Salads, and Sides

In the rush to feed hungry kids, it is often easy to devote too much attention to the idea of a main course, and in the process overlook all the healthy foods that create nutritional balance when included as part of a meal or as a mini-meal. Take soup, for example. It is economical, comforting, and filling, and it requires a boy to sit at the table and focus on what he's eating, providing an opportune time for conversation. Serve it with a hearty bread and support dunking, a good way to win over the soup-suspicious. Try to make soup once or twice a week. If supper is running late, give your son a bowl of it to eat while you finish cooking. Soup is filling, and it is a way to manage portion sizes for the rest of the meal. Canned and packaged rice noodle soups are great time-savers. Check the labels to find those that are free of MSG and trans fats. Shop for organic soups, too, which a number of companies are introducing as healthy alternatives to products loaded with sodium and artificial ingredients.

Incorporating vegetables and grains into daily meals is another important component in good eating. If you build meals around them, you'll create more nutritious fare and find that you are following dietary recommendations to cut back on portions of meat, fish, and chicken.

Set aside a place to store grains in clear jars on the kitchen counter, so you see them, and get into the habit of cooking grains often. Use them to stuff peppers, as a bed for sautéed vegetables, or add them to soups, stews, curries, and salads. Keep canned beans in the cupboard and experiment with ways to use them with grains and other vegetables in side dishes and for main meals. The humble marriage of beans and rice is a complete meal, providing the body with everything it needs to build new protein.

Shop twice a week for lettuce, sprouts, baby spinach, peppers, grape or cherry tomatoes, cucumbers, and avocados, so you'll always have the makings of a good salad. Wash the greens and prepare the salad vegetables as the first step in making dinner, to ensure that it is always part of the meal, and you are not too rushed to bother when the main course is done. Buy fresh and frozen vegetables to avoid running out, and to instill in every family member the habit of eating them every day. Lightly cooked and tossed with a little olive oil and garlic, vegetables go with everything.

Leek and Potato Soup   Serves 6 to 8

Make this soup in the fall or winter, when leeks are easy to find. Wash them carefully by slicing lengthwise and swishing in warm water to remove all the grit that can hide in the layers. Like a lot of soups, this one always tastes best the second day. And it is a fine thing to have on hand as a pick-me-up after a football game or soccer match.

> **2 tablespoons olive oil**
>
> **4 leeks, trimmed and chopped**
>
> **1 stalk celery, finely chopped**
>
> **1 carrot, finely chopped**
>
> **2 potatoes, peeled and diced**
>
> **4 cups chicken stock or broth**
>
> **1 cup half-and-half or milk**
>
> **Salt and freshly ground black pepper**

Heat the oil in a large saucepan or stockpot over medium-low heat. Add the leeks, celery, and carrot and sauté for about 10 minutes, stirring occasionally, until soft. Add the potatoes and chicken stock, turn the heat up to high, and bring to a boil. Turn the heat down to medium-low, cover, and simmer for 20 minutes, or until the potatoes are very soft.

Puree in a food processor or in a food mill. Return to the pot. Add the half-and-half, stir, and cook over medium heat for 5 minutes, or until the soup is steaming. Season with salt and pepper and serve hot.

Zucchini Soup
Serves 6 to 8

The zucchini is well disguised in this fragrant and light soup, which is good hot or cold. Boys tend to love it, especially in the summer when they're hungry but open to lighter fare. Pour it into a thermos, bring it along on a summer picnic, and serve, with spoons, in paper cups. For the best flavor use very fresh, small and tender zucchini.

1 tablespoon olive oil

1 onion, chopped

2 cloves garlic, chopped

2 teaspoons curry powder

4 small zucchini, chopped (about 4 cups)

1 apple, diced

4 cups chicken stock or broth

Salt and freshly ground black pepper

1 cup plain yogurt, to serve

Heat the oil in a large saucepan or stockpot over medium heat. Add the onion and sauté, stirring occasionally, for 5 minutes, or until the onion is soft. Add the garlic and cook for 1 minute. Sprinkle the curry powder on top of the onion and garlic and sauté, stirring constantly, for 1 minute. Add the zucchini and apple, sauté for 2 minutes, and add the chicken stock. Turn the heat up to high and bring the mixture almost to a boil. Turn the heat down to medium and simmer, partially covered, for 15 minutes.

Using a slotted spoon, transfer the zucchini, apple, and onions to a food processor, leaving the stock in the saucepan. Puree and return the mixture to the saucepan. Stir until smooth. Season with salt and pepper. Reheat to serve hot, or pour the soup into a bowl and chill for 2 hours to serve cold. Spoon a dollop of yogurt on top of each serving.

Corn Chowder Serves 4

When it is in season, fresh whole corn can be used to make this quick soup. (You can also use cooked corn-on-the-cob.) With a sharp knife, cut from the tip of the ear down to the stem, removing just the kernels and leaving behind the tough cob. Depending on their size, four or five ears will give you approximately 2 cups of kernels. Bump this soup up to a hearty and nutritious main-course meal by adding 2 cups of chopped cooked chicken along with the half-and-half.

> **1 tablespoon olive oil**
>
> **1 onion, diced**
>
> **1 red bell pepper, diced**
>
> **2 cups peeled chopped potatoes**
>
> **2 cups chicken stock or broth**
>
> **2 cups fresh or frozen corn kernels**
>
> **$1/2$ cup half-and-half or milk**
>
> **2 tablespoons chopped fresh basil**
>
> **Salt and freshly ground black pepper**

Heat the oil in a large saucepan or stockpot over medium heat. Add the onion and pepper and sauté until soft, about 5 minutes. Add the potatoes and chicken stock, turn the heat up to high, and bring just to a boil. Turn the heat down to medium and cook, partially covered, for about 10 minutes, until the potatoes are tender but not mushy. Add the corn and cook for 5 minutes. Turn the heat down to medium-low, stir in the half-and-half and basil, season with salt and pepper, and heat for 5 minutes longer. Serve hot.

Red Clam Chowder Serves 6

Cookbook author Marie Simmons recommends this recipe from her first generation Italian-American mother as a great way to fill up hungry boys. Thickened with barley, it makes a hearty soup and gives the kitchen a lovely fragrance as it cooks. The frozen vegetables turn it into a nutritionally complete meal.

CLAMS

3 pounds littleneck, Manila, or cherrystone clams,
rinsed and scrubbed clean

3 cups water

1 leafy celery top

1 clove garlic, bruised with the side of a knife

1 bay leaf

1 teaspoon salt

CHOWDER BASE

2 strips thick-sliced bacon, diced

1 onion, chopped

1 rib celery, trimmed and chopped

1 carrot, trimmed and chopped

1 clove garlic, minced

1 bay leaf

$1/2$ teaspoon dried oregano

$1/3$ cup pearl barley

1 (28-ounce) can Italian plum tomatoes, with juice

1 cup diced peeled potatoes

1 (10-ounce) package frozen mixed vegetables (optional)

Salt and freshly ground black pepper

To prepare the clams, put them in a large, broad saucepan. Add the water, celery top, garlic, bay leaf, and salt. Cover and bring to a boil over high heat. Turn the heat down to medium-low and simmer until all the clams are opened, about 8 minutes. Remove the pan from the heat. Remove the opened clams with a slotted spoon. If any clams remain unopened, cover the saucepan and simmer 2 to 3 minutes more. Discard any clams that refuse to open. Set aside to cool.

Set a strainer over a deep bowl. Line the strainer with cheesecloth or a paper towel dampened with water. Strain the clam broth. Discard the solids and reserve the broth. Rinse and dry the saucepan.

To prepare the chowder, combine the bacon, onion, celery, carrot, garlic, bay leaf, and oregano in the saucepan. Cook, stirring over low heat, until the bacon begins to give up fat. Then cover and sweat the vegetables until very soft but not browned, about 10 minutes. Add the clam broth and barley. Bring to a boil, cover, turn the heat down to medium-low, and cook until the barley is tender, about 30 minutes.

Meanwhile, empty the can of tomatoes and juice into a bowl. With kitchen shears, snip the tomatoes into $1/2$-inch pieces. Set aside. Pull the clams from their shells and snip into $1/2$-inch pieces. When the barley is tender, add the tomatoes, potatoes, clams, and frozen vegetables, if using. Bring to a boil, turn the heat down, and simmer, uncovered, until the potatoes are soft and the flavors are blended, about 15 minutes. Season with salt and pepper. Serve hot.

VARIATION: Substitute $1/2$ cup bulgur for the barley.

Croutons   Makes about 3 cups; serves 4 to 6

Serve these tasty bits of bread for dunking into any kind of soup. They're an easy way to make use of bread that would otherwise get stale. Shop for a salt-free seasoning blend to add healthy flavor.

4 slices whole-grain bread, any kind

2 tablespoons olive oil

Seasoning blend

Preheat the oven to 350°F.

Brush the bread with olive oil and sprinkle it with the seasoning blend. Cut the bread into 1-inch cubes and spread them out on a baking sheet.

Bake for 10 minutes, or until crispy, turning once or twice with a spatula. Serve in a bowl along with soup.

Ten-Minute Seafood Soup   Serves 4 to 6

Look for packages of frozen seafood blends containing shrimp, scallops, calamari, and other fish to use in this tasty and versatile soup with no unhealthy fat lurking in the bowl. If you keep a bag or two in the freezer and stock your pantry with clam juice and tomatoes, you can put this together anytime. And it offers an economical way to expose your son to seafood. Serve it with crackers or rolls and a green salad.

1 tablespoon olive oil

1 onion, finely chopped

1 clove garlic, minced

2 (8-ounce) bottles clam juice

1 (14.5-ounce) can diced tomatoes, drained

3 sprigs fresh thyme, or 1 teaspoon dried

Juice of $1/2$ lemon

1 pound frozen seafood mixture

Heat the oil in a large saucepan over medium heat. Add the onion and garlic and sauté for 5 minutes, until the onion is soft. Add the clam juice, tomatoes, thyme, and lemon juice. Increase the heat to high and bring the soup almost to a boil. Add the seafood, turn the heat down to medium-low, and simmer for 10 minutes, until the shrimp turn pink and the seafood is cooked. Serve hot.

VARIATIONS:

• Increase the olive oil to 2 tablespoons. Chop 1 carrot and 2 stalks celery and sauté along with the onions and garlic.

• Add up to 2 cups cooked rice or pasta to make a stew.

Hearty Vegetable Soup
Serves 12 to 14

Make this soup on a chilly or rainy day when you have reason to spend a few hours indoors and can keep an eye on it. It makes a big batch, perfect for a casual party or to share with a neighbor. The vegetables melt together as they cook, so boys who say they don't like cabbage won't know it is in there. And the beans deliver plenty of protein. Put the Parmesan cheese in a shaker and pass it at the table. Serve with whole-grain bread.

2 tablespoons olive oil

1 onion, finely chopped

2 stalks celery, finely chopped

2 cloves garlic, minced

1 small zucchini, diced

1 potato, peeled and chopped

4 cups cole slaw mix or chopped cabbage

1 (14.5-ounce) can diced tomatoes with juice

8 cups chicken or beef stock or broth, or a mixture of chicken and beef

1 (10-ounce) package frozen chopped spinach

1 (14-ounce) can cannellini or kidney beans, drained and rinsed

Salt and freshly ground black pepper

Freshly grated Parmesan cheese or crumbled feta cheese

Heat the oil in a large stockpot over medium heat. Add the onion, celery, and garlic and sauté for 5 minutes, or until they are soft. Add the zucchini and sauté for 2 minutes more. Add the potato and cole slaw mix, stir, and cook for 5 minutes, or until the cabbage is wilted. Add the tomatoes, stock, and spinach and bring the soup to a boil. Turn the heat down to low, cover, and simmer for 2 hours.

Add the beans and cook for 20 minutes longer. Season with salt and pepper. Serve garnished with Parmesan or feta cheese.

Carrot-Apple Salad Serves 4

Boys can usually be counted on to like carrots and apples, and this colorful salad tends to be one of their favorites. Use several different kinds of firm apples for a range of flavors. It is a great accompaniment to chicken and pork and goes nicely with omelets and scrambled eggs. Think of it as a replacement for potatoes or bread in a meal that already contains a source of carbs.

2 cups cider

4 apples, peeled and sliced

$1/4$ cup raisins

1 carrot, shredded

Bring the cider to a boil in a medium saucepan. Add the apple slices, turn the heat down to medium, and cook for 1 minute, until the apples are just barely soft. Add the raisins and carrot, remove from the heat, and let sit for 2 minutes.

Place a strainer over a medium saucepan and drain the apple mixture for several minutes. Transfer the apple mixture to a bowl.

Bring the drained juices to a boil over high heat and boil for 3 to 4 minutes, until reduced to about $1/4$ cup. Pour the thickened juice over the apples, stir gently, and cool completely.

VARIATIONS:

- Use dried sweetened cranberries in place of the raisins.
- Add $1/4$ cup chopped walnuts along with the raisins.

Spicy Carrot Salad
Serves 6 to 8

Health professionals urge us to eat plenty of yellow-orange vegetables, which help cells repair themselves and inhibit cancer-producing substances. This salad, adapted from *Toronto Star* writer Jim White's recipe, is a great way to put carrots in their own starring role. It always disappears at potlucks and on buffet tables. Make it in the morning to serve for supper.

> **8 carrots, sliced diagonally**
>
> **2 tablespoons olive oil**
>
> **1 tablespoon fresh lemon juice**
>
> **$1/2$ teaspoon ground cinnamon**
>
> **$1/4$ teaspoon ground ginger**
>
> **$1/4$ teaspoon salt**
>
> **1 teaspoon light brown sugar**
>
> **$1/2$ cup slivered almonds or chopped pecans**
>
> **1 tablespoon chopped fresh parsley or cilantro**

Cook the carrots in boiling water for 6 to 8 minutes, or until crisp-tender. Drain and set the carrots aside in a bowl.

Combine the oil and lemon juice in a bowl and blend with a whisk. Add the cinnamon, ginger, salt, and brown sugar, and blend until smooth. Pour the mixture over the carrots and toss to evenly coat. Refrigerate, covered, for at least 2 hours. Garnish with the almonds and parsley before serving.

Corn and Barley Salad
Serves 4 to 6

This crunchy salad, loaded with flavor and fiber, keeps for up to a week in the refrigerator. It is a good example of how easy it is to combine grains and vegetables into an appealing side dish. Serve it with grilled meats and chicken, or tuck it into wraps and burritos in place of beans.

> **1 cup pearl barley**
>
> **1 cup fresh or frozen, thawed corn kernels**

1 red bell pepper, diced

3 tablespoons olive oil

2 teaspoons balsamic vinegar

1 teaspoon Dijon-style mustard

1 tablespoon chopped fresh basil

Salt and freshly ground black pepper

Bring 3 cups of water to a rolling boil in a medium saucepan. Stir in the barley, turn the heat down to low, cover, and cook for 30 minutes, or until the barley is tender but not mushy. Drain well.

Transfer the barley to a bowl. Add the corn and bell pepper.

In a jar with a tight-fitting lid, combine the oil, vinegar, mustard, and basil and shake until well blended. Pour over the salad. Season with salt and pepper. Let it sit for 1 hour at room temperature or refrigerate overnight and bring to room temperature before serving.

Nutty Napa Salad   Serves 6 to 8

With its delightfully crunchy texture, this salad will quickly disappear when teenagers are around. It is a winner with kids who don't like cabbage and is an easy way to bring a new vegetable taste to your table. It will keep for several days, tightly covered, in the refrigerator, and has been known to make a fine contribution to a sandwich or wrap.

SALAD

1 medium head napa cabbage, sliced into thin shreds

$1/2$ cup chopped pecans

$1/2$ cup slivered almonds

$1/2$ cup unsalted roasted sunflower seeds

DRESSING

$1/3$ cup canola or walnut oil

2 teaspoons soy sauce

2 tablespoons sugar

3 tablespoons cider vinegar

To make the salad, combine the cabbage in a bowl with the pecans, almonds, and sunflower seeds.

To make the dressing, combine the oil, soy sauce, sugar, and vinegar in a small bowl and whisk until smooth, or combine them in a jar with a tight-fitting lid and shake well.

Pour the dressing on the salad, toss, and serve.

Barley-Edamame Pilaf Serves 4 to 6

Soybeans that are harvested when the seeds, or beans, are immature, edamame are high in protein ($^2/_3$ cup contains 10 grams), the type that can lower the "bad" LDL cholesterol. The beans are a beautiful bright green color that perks up the barley in this flavorful, crunchy salad. Allow about 15 minutes to cook, cool, and shell the beans. Serve with roast chicken, broiled salmon, or scrambled eggs.

1 (1-pound) package frozen edamame in pods

1 tablespoon olive oil

2 stalks celery, finely chopped

1 cup pearl barley

3 cups chicken stock, broth, or water

$^1/_2$ cup dried cherries

$^1/_2$ cup chopped walnuts

Salt and freshly ground black pepper

Bring about 4 cups of water to a boil in a saucepan, add the edamame pods, and boil for 4 minutes. Drain in a colander and let sit until cool enough to handle. Remove the seeds by pressing gently on the pods. (You will have about $1^1/_2$ cups.) Set aside.

Heat the oil in a medium saucepan over medium heat. Add the celery and sauté for 6 minutes, or until the celery is very soft. Add the barley and stock, turn the heat to high, and bring just to a boil. Turn the heat down to low, cover, and simmer for about 30 minutes, until the barley is tender but still firm to the bite. Add the cherries, cover, and simmer for 10 minutes longer. Remove from the heat.

Stir in the edamame and walnuts. Season with salt and pepper. Serve warm or cold.

Greens Are the Way to Go

Salads present a great opportunity to get nutritious foods into your son. If eating greens hasn't become a habit for him, start with the dressing and set up a salad experiment. Be open-minded. Buy several different kinds of low-fat, light, or reduced-fat dressings (ideally containing no more than 200 milligrams of sodium or 3 grams of saturated fat per 2 tablespoons). Pour about 2 tablespoons of each into several small shallow bowls or custard cups or a muffin pan. Arrange pieces of crunchy iceberg or romaine lettuce on a plate along with a few carrot and celery sticks and ask your son to dip in and pick his favorite dressing. Make it fun by providing him with a glass of water to clear his palate between bites. Use the occasion to explain the importance of eating salad and tell him that you want him to try a small salad with dinner every night. Make his salad in a separate bowl, using crunchy "white" iceberg lettuce and top it with a tablespoon of *his* dressing. Get him accustomed as well to using a small amount of *his* dressing as a dip for after-school mini-meals containing carrot and celery sticks, raw broccoli, grape tomatoes, and cucumber slices.

Over time, add bits of fresh spinach and other more interesting dark green and red lettuces to his salad bowl. Chances are he will eat anything in the bowl within a month or two if you say no more about it. (Go slowly with onions, which seem to be an acquired taste for many teenage boys. They may prefer them roasted rather than raw.)

Make salad a regular part of every dinner, but vary what goes into it. Think about making it colorful, which will assure a balance of nutrients. To a crisp mix of red and green lettuces, add chopped carrots one day, shredded another. Alternate between red, green, yellow, and orange bell pepper slices, or include two colors for a bright splash. Include chopped or sliced celery, cucumber, avocado, sprouts, olives, hard-cooked eggs, crumbled feta cheese, and fresh herbs. Toss in leftover roasted vegetables, cooked broccoli or green beans, cooked potatoes, rice, or barley. Add whole or chopped unsalted nuts such as walnuts, pecans, almonds, or sunflower seeds, or chop several kinds and sprinkle on top. And turn the salad into a complete meal by adding protein such as tofu, canned beans, shrimp, salmon, or slices of chicken or meat.

Rice and Pepper Salad

Serves 6 to 8

This colorful and light salad is a good way to introduce boys to the world beyond white rice. Serve it with anything. It even works as a topping for a dinner salad (see page 188). Look for blends of brown and wild rice in the supermarket.

4 cups water

1 cup brown and wild rice blend

1 cup white rice

2 scallions, green and white parts, trimmed and chopped

1 red bell pepper, finely chopped

1 orange bell pepper, finely chopped

2 stalks celery, finely chopped

$^1/_2$ cup chopped pecans

$^3/_4$ cup fresh orange juice

1 teaspoon orange oil or canola oil

Salt and freshly ground pepper

Bring 2 cups of the water to a boil in a medium saucepan over high heat. Add the rice blend, turn the heat down to low, cover, and simmer according to the package directions, or for about 40 minutes, until all the water is absorbed. At the same time, bring the remaining 2 cups of water to a boil over high heat in another medium saucepan. Add the white rice, turn the heat down to low, cover, and simmer for 20 minutes, or until all the water is absorbed.

Combine the two types of rice in a large bowl. Add the scallions, bell peppers, celery, and pecans and toss gently. Combine the orange juice and orange oil in a small bowl, stir with a fork, and pour over the salad. Season with salt and pepper and toss again. Serve warm or at room temperature.

VARIATIONS:

• Add $^1/_2$ cup dried cranberries or raisins.

• Add 1 (10-ounce) can mandarin orange segments, drained.

• Turn the salad into a dinner by draining 1 (6-ounce) can tuna or 1 (7.5-ounce) can salmon, adding to the salad along with 2 cups (1 package frozen) cooked, chopped green beans and 1 cup crumbled feta cheese.

• Add a spoonful of leftover salad to a plateful of lettuce or mesclun mix and top with feta cheese, olives, and bottled raspberry vinaigrette dressing.

Four Great Salad Dressings

It's easy to make your own dressings. The flavors will be bright and fresh, you'll know for sure what's in them, and you'll save some money as well. Creating your own blends provides another opportunity to wean boys from sugar, a basic ingredient in many bottled dressings. And if you balance the rest of the meal, you can indulge in using a bit of half-and-half to get a smooth, creamy texture. Whatever dressing you choose, use it sparingly. Just 1 or 2 tablespoons can go a long way. For any of the following, use a whisk to blend the ingredients in a bowl or combine everything in a jar with a tight-fitting lid and shake well. All of these dressings will keep for several weeks, tightly covered, in the refrigerator.

Buttermilk-Herb Ranch Dressing
Makes $3/4$ cup

    $1/4$ cup chopped fresh parsley or basil

    $1/3$ cup half-and-half

    $1/3$ cup buttermilk

    1 tablespoon plain yogurt

    Salt and freshly ground black pepper

Combine all the ingredients and blend or mix well.

Honey-Orange-Mustard Dressing
Makes $1/3$ cup

    2 tablespoons fresh orange juice

    2 tablespoons honey

    1 tablespoon Dijon-style mustard

    1 tablespoon balsamic vinegar

    1 tablespoon canola oil

Combine all the ingredients and blend or mix well.

Lemon-Ginger Dressing
Makes $1/2$ cup

    3 tablespoons soy sauce

    Juice of 1 lemon

    1 (2-inch) piece fresh ginger, peeled and grated (2 teaspoons)

    3 tablespoons olive oil

2 tablespoons canola oil

Salt and freshly ground black pepper

Combine all the ingredients and blend or mix well.

Lemon-Thyme Vinaigrette   Makes ³/₄ cup

2 cloves garlic, minced

1 tablespoon chopped fresh thyme

1 tablespoon chopped fresh parsley

Juice of 1 lemon

¹/₂ cup olive oil

¹/₃ cup freshly grated Parmesan cheese

Salt and freshly ground black pepper

Combine all the ingredients and blend or mix well.

Shopping Tip: There are hundreds of bottled dressings to choose from today. Read the label before you buy. The *Nutrition Action Healthletter* recommends dressings that contain no more than 80 calories, 3 grams of saturated fat, and 200 milligrams of sodium per 2 tablespoons.

Spinach-Orzo Salad

Serves 6 to 8

Orzo is a pasta that looks like tiny footballs. The rainbow mix produces a colorful salad that goes with just about anything. It keeps for 3 days, tightly covered in the refrigerator, and improves in flavor as it sits. Add a spoonful to a plate containing a sandwich or serve it as a healthy alternative to fries.

> **2 cups rainbow orzo**
>
> **4 cups chopped fresh spinach**
>
> **$1/2$ cup sliced kalamata olives**
>
> **$1/2$ cup crumbled feta cheese**
>
> **2 ripe tomatoes, chopped**
>
> **$1/2$ cup Lemon-Thyme Vinaigrette (page 129)
> or a dressing of your choice**

Bring 6 cups of water to a boil in a large saucepan, stir in the orzo, and cook for 6 to 8 minutes, until the orzo is soft but still firm to the bite. While the orzo is cooking, combine the spinach, olives, cheese, and tomatoes in a bowl. When the orzo is cooked, drain it quickly and pour on top of the salad ingredients in the bowl. Let sit for 2 minutes to slightly wilt the spinach and soften the cheese. Pour on the dressing and toss the salad. Serve warm, at room temperature, or cold.

Soba-Vegetable Salad with One-Tablespoon Dressing

Serves 4 to 6

Soba noodles are a type of Japanese buckwheat pasta that keeps its texture when used in cold salads. Unlike wheat pasta, which should never be rinsed after it is cooked, hot soba benefits from a quick rinse in a colander once it has reached the right consistency, to keep it from sticking together. Use any leftover raw vegetables in this accommodating salad and serve it in place of mashed potatoes or bread. Stored in the refrigerator, leftovers make a great after-school mini-meal.

> ONE-TABLESPOON DRESSING
>
> **1 tablespoon peanut oil**
>
> **1 tablespoon canola oil**
>
> **1 tablespoon rice wine vinegar**
>
> **1 tablespoon soy sauce**

SALAD

7 to 8 ounces soba noodles

2 stalks celery, sliced into matchsticks

1 orange bell pepper, seeded and thinly sliced

1 cup frozen petite peas, thawed

To make the dressing, combine the oils, vinegar, and soy sauce in a small bowl and whisk until smooth. Or, combine the ingredients in a jar with a tight-fitting lid and shake well. Set it aside.

Bring a large pot of water to a boil. Add the noodles and cook until tender but still firm to the bite, 6 to 8 minutes. Drain the noodles in a colander, rinse quickly under cold water, shake gently to drain well, and transfer the noodles to a serving bowl.

Add the celery, bell pepper, and peas. Pour on the dressing and toss to mix. Serve warm, at room temperature, or cold.

Bulgur Salad
Serves 4 to 6

Use up whatever leftover fresh vegetables you have on hand to add more flavors to this very quick, high-fiber salad. It makes a great side dish to take to a cookout, or to have on hand on a hot summer day. Serve it in custard cups along with sandwiches in place of chips. Make it with your son's favorite dressing to interest him in giving it a try.

1¹/₂ cups water

1 cup coarse bulgur

2 cloves garlic, minced

1 carrot, diced

1 cucumber, peeled and diced

6 to 8 snap peas, chopped

¹/₄ cup salad dressing

Bring the water to a boil in a medium saucepan. Add the bulgur, cover the pan, and remove from the heat. Let sit for 15 minutes, or until all the water has been absorbed.

Transfer the bulgur to a medium bowl, add the garlic, carrot, cucumber, snap peas, and salad dressing, and toss to mix. Cover and chill for 1 hour before serving.

Guide to Quick and Easy Grains

Wander through a natural foods store, and you'll encounter bags and bins of all kinds of grains. Here are five choices that are the easiest to incorporate into quick meals. They're excellent sources of fiber and, since they are slowly digested, a serving of as little as $1/2$ cup keeps a boy feeling full longer than an equal amount of quickly digested carbohydrate, such as white bread. They are inexpensive and easy to store, too.

Get into the habit of cooking one or two of these grains every week in preparation for upcoming meals. A good time to do this is in the evening, after dinner, as you are feeding the dog and tidying up the kitchen. All keep well for at least 3 days, tightly covered in the refrigerator.

Barley. Pearl or pot barley (rather than instant) is the type you want, since it is only lightly milled and thus contains all of the germ and most of the bran.

To cook: Bring 3 cups of water to a boil in a medium saucepan. Add 1 cup of barley, turn the heat down to medium-low, cover, and simmer for 30 minutes, or until the barley is soft to the bite but not mushy. Drain off any extra water. Makes 3 cups.

Bulgur. Cracked wheat that has been partially cooked and dried, bulgur is available in several grinds. Look for coarse, which has a lot of character. The backbone for tabouli salads, bulgur can also stand in for rice in baked desserts.

To cook: Bring $1^1/2$ cups of water to a boil in a medium saucepan. Add 1 cup of bulgur, cover the pan, remove from the heat, and let sit for 15 minutes, or until all the liquid is absorbed. Makes 4 cups.

Couscous. Buy the quick-cooking kind, which means the wheat berries have been ground, steamed, and dried into tiny round pellets. It is available as whole wheat, too.

To cook: Bring $1^1/2$ cups of water to a boil in a saucepan. Add 1 cup couscous, cover the pan, and simmer for 5 minutes. Remove from the heat and let sit for 5 minutes longer. Makes 3 cups.

Quinoa. Not really a grain, quinoa is actually a seed, but it behaves like a grain when cooked and can be used in all the same ways. Quinoa is high in protein, calcium, and iron and is a source of all eight essential amino acids. The most common type sold in America is a pale whitish-yellow; some stores also carry red and black quinoa. Be sure to rinse it well to remove the bitter seed coating before cooking. And put on your glasses if need be to take a good look at the beauty of cooked quinoa; the outer germ spirals out around each kernel, giving the cooked seeds a lovely lacy effect. Pair it with beans, or use in place of couscous or rice.

To cook: Bring 2 cups of water to a boil in a medium saucepan. Put 1 cup of quinoa in a strainer or sieve and rinse several times. Add it to the boiling water, turn the heat down to low, cover, and simmer for 20 minutes, or until all the water is absorbed. Makes 4 cups.

Rice. There are many varieties of rice. One cup of any kind provides about 4 grams of protein and 160 to 180 calories. Brown rice contains intact bran and germ layers along with nutritionally important fiber, vitamins, and minerals, making it the best choice in terms of nutrition. Long-grain white or brown rice and white or brown basmati rice cook up with separate grains and are the best choices for salads. Short-grain brown rice tends to be stickier.

To cook: For long-grain, combine 1 cup rice and 2 cups water in a saucepan with a tight-fitting lid. Bring to a boil, stir, turn the heat down to low, cover, and simmer for 15 to 20 minutes for white rice or 30 to 45 minutes for brown rice, or until all the liquid has been absorbed. (To cut down on the cooking time for brown rice, soak it for at least 2 hours or as long as overnight in water to cover, then drain and proceed with the previous instructions, cooking it for about 15 minutes.) Makes 3 cups.

Quinoa-Vegetable Casserole

Serves 4 to 6

Quinoa is a seed that is very nutritious, providing 11 grams of protein and 5 grams of fiber per half-cup. Its nutty flavor makes it a good substitute for pasta and potatoes, which add more carbohydrates to a meal. Here it is combined with cooked vegetables to reheat quickly in the oven. Add any other bits of leftover fresh or cooked vegetables to the filling, and season it as you wish with finely chopped fresh herbs; add about 1 tablespoon just before you put the vegetables in the bottom crust. Serve it with a big spoon.

> 2^1/$_2$ cups cooked quinoa (page 133)
>
> 3 tablespoons freshly grated Parmesan or Romano cheese
>
> 2 tablespoons olive oil
>
> 2 cups (10 ounces) chopped fresh mushrooms
>
> 4 scallions, chopped
>
> 1 small red bell pepper, diced
>
> 2 cups chopped fresh spinach or 1 (10-ounce) package frozen chopped spinach, thawed and squeezed dry
>
> 1 (14.5-ounce) can diced tomatoes, with juice

Preheat the oven to 350°F.

Put 1 cup of quinoa and 1 tablespoon of cheese into a 9-inch pie pan and mix gently with a fork. Spread the mixture into an even layer. Set aside.

Heat the oil in a large frying pan over medium heat. Add the mushrooms, scallions, and bell pepper, and sauté, stirring occasionally, for 5 minutes, until the vegetables are soft. Stir in the spinach and cook for 3 minutes longer, until the spinach wilts. Stir in the tomatoes and cook for 5 minutes, until the mixture is heated through.

Spoon the vegetable mixture into the pie shell (it should be very juicy). Spoon the remaining 1^1/$_2$ cups of quinoa on top of the vegetables, forming an even top layer. Sprinkle the top with the remaining 2 tablespoons of cheese.

Bake for 20 minutes, or until the top is browned. Serve hot.

Grits with Spinach

Serves 6 to 8

Grits, the big-grained cousin to cornmeal, are popular throughout the South as a cheap and long-keeping pantry staple. They provide carbs without added fat or sugar; 1 cup of cooked grits contains 130 calories, 29 grams of carbs, and 3 grams of protein. Supermarkets generally sell three types: instant, quick-cooking, and regular. Any of them will work for this recipe, but the cooking times will vary, so check the package directions.

> **1 (10-ounce) package frozen chopped spinach, thawed**
>
> **3¹/₂ cups water**
>
> **1 cup quick-cooking grits**
>
> **2 eggs**
>
> **¹/₃ cup milk**
>
> **1 cup shredded cheddar cheese**
>
> **Salt and freshly ground black pepper**

Preheat the oven to 350°F.

Squeeze the spinach to remove as much water as possible and set aside.

Bring the water to a boil in a medium saucepan and add the grits. Turn the heat down to medium-low and simmer for 8 to 10 minutes, stirring frequently, until the grits are very thick. Remove the pan from the heat and stir in the spinach. Set aside. Combine the eggs and milk in a 1-quart greased ovenproof casserole and beat with a whisk until smooth. Add the grits and spinach mixture to the casserole along with the cheese and stir until smooth. Season with salt and pepper.

Bake for 50 to 60 minutes, until the top is browned and the grits are firm. Serve hot or warm.

Cogswell Pudding   Serves 6 to 8

The ultimate comfort food, this simple, savory side dish goes with everything, from chili to roast chicken. It is a great choice for a cold night when everyone wants to feel warmer. And cooled slightly, it is the perfect food to serve a boy who is just starting to eat again after having his wisdom teeth out. Reheat leftovers in the microwave.

> **4 cups milk**
>
> **²/₃ cup farina (creamed wheat)**
>
> **2 tablespoons butter**
>
> **2 eggs**
>
> **5 tablespoons freshly grated Parmesan cheese**

Preheat the oven to 425°F.

Scald the milk in the top of a double boiler over simmering water. Gradually add the farina and cook, stirring frequently, for 6 minutes, or until the mixture begins to thicken. Add the butter and stir. Beat the eggs and stir into the pudding, along with 1 tablespoon of the cheese. Pour the mixture into a 7 by 11-inch greased baking dish. Sprinkle the remaining 4 tablespoons Parmesan cheese over the top.

Bake for 10 to 15 minutes, until the top is browned and the pudding is set. Serve hot or warm with a spoon.

VARIATION: For a firmer, brown top, put the pudding under the broiler for a few minutes after it has set.

Zucchini Couscous   Serves 4

Shredded zucchini, which you can make in seconds with a box grater or a food processor, cooks quickly and releases moisture that adds flavor to this quick recipe. It is a good way to introduce your family to grains beyond rice. Turn it into a main dish by adding 1 cup of chopped cooked chicken or shrimp.

1 tablespoon olive oil

1 onion, diced

1 to 2 teaspoons curry powder

1 medium zucchini, shredded

2 cups cooked couscous (see page 132)

2 tablespoons freshly grated Parmesan cheese

Freshly ground black pepper

Heat the oil in a large frying pan over medium heat. Add the onion and sauté for 5 minutes, or until the onion is soft but not brown. Stir in the curry powder and cook for 1 minute longer to release its fragrance. Add the zucchini, stir, and cook for 4 minutes, or until the zucchini softens and releases moisture. Add the couscous, toss with a fork to blend well, and cook for 3 minutes. Add the cheese and cook for about 2 minutes longer, just until the mixture is heated through. Serve hot or warm.

VARIATION: Add 1 cup diced red, yellow, orange, and/or green bell pepper along with the onion. Before serving, top with 1 tablespoon chopped fresh basil or parsley and 2 tablespoons chopped toasted pecans.

Lentil and Rice Salad

Lentils are an inexpensive powerhouse food. Just $1/4$ cup cooked contains 130 calories, 11 grams of fiber, and 8 grams of protein. Plus, they're high in folic acid and iron. For this salad use the tiny dark green or French lentils, which hold their shape well and cook quickly. There's no need to cook the peas, which will thaw right in the bowl. Serve with sliced tomatoes. Use leftovers as fillings in pita bread or wraps.

- 1 cup French lentils
- 1 cup cooked brown rice
- $1/3$ cup crumbled feta cheese
- $1/3$ cup chopped kalamata olives
- $1/3$ cup chopped walnuts
- 2 cups frozen baby peas
- 2 tablespoons olive oil
- 1 tablespoon white balsamic vinegar
- Salt and freshly ground black pepper

Put the lentils in a medium saucepan, cover with water to about 2 inches above the level of the lentils, and bring to a boil over high heat. Turn the heat down to medium-low and simmer for 20 minutes, or until the lentils are soft, but still slightly chewy. Drain well and transfer to a bowl.

Add the rice, feta, olives, walnuts, and peas. Toss gently to mix and let sit at room temperature for about 10 minutes.

Combine the olive oil and vinegar in a small bowl and blend with a whisk until smooth. Pour the dressing over the salad and toss gently. Season to taste with salt and pepper. Serve warm, at room temperature, or cold.

Perfect Cornbread

This quick bread goes with just about everything, for breakfast, lunch, or dinner. Make it with stone-ground whole-grain cornmeal, a better choice for fiber and protein than enriched white cornmeal. Serve hot with butter, honey, or jam to make a simple meal seem special.

Combine the dry ingredients in a bowl the night before to save time. Wrapped tightly in a plastic bag, the baked cornbread will keep for several days at room temperature. To serve leftover cornbread, split, lightly butter, and toast.

1 cup all-purpose flour

1 cup whole-grain cornmeal, preferably medium grind

2 tablespoons light brown sugar

1 teaspoon baking powder

$1/2$ teaspoon baking soda

3 tablespoons vegetable oil

$1^1/2$ cups buttermilk

2 eggs, beaten

Preheat the oven to 375°F. Grease an 8 by 8-inch baking pan or a 10-inch cast-iron frying pan.

Combine the flour, cornmeal, sugar, baking powder, and baking soda in a medium mixing bowl and blend with a whisk. Add the oil, buttermilk, and eggs, and blend with the whisk until smooth. Let the mixture sit for about a minute and blend again. Pour the batter into the prepared pan.

Bake for 25 to 30 minutes, until the top is lightly browned and the center bounces back when you press it gently with your finger. Cut into squares or rectangles and serve hot.

Sweet Potato Pudding   Serves 6

This recipe is adapted from Dara Goldstein's *The Vegetarian Hearth*. It is a fine way to serve sweet potatoes to teenagers who may think they don't like them.

Allow time to bake the sweet potatoes before you assemble the pudding. You can also bake them ahead and refrigerate them for up to 2 days before you make the pudding.

4 sweet potatoes

2 tablespoons butter

3 tablespoons light brown sugar

$1/2$ teaspoon ground cinnamon

4 small, seedless tangerines or mandarins, peeled

2 tablespoons chopped pecans

Preheat the oven to 400°F.

Place the sweet potatoes in a baking dish and bake for 30 minutes, or until soft through when pierced with a fork. Let them cool for 15 minutes, or until you can handle them.

Turn the oven temperature down to 350°F. Grease a 1-quart soufflé or baking dish.

Cut the sweet potatoes in half lengthwise and scoop the flesh out into a bowl. Mash it lightly. Discard the skins. Stir in the butter, 2 tablespoons of the brown sugar, and the cinnamon. Cut the tangerines in half through the middle, so each segment becomes two pieces. Remove any seeds. Gently stir the tangerines into the pudding. Transfer the mixture to the prepared dish. Combine the remaining 1 tablespoon brown sugar with the pecans and sprinkle the mixture over the top of the pudding.

Bake for 30 minutes, or until the top is browned. Serve hot or warm.

Sweet Potato Fries

Serves 2 to 4

A healthy change from french fries, these oven-baked treats are truly addictive. Scrub the potatoes but don't peel them, to retain the nutrients that lurk just underneath the skin. Broil leftovers for about 3 minutes, until they become crisp.

1 tablespoon olive oil

1 teaspoon taco seasoning

2 large sweet potatoes

Preheat the oven to 400°F.

Combine the oil and taco seasoning in a large bowl and blend with a whisk until smooth. Cut each sweet potato in half, and then slice into thin matchstick pieces. Toss in the seasoned oil until well coated.

Arrange the sweet potatoes in a single layer on a baking sheet and bake for 10 minutes, or until slightly crispy. Serve hot.

VARIATION: Prepare 2 Yukon gold or russet potatoes and 1 large sweet potato as above. Toss the white potatoes in the seasoned oil and bake for 5 minutes. Toss the sweet potato in the remaining oil in the bowl (add a bit more oil if necessary), add to the Yukon gold potatoes, and bake for 10 minutes longer.

Smashers

Serves 4 to 6

Tiny red potatoes, easiest to find in the spring or fall, deliver the best flavor to this very easy recipe. The name is sure to stick in your family's collective memory, and if you ask your son to help with the smashing, he will probably be only too happy to say yes. Instruct him not to be too exuberant. The idea is to leave the potatoes in small chunks. They're a nice change from conventional mashed potatoes. If you have any leftovers, put them in a pie pan, add a little milk, dot with about 1 tablespoon of butter, and bake in a preheated 350°F oven for 20 minutes, or until lightly browned.

2 pounds tiny whole red potatoes (about 20)

1 teaspoon salt

2 tablespoons butter

$1/3$ cup milk

Salt and freshly ground black pepper

Cut the potatoes in half, put them in a large, heavy saucepan, and add the salt and enough cold water to cover them by about an inch. Bring to a boil over high heat, turn the heat down to medium-low, and cook for 15 to 20 minutes, until the potatoes can be pierced easily with a knife. Drain the potatoes and quickly return them to the pan to keep them as hot as possible. Add the butter and milk and smash them gently with a masher or fork. Season with salt and pepper. Serve hot.

Crispy Mustard-Potato Wedges Serves 4

Bake the potatoes for this recipe in advance (up to 24 hours before mealtime) so they have time to cool and are easy to slice into wedges. The mustard caramelizes as they cook the second time, giving them a crisp texture as well as a spicy flavor. Since they're cut into wedges, this is a good recipe for practicing portion control. Serve two per person and save leftovers to reheat in the microwave. Serve with chicken, meat, fish, or egg dishes.

2 large russet potatoes (12 to 14 ounces each)

$1/2$ cup Dijon-style mustard

2 tablespoons olive oil

1 tablespoon minced fresh thyme, or 1 teaspoon dried thyme

Coarse salt and freshly ground black pepper

Preheat the oven to 400°F. Scrub the potatoes and prick in several places with a fork. Place directly on the oven rack and bake for about 40 minutes, or until they give a bit when pressed but are not completely soft throughout. Let cool for about 15 minutes. (If baking them 1 day ahead, refrigerate them after they have cooled completely.)

With a large knife, slice each baked potato into four lengthwise wedges. Combine the mustard, olive oil, thyme, salt, and pepper in a large mixing bowl. Add the potato wedges and toss gently to coat with the mustard mixture. Arrange the mustard-coated potatoes on a baking sheet and bake for 10 minutes, turning several times. Serve hot.

VARIATION: Cook the baked potatoes over a medium fire on the grill along with steaks or burgers. Oil the grill grate. Using tongs, arrange the prepared wedges on the grate. Cover the grill and cook the wedges, turning every 5 minutes, for about 15 minutes, until tender and evenly browned. Serve hot or warm.

Twice-Baked Potatoes
Serves 6 to 8

Use large, firm Idaho baking potatoes for the best flavor. Don't bake them in aluminum foil, which gives them an insipid consistency. Stuff more potatoes than you need for one meal, cool, and freeze, wrapped in aluminum foil. To reheat, unwrap and bake in a preheated 300°F oven for about 30 minutes.

> 4 medium baking potatoes (about 8 to 9 ounces each)
>
> 1 tablespoon olive oil
>
> 2 medium onions, finely chopped
>
> 1 cup sour cream or Yogurt Cheese (page 108)
>
> Salt and freshly ground black pepper
>
> 4 slices turkey bacon, cooked and crumbled

Preheat the oven to 400°F. Prick the potato skins with a sharp-tined fork and bake directly on the middle oven rack for 1 hour, or until the potatoes feel very soft when stabbed with a sharp knife.

While the potatoes are baking, heat the oil in a large frying pan over medium heat. Add the onions and sauté for 5 minutes, until soft. Remove the pan from the heat and set aside.

When cooked, transfer the potatoes to a cutting board. Turn the oven temperature down to 350°F.

Slice each potato in half lengthwise. Using an oven mitt, pick up one half and with a tablespoon carefully scrape the potato pulp into a large bowl, leaving the skins intact. (It is okay to leave a bit of potato clinging to the skin.) Repeat until all the potato pulp is in the bowl. Arrange the skins in a flat ovenproof baking dish. Add the sour cream to the potato pulp and mash well.

Season to taste with salt and pepper. Spoon the mashed mixture back into the skins and top with the turkey bacon.

Bake for 10 to 15 minutes, until hot. Serve immediately.

VARIATION:

• Substitute $1/4$ cup chopped scallions or chives for the turkey bacon.

• Reduce the sour cream to $1/2$ cup and add $1/2$ cup mashed, cooked pinto beans.

Spinach Casserole   Serves 6 to 8

This quick and easy combination makes a tasty side dish for any kind of supper. Blocks of frozen, chopped spinach work very nicely; thaw at room temperature for several hours or in the refrigerator overnight. Turn to this recipe when you have a few slices of bread threatening to get stale; just about any kind complements the spinach flavor. Grind the bread into crumbs in a few seconds in the food processor and store what you don't need in the freezer.

2 (10-ounce) packages chopped frozen spinach, thawed,
    or 8 cups fresh spinach, chopped

5 tablespoons olive oil

1 onion

3 cloves garlic, minced

1 cup whole-wheat bread crumbs, fresh or frozen

$1/2$ cup freshly grated Parmesan or Romano cheese

Salt and freshly ground black pepper

Put the thawed spinach, if using, in a colander in the sink and squeeze out the excess water with your hands or by pressing it down with a large kitchen spoon.

Heat 1 tablespoon of the oil in a large skillet over medium heat. Add the onion and garlic and sauté for 5 minutes, or until soft but not brown. Add the drained frozen spinach, or fresh spinach if using, turn the heat down to medium-low, cover, and cook for 5 minutes. Stir in the bread crumbs and cook, covered, for 4 minutes, or until the crumbs have absorbed any juices and are very soft. Sprinkle in the cheese, drizzle with the remaining 4 tablespoons of oil, and cook, uncovered, for 3 minutes longer. Season with salt and pepper. Serve warm. Or, spoon the finished mixture into a covered glass casserole dish and refrigerate; at serving time reheat in the microwave.

The Magic of Peanut Sauce

With its sweet-sour flavor and its familiar taste of peanut butter, a spicy peanut sauce often helps reluctant boys begin sampling vegetables they might otherwise avoid. Here's an easy recipe for making your own. You can also find a number of different brands at the store. Try it on pasta or steamed broccoli or as a dip for raw vegetables, or dilute it with 2 tablespoons of water and toss with 4 cups of packaged tri-color cole slaw mix or broccoli slaw. Thinned, it works as a marinade for pork, chicken, or shrimp. It also tastes great on crackers or rice cakes.

Peanut Sauce   Makes 2 cups

- 1 cup unsweetened chunky peanut butter
- $1/4$ cup fresh lime juice
- $1/4$ cup soy sauce
- $1/4$ cup water
- 2 tablespoons walnut or canola oil
- 1 tablespoon light brown sugar
- 1 tablespoon grated fresh ginger (from a 2-inch piece)
- $1/4$ teaspoon crushed red pepper flakes, or more to taste
- $1/2$ cup finely chopped fresh cilantro

Combine the peanut butter, lime juice, soy sauce, water, oil, brown sugar, ginger, and red pepper flakes in a food processor and process until smooth. Spoon the mixture into a bowl and stir in the cilantro. (The sauce will turn an odd green color if you put the cilantro in the food processor.)

Use 1 cup of this sauce for 4 cups of cole slaw and keep the rest on hand to serve over pasta or with vegetables. It will keep, covered in the refrigerator, for up to a week.

CHAPTER 6

Make-Ahead Main Dishes and Fast, Easy Dinners

You walk through the door after work, and it is time for dinner. Everyone is hungry. What do you do? Try not to head out to the closest fast-food emporium. Instead, pull together something, anything, from what you have on hand. Use the opportunity to make the point that home is where you eat, and show your son that making dinner is easy, not stressful. Ask him to set the table and cut up some carrots while you cook some pasta, drizzle it with olive oil, and dust it with grated cheese, or make an omelet or frittata, or broil up some tuna melts. Toss together a salad. Reheat leftovers. Keep it simple. Then sit down with your family and talk as you eat.

Remember that practice makes perfect. Good food is surprisingly easy to prepare, in part because it usually needs very little cooking to taste its best. (A piece of fresh fish bakes in about 10 minutes.) But you've got to dig in and make it happen.

Too many of today's parents don't cook. We've become a nation of fast-food junkies. If your son grows up in a world where food is rarely cooked or eaten at home, you'll cheat him out of an important part of life. "Feeding is about the love and connection between you and your child," points out nutritionist Ellyn Satter in *Secrets of Feeding a Healthy Family.* "Meals provide us all with reliable access to food, and they provide children with dependable access to their parents and to caring. Without meals, a home is just a place to stay."

So make a list, buy some food, and start cooking dinner. Keep the house stocked with possibilities—whole grains, eggs, pasta, fresh and frozen vegetables, canned tomatoes, tuna, cheese, and fresh and frozen fruit provide the makings of a number of meals. Be ever on the look-out for ways to stretch one meal into two or three. Cook something special on Monday and Thursday nights and turn to easy pantry meals (see page 176) on the other weeknights to give yourself a break.

When a weekend rolls around, or you have some time to spend in the kitchen, try one of the recipes in this chapter that takes more than 15 minutes. They're not difficult, but they require extra time—for marinating ingredients, letting pastry chill, or giving slow-cooked foods a chance to develop great flavor. Use weekend time to get ahead, too, by making one of the recipes that tastes best the second day, or that's easy to freeze. Devoting a few hours of weekend time to cooking beef or pork roasts, ham, turkey breasts, or whole chickens makes a lot of sense when you are feeding teenage boys. Pound for pound they're a better deal than buying deli meats, they're far better tasting, and they give you lots of leftovers upon which you can build other meals.

Oven-Fried Chicken   Serves 4

Avoid fried chicken from fast-food restaurants. It almost always has been cooked in unhealthy trans fats and is high in calories. Even if you fry it at home, one serving (3.5 ounces) of breast meat contains 13 grams of fat, 3.5 of them saturated fat. Here's a way to serve your family a healthier meal—something that looks fried, but isn't. One piece provides about 160 calories and just over 3 grams of fat. Serve with steamed broccoli, a green salad, and sliced apples.

> **1 cup plain yogurt**
>
> **1¹/₂ cups fine dry bread crumbs**
>
> **1 teaspoon ground cumin**
>
> **¹/₂ teaspoon dried oregano**

Salt and freshly ground black pepper

4 boneless, skinless chicken breast halves, 1 to 1$^{1}/_{4}$ pounds

Preheat the oven to 400°F.

Put the yogurt in a shallow dish. Combine the bread crumbs, cumin, oregano, salt, and pepper in a shallow bowl and stir gently with a fork to mix. Dip a chicken breast half into the yogurt mixture, turn to coat both sides, and dip into the crumb mixture, turning again to coat both sides. Place the chicken on a greased or parchment paper–lined baking sheet. Repeat with the other three halves.

Bake for 10 minutes, turn the pieces over with tongs, and bake for 10 to 15 minutes longer, until the coating is lightly browned and slightly crispy. Serve hot.

Potato, Chicken, and Green Bean Salad   Serves 4 to 6

Turn a classic, all-American side dish into a nutritious dinner. The secret to the best flavor is combining the ingredients while they're still warm, and eating the salad at room temperature. Use new red potatoes or Yukon golds, all about the same size so they'll cook in the same amount of time. Serve with breadsticks or whole-grain crackers and fresh fruit for dessert.

$^{1}/_{2}$ cup olive oil

$^{1}/_{4}$ cup white wine vinegar

1 clove garlic, minced

Salt and freshly ground black pepper

1 pound potatoes

4 boneless, skinless chicken breast halves

1 pound fresh or frozen green beans, cut into 2-inch pieces

1 cup cherry tomatoes, cut into halves

$^{1}/_{4}$ cup chopped fresh parsley

$^{1}/_{4}$ cup chopped red onion (optional)

Heat the grill to medium or preheat the broiler.

Combine the oil, vinegar, garlic, salt, and pepper in a small bowl and whisk until smooth. Set aside.

Put the unpeeled potatoes in a large saucepan, cover with water, and bring to a boil over high heat. Turn the heat down to medium and boil for 15 to 20 minutes, until the potatoes can be easily pierced with a knife.

While the potatoes are cooking, grill or broil the chicken breasts for about 3 minutes per side, until they are no longer pink on the inside.

Cook the beans in a steamer over boiling water or drop them into boiling water for 3 minutes, until they are crisp-tender. Drain if necessary and put them in a medium bowl.

Drain the potatoes and let them sit for a few minutes, until they are just cool enough to handle. Slice them into the bowl with the beans, add the dressing, and toss. Slice the chicken and add it to the potatoes and beans along with the tomatoes. Toss gently with the tomatoes, parsley, and onion, season with salt and pepper, and serve.

Chicken Curry for the Baseball Team — Serves 12 to 14

This quick and tasty curry feeds a hungry gang. Make it for your son's teammates to give him the opportunity to experience the pleasure of sharing a meal at home with friends—and to give his buddies a break from pizza at team meals. Since it is very mild, it appeals to every palate. And the flavors improve as it sits, so make it a day ahead if you can. If you need to double the recipe, make two batches. Serve with rice, a bowl of chutney, and a green salad.

3 tablespoons peanut oil

4 pounds boneless, skinless chicken breasts,
    cut into bite-size pieces

3 onions, sliced

4 cloves garlic, diced

2 large potatoes, peeled and diced

3-inch piece of fresh ginger, peeled and grated

2 tablespoons curry powder

1 teaspoon ground cumin

4 (14.5-ounce) cans diced tomatoes, with juice

1 cup coconut milk

Heat 1 tablespoon of the oil in a Dutch oven over medium-high heat. Add half the chicken and sauté, turning several times, until it is no longer pink, about 5 minutes. Remove the chicken from the pan with a slotted spoon and put it in a bowl. Add another tablespoon of the oil, sauté the remaining chicken, and add it to the bowl. Add the remaining 1 tablespoon of oil to the pan and sauté the onions for 3 minutes. Add the garlic and potatoes and cook, stirring, for

2 minutes longer. Add the ginger, curry powder, and cumin and cook, stirring frequently, for 2 minutes more, or until the spices are fragrant. Add the tomatoes and the coconut milk and bring the mixture almost to a boil. Turn the heat down to medium and simmer for 10 minutes, or until the potatoes are cooked but still firm. Return the chicken to the pan and simmer for 10 minutes. Serve hot.

NOTE: If you are planning to serve this the night you make it, before starting the curry, combine 2 cups brown or white basmati rice with 4 cups water. Bring to a boil, turn the heat down to low, cover, and cook for 20 minutes for the white rice, 30 to 45 minutes for the brown rice, or until all the water has been absorbed. Makes 6 cups.

Chicken-Pepper Stir-Fry   Serves 4

Allow about 10 minutes to prepare and line up all the ingredients, and another 8 to 10 minutes to complete the cooking. This recipe also will work well with about 8 ounces of pork, beef, or tofu. Chop and use any other vegetables you prefer. Serve with rice, a green salad, and fresh pineapple.

BROWN SAUCE

$^1/_3$ cup water or chicken stock or broth

2 tablespoons hoisin sauce

1 tablespoon soy sauce

1 tablespoon rice wine vinegar

STIR-FRY

2 tablespoons peanut oil

3 cloves garlic, minced

1 tablespoon grated fresh ginger

2 boneless, skinless chicken breasts, cut into bite-size pieces

1 stalk celery, sliced

1 red bell pepper, chopped

1 onion, chopped

$^1/_2$ cup chopped peanuts

To make the sauce, combine the water, hoisin sauce, soy sauce, and vinegar in a small bowl and blend with a whisk until smooth. Set aside.

To make the stir-fry, heat a wok or heavy frying pan over medium-high heat. Add the oil and heat. Add the garlic and ginger and stir-fry for about 1 minute, until sizzling and fragrant. Add the chicken and stir-fry until it is no longer pink, about 4 minutes. Push to the sides of the pan. Add the celery, bell pepper, and onion and stir-fry for 2 to 3 minutes, until the vegetables are crisp-tender. Add the sauce, stir, and cook until all the ingredients are well coated. Add the peanuts and toss. Serve hot.

Saved by a Stir-Fry

One of the fastest ways to get dinner on the table in a hurry, a stir-fry is nothing more than cooking a few fresh ingredients in a small amount of hot oil, tossing them frequently over high heat to lift them out of the oil and let them fall back down into it. This helps them cook evenly and quickly, keep their flavor, and retain lots of nutrients. It is important to be organized before you begin by chopping everything you want to include and lining it up in bowls; once the pan is hot there's no time to hunt around for a carrot or a few mushrooms.

To save time, look in your supermarket for vegetables, beef, and chicken precut and ready to go for stir-fries. And check out the selection of marinades and sauces. The best choices don't contain high-fructose corn syrup or partially hydrogenated oils, and they'll have no more than 400 milligrams of sodium per 2 tablespoons. Use reduced-sodium soy sauce as well.

There's no need to rush out and buy a wok. Unless you have a fancy restaurant-quality stovetop, you probably don't have a source of enough heat to use one. Better choices are a heavy 12- or 14-inch stainless steel frying pan with sloping sides or a large cast-iron frying pan. You can also buy a rounded 10-inch, stainless steel wok-shaped pan with a flat bottom suitable for one or two-person stir-fries.

Teach your son how to cook this way. Teenagers are attracted to the excitement of the sizzling food and the quick turning, and once they learn the technique, they can make a meal for themselves or dinner for the whole family. (Remember that practice makes perfect; encourage experiments with the less-expensive vegetables and expect a few anomalies in the learning curve.) In fact, it is often easier to make a stir-fry for just one or two people.

Since it is possible to combine a number of vegetables in a stir-fry, the method is a great way to get variety into a meal and cut back on the amount of meat you are serving without sacrificing flavor. You can get by with as little as 2 ounces of red meat, chicken, or shrimp per person— a budgetary consideration, too. Choose from a wide variety of vegetables, including bell peppers, hot peppers, carrots, celery, beans, mushrooms, zucchini, snow peas, and bean sprouts. Dense vegetables, such as beets, potatoes, winter squash, and parsnips don't work as well, but if you want to use them, cook them separately by boiling or steaming and add them at the end of the cooking time. You can also add noodles; look for a label that indicates they'll work in a stir-fry and follow the package directions.

Here are the basic steps:

1. Assemble, chop, and line up all the ingredients.

2. Heat the pan over medium-high heat until it is hot. You'll be able to smell it, and a few drops of water flicked onto the surface will vaporize in 2 seconds.

3. Add the oil (peanut is one of the best because it holds up to high heat), swirl to coat the cooking area, and heat for a few seconds.

4. Add the garlic, onions, chiles, or other aromatic ingredients and stir-fry for about 10 seconds.

5. Add the meat, chicken, seafood, or tofu; stir-fry for about 3 minutes, until evenly cooked on the outside, and push it to the sides of the pan, where it will continue to cook without browning. (Marinate ahead of time for added flavor.)

6. Add the vegetables in order of how fast they will cook and stir-fry for about 2 to 3 minutes total, until crisp-tender.

7. Add any sauce you want to use and stir until it coats all the ingredients and is heated through.

Shrimp and Snow Pea Stir-Fry

Serves 4

It is fine to use frozen shrimp for this colorful dish. Soak them in water to cover for about 10 minutes to thaw, and then peel them. If you are in a hurry, or are teaching your son to make a meal, use unthawed, frozen cooked and peeled shrimp, and toss them just until they are heated through. Serve with rice, bulgur, or couscous.

> 1 tablespoon peanut oil
>
> 2 cloves garlic, minced
>
> 2 teaspoons grated fresh ginger
>
> 1 pound medium raw shrimp, peeled and deveined
>
> 8 ounces snow peas
>
> 1 carrot, sliced lengthwise with a cheese slicer into long "tongues"
>
> 2 tablespoons soy sauce
>
> 2 scallions, minced

Heat a wok or heavy frying pan over medium-high heat. Add the oil and heat. Add the garlic and ginger, and stir-fry for about 1 minute, until sizzling and fragrant. Add the shrimp in a single layer and stir-fry for 2 minutes, just until they turn pink. Push to the sides of the pan. Add the snow peas and carrot and stir-fry for 2 minutes. Add the soy sauce and stir-fry for 1 minute. Stir in the scallions and serve.

Maple-Barbecue Chicken Thighs

Serves 6 to 8

Make this tasty finger food when you have another reason to be in the kitchen for a while. It requires being attentive to the broiler. Consider doubling the quantities for a team party or a potluck. The pieces shrink considerably as they cook. Chicken thighs are higher in fat than chicken breast meat, but they're a good source of protein. They taste great warm, at room temperature, or cold. Allow about two per person, depending on the size. Serve with raw veggies and Yogurt Feta Dip (page 106).

> 1/4 cup bottled barbecue sauce
>
> 2 tablespoons pure maple syrup
>
> 2 tablespoons cider vinegar
>
> 4 pounds skinless chicken thighs, with bones

Preheat the broiler and arrange the rack as far as possible from the heat source.

Combine the barbecue sauce, maple syrup, and vinegar in a small mixing bowl and blend with a whisk. Arrange the chicken in a single layer on a broiling pan. Broil for 10 minutes. Turn and broil for another 10 minutes. Turn, brush liberally with sauce, and broil for 5 minutes. Repeat turning, brushing and broiling for 5 minutes three more times, until the chicken is well glazed and just starting to turn dark brown.

Serve with extra paper napkins.

VARIATION: Use chicken wings instead of thighs. If they're hinged, cut them into two pieces with a large sharp knife.

Slow-Cooker Pineapple-Teriyaki Drumsticks   Serves 4 to 6

Don't be afraid to stray from skinless chicken breasts on occasion. Drumsticks are cheaper and provide iron and protein. Use a slow-cooker to gently simmer the flavorful meat until it is literally falling from the bone and needs to be eaten with knife and fork. Toss all the ingredients together in the slow-cooker in the morning and leave a note telling your son to help himself when he comes home from school, or serve as a quick evening meal with whole-grain bread, a green vegetable, and salad.

> **1 cup pineapple juice**
>
> **$1/2$ cup teriyaki marinade**
>
> **10 to 12 chicken drumsticks (about 3 pounds)**

Combine the pineapple juice and marinade in the slow-cooker and stir to blend. Add the chicken and gently stir to coat with the sauce. Cover and cook on low for 6 to 8 hours. Serve hot or warm.

Chicken Fajitas   Serves 4 to 6

Traditionally, and to be true to the name, fajitas are made with marinated grilled steak. This recipe departs from convention by using lower-fat chicken, marinated for a short time in a seasoning blend. Keep frozen chicken tenderloins and frozen pepper strips in the freezer so you can make fajitas quickly. Neither requires thawing to cook. Bake the frozen tenderloins according to package directions and then slice. (It is easy to double this recipe to feed a gang of boys. If you do, wrap a dozen flour tortillas in aluminum foil and let the stack heat in the oven for 15 to 20 minutes. Cook the chicken, peppers, and onions in batches if necessary.) Serve with corn, black beans, and rice.

> 1 tablespoon fajita seasoning
>
> 2 tablespoons fresh lime juice
>
> 5 tablespoons olive oil
>
> 1 pound boneless, skinless chicken breasts,
> cut into thin strips
>
> 6 (8-inch) whole-wheat tortillas
>
> 2 red or green bell peppers, cut into thin strips
>
> 1 large onion, thinly sliced
>
> Guacamole, sour cream, and/or salsa, for topping

Combine the fajita seasoning, lime juice, and 3 tablespoons of the oil in a bowl and blend with a whisk until smooth. Put the chicken in a zippered plastic bag, add the marinade, seal, and gently move the chicken strips around inside the bag until they are evenly coated with marinade. Let sit for 30 minutes.

Preheat the oven to 325°F and arrange the tortillas in a single layer on a baking sheet. (They will hang over the edges a bit.)

Heat the remaining 2 tablespoons of oil in a large frying pan over medium-high heat. Using tongs, remove the chicken from the marinade, add to the pan, and sauté for about 5 minutes, until cooked through. Remove to a platter and cover with foil to keep warm. Add the peppers and onion to the pan and sauté for 4 minutes, or until they just start to turn brown.

Make Your Own Chicken Stock

Save all the bones and skin from the chicken and put them in a large pot. Cover with water and add 2 chopped carrots; 2 stalks celery; 1 unpeeled onion, cut in half; 2 teaspoons of peppercorns; and a few parsley sprigs. Bring just to a boil, turn the heat down to low, and simmer, partially covered, for 2 hours. (Or, put everything in a slow-cooker and cook on high for 5 hours.) Strain and cool. Ladle into 1-quart yogurt containers and freeze. Thaw in the refrigerator and skim the fat from the top before using.

Return the chicken and any juices to the skillet and heat through, tossing gently with the peppers and onion. Put the tortillas in the oven for 1 minute. Using tongs, serve the chicken mixture on the warm tortillas, topped with guacamole, sour cream, and/or salsa.

Whole Roast Chicken
Serves 6 to 8

One of the easiest main courses you can make, a roast chicken also gives you bones for stock and enough meat for several meals. Serve the meat sliced and hot the first night, and then use for sandwiches, wraps, fried rice, or chicken salad. For extra flavor, stuff the cavity with a lemon or with a handful of herbs, such as fresh lovage or fresh tarragon.

1 roasting chicken, 3 to 4 pounds

Salt and freshly ground black pepper

Preheat the oven to 400°F. Season the chicken with salt and pepper and place it on a rack in a roasting pan. Roast for $1^1/4$ hours, or until an instant-read thermometer registers 180°F when inserted in the breast. Remove from the oven, cover loosely with aluminum foil, and let rest for 15 minutes before carving.

Chicken Pot Pie
Serves 6

The little packaged pies sold in the supermarket freezer case bear no resemblance to this down-home delight, a great dish to serve to your family or company. It tends to be a boy's favorite. Use leftover roast chicken, or buy 1 whole, large chicken breast and poach in water to cover for 20 minutes to have enough meat. Tinker with the vegetables that go in under the crust: fresh or frozen peas, chopped green beans, peppers, and corn can all be used. Resist the urge to chop the chicken with a knife, which gives the pie a processed look. Instead, pull it into large shreds. Since this dish uses butter in both the gravy and the crust, balance your meal by serving it with a simple green salad and fruit for dessert.

Chicken Pie Pastry (recipe follows)

2 carrots, sliced

2 stalks celery, sliced

3 cups cooked skinned and shredded chicken

2 tablespoons butter

2 tablespoons all-purpose flour

1¹/₂ cups chicken stock or broth (see page 154)

2 teaspoons dried tarragon

Salt and freshly ground black pepper

Make the pastry and chill it.

Preheat the oven to 425°F.

Combine the carrots and celery in a vegetable steamer or a saucepan containing 1 cup of water and cook for about 4 minutes, until the vegetables are crisp-tender. Drain.

Arrange the vegetables in a single layer in the bottom of a 9-inch pie pan. Put the chicken in a layer on top of the vegetables.

Melt the butter in a saucepan over low heat, add the flour, and stir with a whisk for several minutes, to let the flour absorb the fat and brown slightly. Add the chicken stock, turn up the heat to medium-high, and cook for 3 minutes, stirring with a whisk, to make a smooth gravy. Cook for 4 minutes longer, or until slightly thickened. Add the tarragon and season with salt and pepper.

Pour the gravy over the chicken and vegetables and set it aside to cool for 5 minutes. Roll out the pastry into an 11-inch round and fit it over the filling. Crimp the edges and cut vents to allow steam to escape.

Bake the pie for 10 minutes. Turn the heat down to 325°F and bake for 30 minutes longer, or until the top is lightly browned and the gravy is bubbling at the vents. Let sit for 5 minutes before serving.

VARIATION: Instead of the pastry, top the pie with about 2 cups mashed potatoes, thinned with milk to make them soft enough to spread. Bake in a preheated 350°F oven for 20 minutes, or until the gravy is bubbling up around the edges and the top is just starting to brown.

Chicken Pie Pastry   Makes pastry for 1 pie

1¹/₂ cups all-purpose flour

1/₂ teaspoon salt

1/₂ cup cold unsalted butter, cut into chunks

1/₄ cup cold water

Combine the flour and salt in a food processor and pulse to blend. Add the butter and pulse again until the mixture is crumbly. With the motor running, add the water and blend just until the mixture starts to clump together. Turn the dough out onto a sheet of wax paper, form it into a disk, and refrigerate for 30 minutes.

Roast Turkey Breast   Serves 6 to 8

Providing plenty of tasty meat for supper and leftovers for sandwiches, turkey breast is easy to cook and inexpensive. If you buy a frozen one, allow 2 days for it to thaw in the refrigerator, or soak it in brine (see below), which improves the flavor and keeps the meat juicy. Ask your son to carve it into thin slices, to give him some practice without holiday-meal pressure, and to teach him about alternatives to sliced deli meat.

1 turkey breast, approximately 5 to 6 pounds

Preheat the oven to 400°F.

Set the turkey breast in a roasting pan and roast for 1 hour, or until an instant-read thermometer registers 170°F when stuck into the thickest part. Remove from the oven, cover with aluminum foil, and let sit for 15 minutes before carving.

VARIATIONS:

• Before roasting, rub the turkey breast with $^1/_4$ cup of Pesto (page 96) or 2 tablespoons of spice rub combined with 3 tablespoons of olive oil.

• To coax extra flavor out of a frozen turkey breast, let it sit for at least 6 hours in a brine (see recipe below). This easy extra step also provides flexibility, since the turkey can sit in the brine for up to 48 hours if need be. If using a frozen breast, add it to the brine without thawing and soak for 48 to 60 hours.

Turkey Brine

$^1/_2$ **cup kosher or coarse salt**

$^1/_2$ **cup firmly packed light brown sugar**

$^1/_2$ **cup cider vinegar**

2 bay leaves

4 cloves garlic, peeled and smashed

1 tablespoon celery seeds

8 cups water

Combine all the ingredients in a large stainless steel or enameled pot. Add the turkey breast, cover, and refrigerate, preferably overnight. Drain the turkey breast, pat dry with paper towels, and roast.

Turkey Chili   Serves 6 to 8

Make this flavorful, healthy chili on a busy night when you want to pull supper together in less than 30 minutes. Use ground white or dark turkey meat, or a combination of the two, and keep an eye on it as it cooks in the oil, since it can dry out quickly. Serve with rice or couscous. If you want to make this ahead of time and have it ready for dinner, bake the chili in a heavy, ovenproof casserole dish, cover, and keep warm in a 200°F oven for up to an hour.

- **1 pound ground turkey**
- **1 tablespoon olive oil**
- **1 onion, chopped**
- **2 stalks celery, chopped**
- **2 teaspoons chili powder, or more to taste**
- **2 (14.5-ounce) cans diced tomatoes, with juice**
- **1 (15-ounce) can kidney beans, drained and rinsed (about 2 cups)**

If the turkey is in long strands, place it on a cutting board and chop it well.

Heat the oil in a large frying pan over medium heat, add the turkey, and cook for about 5 minutes, breaking it up with a spoon as necessary and stirring until it is crumbly and no pink is showing. Using a slotted spoon, transfer the turkey to a bowl. Add the onion and celery to the pan and sauté for 5 minutes, or until the vegetables just start to turn soft. Sprinkle in the chili powder and cook, stirring frequently, for 2 minutes. Add the tomatoes, beans, and turkey, turn the heat down to low, and simmer for 10 minutes. Serve hot.

VARIATIONS:

- Substitute 1 (14-ounce) package GimmeLean soy protein for the turkey and cook it the same way, being more aggressive about breaking it up into small bits as it cooks.

- Substitute 1 pound lean ground beef for the turkey. To remove as much saturated fat as possible, drain the cooked beef in a colander and rinse it quickly under hot water before returning it to the pan with the remaining ingredients.

Turkey Lasagna

Serves 10 to 12

Ground turkey gives this classic recipe a sweet, appealing flavor, adding very little saturated fat and more than 26 grams of protein per serving. If you have time, put the turkey in the freezer for about 2 hours before you use it, to make chopping it easier. Store leftover lasagna in the refrigerator for up to 3 days or wrap tightly in aluminum foil and freeze.

1 pound ground turkey

2 teaspoons olive oil

2 eggs

$1^1/4$ cups freshly grated Parmesan or Romano cheese

2 cups (16 ounces) cottage cheese

$^1/4$ cup finely chopped fresh basil

1 (28-ounce) jar pasta sauce

1 tablespoon salt

1 pound lasagna noodles

3 cups shredded mozzarella

Preheat the oven to 350°F.

If the turkey is in long strands, place it on a cutting board and chop it well. Heat the oil in a large frying pan over medium heat, add the turkey, and cook for about 5 minutes, breaking it up with a spoon as necessary and stirring until it is crumbly and no pink is showing. Drain well and return to the skillet.

Put the eggs in a medium bowl and blend with a whisk until smooth. Reserve $^1/4$ cup of the Parmesan. Add the remaining 1 cup of Parmesan and the cottage cheese to the eggs and beat with a spoon until smooth. Stir in the basil.

Reserve $^1/4$ cup of the pasta sauce. Add the rest to the turkey in the skillet, stir to mix, and simmer over low heat for 10 minutes. While the turkey mixture simmers, bring a large pot of water to a boil. Add the salt, then the lasagna noodles, and cook for 6 to 8 minutes (stirring for the first 2 minutes), until the noodles are tender but still firm to the bite. Drain in a colander.

Spread $^1/3$ cup of the turkey-tomato sauce on the bottom of a 9 by 13-inch baking dish. Add a layer of pasta strips. Spread half of the egg and cheese mixture evenly over the pasta, add half of the turkey-tomato sauce, and top that with half of the mozzarella. Repeat the layers, and cover the top with another layer of noodles. Spread the reserved $^1/4$ cup of tomato sauce over the top and sprinkle on the reserved $^1/4$ cup of Parmesan.

Bake for 30 minutes, or until the juices bubble around the edges. Remove from the oven and let sit for 10 minutes before serving.

Turkey Roll   Serves 8 to 10

Here is a good way to put some new life into turkey meatloaf, which is lower in fat than a beef-based meatloaf, but tends to be a bit bland. The possibilities for "fillings" are varied. Consider any colorful seasonal vegetables that can be cut into thin strips and that will serve up a surprise at the table. This meatloaf is suitable for a flexible dinner hour, since it is good hot, at room temperature, or cold. Leftovers make great sandwiches.

1 pound ground turkey

$1/2$ cup old-fashioned rolled oats

1 cup fresh whole-wheat bread crumbs

1 onion, diced

2 stalks celery, diced

3 cloves garlic, minced

1 tablespoon Dijon-style mustard

1 teaspoon Worcestershire sauce

20 whole green beans

1 large red, yellow, or orange bell pepper, cut into thin strips

Preheat the oven to 375°F.

Combine the turkey, oats, bread crumbs, onion, celery, garlic, mustard, and Worcestershire sauce in a large bowl. Mix with your hands.

Lay a piece of wax paper about 18 inches long out on the counter. Transfer the meatloaf mixture onto the wax paper and, using the palms of your hands, pat it into a rectangle approximately 10 by 12 inches. Lay the green beans out horizontally in the center of the rectangle, forming a band of them about four deep. It is okay if they overlap a bit. Arrange the pepper strips on top of the beans. Lift the wax paper and roll the meatloaf up from the long side into a cylinder. Place a sheet of aluminum foil about 20 inches long on the counter. Pick the meatloaf up by the ends of the wax paper and transfer it to the foil. Leaving the wax paper covering in place, roll up again so the meatloaf is completely enclosed in foil. Place the wrapped meatloaf on a baking sheet.

Bake for 1 hour. Let cool for 15 minutes before uncovering and slicing.

Baked Fish

Get into the habit of serving fish to your family at least once a week. It is a good source of protein and will expose your son to the world beyond burgers. Serve with rice, steamed broccoli, and a green salad.

> **1 pound fresh pollock or cod fillets or salmon steaks**
>
> **2 teaspoons olive oil**
>
> **1 teaspoon dried thyme**

Preheat the oven to 425°F.

Rub both sides of the fish with the oil and place the fish in a flat baking dish, skin side down, if the skin is on the fish. Sprinkle the top with thyme. Bake for 5 to 10 minutes depending on the thickness, until the fish flakes easily with a fork and is hot through. Serve immediately.

VARIATIONS:

- Sprinkle the fish with 1 teaspoon grated Parmesan cheese before baking.
- Cut the fish into four equal portions. Put several tablespoons of milk into a flat dish and several tablespoons of dry bread crumbs into another flat dish. Holding the pieces skin side up, dip them into the milk and then into the bread crumbs, gently pressing down so the crumbs adhere. Turn the pieces over and arrange in the baking dish skin side down, crumb side up. Bake as above.
- Broil the fillets about 4 inches from the heat source for 3 to 6 minutes.

Crab Cakes

While fresh crabmeat is wonderfully tasty, canned crabmeat is inexpensive and a good pantry staple. Here it is combined with a few other kitchen basics for a quick and healthy meal that works well for a weeknight supper. Serve with cole slaw and a dish of fresh pineapple chunks.

> **1 egg**
>
> **1 (6-ounce) can crabmeat, drained**
>
> **$1/2$ cup fresh bread crumbs**
>
> **2 teaspoons Dijon-style mustard**
>
> **1 stalk celery, diced**
>
> **2 tablespoons mayonnaise**
>
> **1 tablespoon olive oil**

Break the egg into a small bowl and beat with a fork. Add the crabmeat, bread crumbs, mustard, celery, and mayonnaise. Toss gently with a fork until mixed. Let stand for 10 minutes or, if you have time, chill for 30 minutes.

Using your hands, shape the mixture into two patties, each about $1/2$ inch thick. Heat the oil in a medium frying pan over medium heat. Add the crab cakes and cook for 3 minutes. Turn and cook on the other side for 3 minutes, or until lightly browned. Serve hot.

Surprise Packages

When you are in a hurry to fix dinner turn to this easy method: Preheat the oven to 400°F. Tear off a 12-inch square of aluminum foil for every family member. Grease it lightly with olive oil. In the center, add about 3 ounces of seafood or $1/2$ cup of thinly sliced chicken, meat, or canned beans. Top with a selection of thinly sliced vegetables, such as carrots, celery, mushrooms, snow peas, or onions. Sprinkle on 1 or 2 teaspoons of dried herbs, herb blend, or seasoning mix. Add 2 teaspoons of olive oil and season with salt and pepper. Fold up the edges of each packet to form a tight seal. Arrange the packets on a baking sheet. Bake for 20 minutes. Serve on dinner plates (recommend opening them slowly) along with rice, couscous, or bulgur and a green salad.

Salmon Patties   Serves 4 to 6

Deceptively simple, these are the ultimate in comfort food and a good reason to keep a few cans of salmon in the pantry. They're also nutritious, offering plenty of protein and omega-3 fatty acids to stimulate brain function, making them a good choice for dinner the night before the SATs. They'll taste best if you make your own mashed potatoes rather than relying on instant. Serve with green beans and sliced apples.

4 potatoes

2 tablespoons butter

$1/3$ cup milk

Salt and freshly ground black pepper

1 (7.5-ounce) can pink salmon, drained

1 tablespoon olive oil

Peel the potatoes, cut them into large chunks, and put them in a large pan of water. Bring to a boil, turn the heat down to medium-low, and simmer for 15 minutes or until the potatoes can be pierced easily with a knife.

Meanwhile, combine the butter and milk in a small saucepan and heat until the butter melts. Set aside.

Drain the potatoes and press them through a ricer or mash them in the pan. Add the milk and butter mixture and stir until smooth. Season with salt and pepper.

Add the salmon to the potatoes, and stir until well blended. Form the mixture into six patties, each about 3 inches in diameter.

Heat the oil in a large frying pan over medium heat. Add the patties and cook for 5 minutes, or until browned. Turn and cook on the other side for 5 minutes. Serve hot.

Salmon with Thai Lemongrass Marinade   Serves 3 to 4

The marinade, created by spicy food mavens Dave DeWitt and Nancy Gerlach, is so delicious you'll be tempted to drink it. Allow about 20 minutes to make it and another 30 minutes for the fish to sit in it. The chiles give it considerable heat. Reduce the quantity or omit them altogether if you want a milder flavor. Use the marinade to marinate chicken or seafood before baking or stir-frying, or as a sauce for rice or noodles.

1 or 2 salmon fillets, about 1 pound total

1 cup Thai Lemongrass Marinade (recipe follows)

Place the fish in a shallow glass baking dish and pour the marinade over the top. Turn the fish so both sides are coated with marinade. Cover and refrigerate for 30 minutes to 2 hours.

Remove the dish from the refrigerator about 10 minutes before baking. Preheat the oven to 425°F.

Bake the fish, skin side down, for 10 minutes per inch of thickness, or until it flakes easily. Serve hot.

Thai Lemongrass Marinade

1 stalk lemongrass

$^1/_2$ cup coconut milk

8 Thai or 4 serrano chiles, stems removed and flesh chopped

2$^1/_2$ tablespoons fresh lime juice

3 tablespoons light brown sugar

1 shallot, sliced

1 tablespoon Asian fish sauce

1 tablespoon soy sauce

1 tablespoon fresh chopped cilantro

1 teaspoon grated fresh ginger

Cut off and discard the green top of the lemongrass and the root end, leaving about a 6-inch stalk. Remove any tough outer leaves, cut the stalk into 1-inch pieces, and lightly pound the pieces with the knife handle to release the flavor. Combine the lemongrass with the coconut milk in a small saucepan and simmer over medium-low heat for 10 to 15 minutes, until the mixture is very fragrant. Do not let it boil. Remove the pan from the heat and strain into a bowl, pressing gently on the lemongrass. Discard the lemongrass.

Pour the hot coconut milk into a food processor or blender. Add the chiles, lime juice, brown sugar, shallot, fish sauce, soy sauce, cilantro, and ginger and puree until smooth. Use as above or transfer to a glass jar with a tight-fitting lid and store in the refrigerator, where it will keep for 1 week.

Beef Ribbons

Ask the boys in your life to help you prepare and cook these skewers, and you will get them interested in grilling. They seem to enjoy the work, perhaps because threading the meat onto the skewers is a bit like putting a worm on a fishing hook, since the meat is sliced in long, thin strips. Get the meat marinating in the early afternoon if you can, since it adds a nice bit of flavor. Skip the marinade if you are in a hurry. Use leftovers in sandwiches or tacos.

2 pounds sirloin steak

Juice of 1 large lemon

$^1/_4$ cup soy sauce

Trim the fat from the outer edges of the sirloin, and slice it lengthwise into $^1/_4$-inch-thick strips. Combine the lemon juice and soy sauce in a large, flat glass or stainless steel baking dish and stir with a whisk until blended. Arrange the steak strips in a single layer in the marinade and turn once with a fork so both sides are coated. Cover the dish with plastic wrap and chill for 2 to 4 hours, turning once with a fork about halfway through the marinating time.

Build a medium fire in a charcoal grill or heat a gas grill to 350°F. While the grill is heating, thread several pieces of beef onto each skewer, forming each into an "S" shape and piercing it every inch or two. Discard the marinade. Lightly brush the grill grate with olive oil, arrange the skewers on the grill, and grill for 3 minutes per side, or until the meat is browned and beginning to sizzle. Transfer the skewers to a platter. Using a fork, slide the meat off the skewers and onto a serving platter.

Rib-Eye Steaks   Serves 4 to 6

Although they cost anywhere from $8 a pound and up, thick boneless rib-eyes are flavorful and juicy, making them a special treat for carnivores. Most rib-eyes weigh more than half a pound, and even though they shrink by about 15 percent during cooking, you need to be vigilant to keep the portion size to 3 ounces, which has approximately 6.4 grams of fat. Hold some back as leftovers to use for making Fried Rice (page 189) and dinner salads (page 188). This cooking method will also work for Delmonico, strip, and top loin steaks.

1 tablespoon olive oil or butter

2 rib-eye steaks (12 to 14 ounces each)

Salt and freshly ground black pepper

Preheat the oven to 425°F.

Heat the oil in a cast-iron frying pan large enough to hold both steaks over medium-high heat. Add the steaks and cook them for about 3 minutes on each side, until they are browned.

Transfer the pan to the oven and bake for 10 minutes, or until a slice shows that the meat is cooked to your preference. Cover with aluminum foil and let the steaks sit for 5 minutes before slicing.

Satay

These Indonesian-inspired tidbits, threaded on skewers, acquire deeper flavor if you give them time to marinate for several hours. Make your own marinade (recipes follow) or buy one at the store. The pieces of chicken, beef, or pork don't need to swim in the marinade; use just enough to coat them. Serve with a spicy peanut sauce for dipping. Instead of broiling, you can thread the meat on skewers that have soaked in cold water for about 30 minutes, then grill over medium heat.

Chicken Satay

> 2 cloves garlic, minced
>
> 1 tablespoon soy sauce
>
> 1 tablespoon grated fresh ginger
>
> 1 teaspoon light brown sugar
>
> Juice of 1 lime
>
> 1 tablespoon olive oil
>
> 1 pound boneless, skinless chicken breasts
>
> Peanut Dipping Sauce, to serve (recipe follows)

Combine the garlic, soy sauce, ginger, brown sugar, lime juice, and oil in a flat baking dish and blend with a whisk until smooth. Cut the chicken into $1/2$-inch cubes and toss in the marinade. Turn several times with a spatula to coat the chicken on all sides. Cover tightly and refrigerate for 30 minutes to 2 hours.

Beef Satay

> 2 cloves garlic, minced
>
> 1 tablespoon soy sauce
>
> 1 teaspoon honey
>
> 1 teaspoon ground cumin
>
> 2 tablespoons olive oil
>
> 1 pound top beef sirloin or top beef loin steak
>
> Peanut Dipping Sauce, to serve (recipe follows)

Combine the garlic, soy sauce, honey, cumin, and oil in a flat baking dish and blend with a whisk until smooth. Cut the steak into $1/2$-inch cubes and toss in the marinade. Turn several times with a spatula to coat the meat on all sides. Cover tightly and refrigerate for 30 minutes to 2 hours.

Pork Satay

2 cloves garlic, minced

2 tablespoons soy sauce

1 teaspoon light brown sugar

2 tablespoons creamy peanut butter

Juice of 1 lemon

$1/4$ teaspoon cayenne

1 pound pork sirloin or pork loin

Peanut Dipping Sauce, to serve (recipe follows)

Combine the garlic, soy sauce, brown sugar, peanut butter, lemon juice, and cayenne in a flat baking dish and blend with a whisk until smooth. (The marinade will be lumpy at first. Keep stirring until it becomes smooth.) Cut the pork into $1/2$-inch cubes and toss in the marinade. Turn several times with a spatula to coat the meat on all sides. Cover tightly and refrigerate for 30 minutes to 2 hours.

To cook the satay, preheat the broiler. Thread the chicken, beef, or pork onto thin bamboo skewers, using about 6 to 8 pieces per skewer, and 6 to 8 skewers per pound of meat. Spread the pieces out a bit on each skewer rather than bunching them up, so they will cook evenly and quickly. Arrange the skewers on a broiler pan and cook about 6 inches from the heat for 4 minutes. Turn and cook for another 4 minutes, or until the meat is thoroughly cooked. Serve hot, with dipping sauce.

Peanut Dipping Sauce
Makes 1 cup

$1/2$ cup smooth or crunchy unsweetened peanut butter

$2/3$ cup coconut milk

Juice of 1 lime

2 tablespoons soy sauce

1 tablespoon Asian fish sauce

1 tablespoon honey

$1/4$ teaspoon cayenne, or more to taste

Combine all the ingredients in a small bowl and stir until smooth. Serve with the satay or store in the refrigerator, tightly covered, for up to 2 weeks.

The Leanest Cuts

The following cuts of meat meet the current government standards for lean, which means that a 3-ounce serving contains less than 10 grams of total fat, 4.5 grams or less of saturated fat, and less than 95 milligrams of cholesterol. When you are cooking and serving meat, pay close attention to the portion size. That 3 ounces is about the size of a deck of cards—not a steak that covers a dinner plate.

Fat grams are based on a 3-ounce serving.

3-Ounce Serving	Saturated Fat	Total Fat
Eye round	1.4 g	4 g
Top round steak	1.6 g	4.6 g
Bottom round	1.7 g	4.7 g
Top sirloin	1.9 g	4.9 g
Round tip	1.8 g	5 g
Ground beef (95% lean)	2.4 g	5 g
Brisket (flat half)	1.9 g	5.1 g
Chuck shoulder roast	1.8 g	5.7 g
Chuck shoulder steak	1.9 g	6 g
Top loin (strip) steak	2.3 g	6 g
Flank steak	2.6 g	6.3 g
Rib-eye (small end)	2.4 g	6.4 g
Rib steak (small end)	2.5 g	6.5 g
Tri-tip	2.6 g	7.1 g
Tenderloin	2.7 g	7.2 g
T-bone	3 g	8.2 g

Zheng He Beef

Although this combination of ingredients may seem unconventional, the final result is reminiscent of egg roll filling. It is wildly popular with teenagers, and an easy dinner to make when you are expecting a number of boys. Make the filling ahead of time and reheat it in the microwave just before dinner, or keep it warm, covered, in a 200°F oven.

- 1 pound lean ground beef
- 1 tablespoon olive oil
- 8 scallions, white part only, minced
- 3 cloves garlic, minced
- 1 (1-pound) package cole slaw mix
- 1 cup diced fresh pineapple
- $1/4$ cup vinegar (any kind)
- 2 tablespoons ketchup
- 2 tablespoons soy sauce
- 1 tablespoon light brown sugar (optional)
- 8 to 10 (8-inch) tortillas

Preheat the oven to 325°F. Heat a Dutch oven over medium heat. Add the ground beef and cook, stirring frequently, until no pink is showing, about 6 minutes. Drain well and set aside. Wipe out the pan.

Return the Dutch oven to medium heat and heat the oil. Add the scallions and garlic, and cook, stirring frequently, for 2 minutes. Add the cole slaw and cook for 5 minutes, tossing it several times to mix in the scallions and garlic.

Return the meat to the pan, turn the heat down to low, cover, and cook for 5 minutes, until the cabbage is wilted.

Arrange the tortillas in a stack, wrap in aluminum foil and put in the oven to bake for 15 to 20 minutes, until warm. Combine the pineapple, vinegar, ketchup, and soy sauce in a small bowl and stir until blended. Taste it. If you'd like more of a sweet-sour combination, add the brown sugar. Pour the mixture over the cabbage and beef and cook for about 10 minutes longer, stirring occasionally, until the cabbage is very soft. Using a slotted spoon, fill each tortilla with the beef mixture, roll up, and serve hot.

Savory Meat Loaf

Serves 8 to 10

This all-American classic never goes out of style, and leftovers make great sandwiches. Use ground beef that is 95 percent lean, and drain the pan twice to remove as much fat as possible. This version, created by the late Verna Ditcher, won a blue ribbon at the Hamburg, New York, fair.

> **2 pounds lean ground beef**
>
> **$1/2$ cup old-fashioned rolled oats**
>
> **$1/4$ cup barbecue sauce**
>
> **$1/2$ teaspoon dry mustard**
>
> **$1/2$ cup toasted wheat germ**
>
> **2 eggs**
>
> **1 onion, minced**
>
> **1 teaspoon salt**

Preheat the oven to 350°F.

Combine all the ingredients in a large bowl and using clean hands, mix them well. Pat the mixture into a 9 by 5-inch loaf pan.

Bake for 1 hour. Using oven mitts, carefully tip the pan into the sink and drain off the fat. Cool for 10 minutes and drain again.

Serve warm. Allow any leftover meatloaf to cool completely and wrap in aluminum foil. Refrigerate for up to 3 days.

Quick Pork Stew

Serves 4 to 6

Pork tenderloin cooks quickly, making it a good choice for a weeknight supper. Buy it unseasoned; cuts sold packaged in marinades are usually very high in sodium (check the labels). You can make this tasty and colorful stew in less than half an hour. Serve in bowls with cornbread or hot rolls and a salad.

> **2 potatoes, peeled**
>
> **1 tablespoon olive oil**
>
> **1 onion, chopped**
>
> **1 red or green bell pepper, chopped**
>
> **2 cloves garlic, minced**
>
> **1 teaspoon ground cumin**

1 pork tenderloin (6 to 8 ounces), cut into small cubes

1 (14.5-ounce) can diced tomatoes with juice

Salt and freshly ground black pepper

$^1/_2$ cup chopped fresh parsley

Cut the potatoes into big chunks, put in a medium saucepan, and cover with water. Bring to a boil over high heat, reduce the heat to medium, and cook for 15 minutes, until they are soft when pierced with a knife. Drain and set aside to cool.

Heat the oil in a large frying pan over medium heat. Add the onion and pepper and sauté, stirring occasionally, for 6 minutes, until the vegetables are soft. Add the garlic and cook for 1 minute. Add the cumin and cook, stirring, for 1 minute. Add the pork and cook for 2 minutes, stirring constantly, until it is no longer pink. Add the tomatoes, cover the pan, and simmer for 10 minutes. Dice the potatoes, add to the stew, and cook for 5 minutes longer. Season with salt and pepper, sprinkle with parsley, and serve hot.

VARIATION: To make a vegetarian version, omit the pork. Drain and rinse 1 (15-ounce) can garbanzos and add along with the tomatoes.

Oven-Baked Ribs

Serves 4

Boys love to pick up ribs and gnaw on them. Allow several hours to cook ribs in the oven. Use the quick sauce below to season them, or open a bottle of your favorite barbecue sauce. Apply it after the ribs are almost cooked to avoid burning them. For instant ribs, buy precooked, seasoned ribs and reheat them according to the package directions. Serve with plenty of paper towels, and well away from Grandma's antique damask tablecloth.

1 rack baby back ribs (approximately 2$^1/_2$ pounds)

$^1/_4$ cup ketchup

1 tablespoon soy sauce

2 teaspoons cider vinegar

Preheat the oven to 325°F.

Arrange the ribs in a large baking dish, cover with aluminum foil, and bake for 30 minutes. Turn the ribs, cover again with the foil, and bake for 30 minutes longer. In a small bowl combine the ketchup, soy sauce, and vinegar.

Increase the oven temperature to 400°F. Brush some of the sauce on the ribs and bake, uncovered, for 20 minutes. Turn the ribs over, brush them with some more of the sauce, and bake, uncovered, for 20 minutes longer.

Increase the heat to 500°F. Brush the ribs again with sauce and bake for 5 minutes. Turn the ribs, brush with the remaining sauce, and bake for 5 minutes longer. Cut into sections of 3 to 4 ribs and serve hot.

Rib Jargon

It is easy to get confused when shopping for ribs. Here's a quick guide to some of the terms:

Spareribs, from the belly, have the best flavor. Restaurant menus offer St. Louis–style ribs, cut to expose the cartilage on the brisket bone side, usually basted with a sauce as they cook; and Memphis-style ribs, which are rubbed with dry spices before cooking. Both of these styles of ribs are best cooked very slowly in a smoker.

Baby back ribs, also called pork loin ribs, come from the vertebrae. They tend to have less meat than spareribs and can be the most expensive, but they also yield the best results when cooked in the home oven.

Country-style ribs are not ribs. They are cut from the pork loin to look like ribs. And while they will behave like ribs when cooked and basted with sauce, they don't have the meaty flavor of true ribs.

Roast Pork Loin   Serves 10 to 12

Boned pork loin roasts, which are easier to carve than roasts with the bone in, taste great hot, at room temperature, or cold. (Don't confuse pork loin with pork tenderloin, a smaller and leaner cut that cooks in one-third the time.) A pork loin roast is a flexible dinner choice when family members are coming home, hungry, at different times, since once it is cooked, you can simply carve off a few slices as needed. Watch for sales on pork roasts, when large cuts weighing up to 8 pounds are priced at under $3 per pound. Cut large uncooked roasts into two or three pieces, wrap tightly in aluminum foil, and freeze. Serve with applesauce, broccoli, and roasted sweet potatoes.

1 boneless pork loin roast, about 3 to 4 pounds

4 to 5 cloves garlic, cut into slivers

1 tablespoon Dijon-style mustard

Preheat the oven to 425°F.

With a sharp knife cut 1-inch slits randomly in the fatty top of the roast and insert a sliver of garlic in each slit. Spread the mustard over the roast.

Roast for 50 to 60 minutes, uncovered, until an instant-read thermometer registers 160°F. Remove the roast from the oven, cover with aluminum foil, and let sit for 15 minutes before carving.

VARIATION: The day before cooking, pour 1 (12-ounce) can of frozen, thawed apple juice concentrate into a shallow roasting pan. After inserting the garlic, put the pork loin in the pan, fat side up. Cover the roast with aluminum foil and marinate in the refrigerator for at least 12 and up to 24 hours, turning the roast several times so it marinates evenly. Drain off the apple juice before cooking.

Lamb and Eggplant Pie
Serves 6 to 8

Here is a great meal to make when kids may be coming home late. You can't overcook it. The flavors simply meld together. It is fabulous left over, too. Substitute zucchini for the eggplant and ground beef for the lamb if you wish.

2 eggplants

5 tablespoons olive oil

1 onion, diced

1 pound ground lamb

^{1}/$_2$ cup Pesto (page 96)

1 (28-ounce) jar tomato sauce

^{1}/$_2$ cup freshly grated Parmesan cheese

Cut the eggplants into ^{1}/$_4$-inch slices. Arrange them in layers in a colander in the sink, salting each layer liberally. Let sit for 15 minutes.

Heat 1 tablespoon of the oil in a medium frying pan over medium heat. Add the onion and sauté for 5 minutes, stirring several times, until the onion is soft but not brown. Add the ground lamb and cook, stirring frequently, for about 5 minutes or until the meat is brown and no pink is showing. Drain well and set aside.

Rinse the eggplant slices under cold water and pat dry with paper towels. Preheat the broiler.

In a small bowl, combine the pesto with the remaining 4 tablespoons of oil. Arrange the eggplant slices on a baking sheet and brush each slice with the pesto-oil mixture. Broil for 2 to 3 minutes, until the eggplant slices are lightly browned. Turn the slices over, brush the other sides with the pesto-oil mixture, and broil for 2 to 3 minutes longer, until lightly browned. Transfer the cooked slices to a platter. Continue broiling the eggplant until all the slices are cooked.

Preheat the oven to 325°F. Spoon about $1/4$ cup of the tomato sauce into the bottom of a large glass or stainless steel baking dish. Arrange half of the eggplant slices in the bottom of the dish so they just overlap. Cover the eggplant with the lamb and onion mixture, spreading it out with a spoon to form an even layer. Spoon about half of the tomato sauce over the lamb layer and gently smooth it with a spoon. Cover this layer with the remaining eggplant slices. Add the remaining tomato sauce and smooth it with a spoon. Sprinkle the cheese evenly over the top. Cover with aluminum foil.

Bake for 30 minutes, or until the juices are bubbling around the edges and the cheese is melted. If you need to hold dinner for a while, keep it warm at 200°F.

VARIATION: To make a vegetarian version, substitute 1 cup cooked bulgur or barley for the lamb.

Lamb Stew
Serves 6 to 8

Make this straightforward stew on a weekend, and you can enjoy it for at least two days. It is fragrant and warming, and an easy sell to hungry boys. Buy a butterflied lamb leg and cut it into cubes. Or, reduce the amount of meat in the recipe by cutting pieces from four or five lamb chops. Serve with crusty, whole-grain rolls and a green salad.

3 tablespoons olive oil

2 carrots, finely chopped

1 onion, finely chopped

4 cloves garlic, minced

3 tablespoons all-purpose flour

Salt and freshly ground black pepper

$1^1/2$ pounds lamb, cubed (about 3 cups)

1/2 cup dry red or white wine

Juice of 1 lemon

1 tablespoon light brown sugar

1 (14.5-ounce) can diced tomatoes, with juice

2 cups beef stock or broth

1 (28-ounce can) or 2 (15.5-ounce) cans cannellini or small white
   beans (about 4 cups), drained and rinsed

5 sprigs fresh thyme

Freshly grated Parmesan cheese, for garnish

Preheat the oven to 350°F.

Heat 1 tablespoon of the oil in a heavy Dutch oven over medium heat. Add the carrots, onion, and garlic and sauté for about 5 minutes, until the vegetables are soft. Using a slotted spoon, transfer the vegetables to a bowl.

Put the flour in a large, shallow dish and season with salt and pepper. Add the lamb cubes and toss until they are evenly coated.

Heat the remaining 2 tablespoons of oil in the Dutch oven over medium heat. Add the lamb in two batches and sauté, turning, for about 4 minutes, until browned on all sides. Using the slotted spoon, transfer the lamb to the bowl with the vegetables.

Add the wine, lemon juice, and brown sugar to the pan and stir with a wooden spoon, incorporating all the browned flour into the liquid. Bring to a boil and cook for 1 minute. Season with salt and pepper. Add the tomatoes and beef stock and bring just to a boil. Remove from the heat and add the vegetables, lamb, and beans. Stir gently to mix. Arrange the thyme on top of the stew, cover, and bake for 1 hour. Serve in bowls, sprinkled with cheese.

Slow-Cooker Vegetable Chili   Serves 6 to 8

There are several ways to serve this chili, which only takes 10 minutes to assemble. Prepare it for a weeknight supper and serve topped with cottage or feta cheese or sour cream and a sprinkling of fresh cilantro or parsley; put a spoonful in a bun and call it a sloppy joe; let it cool and use as a filling for wraps; fold it into an omelet; or toss a few cups with cooked rice or bulgur. To give it color, use several different bell peppers (red and yellow, orange and green) and a combination of canned beans. And if you have had your chili powder for more than 6 months, toss it out and buy a fresh one for the best flavor.

2 tablespoons olive oil

2 onions, finely chopped

2 bell peppers, seeded and finely chopped

1 stalk celery, diced

3 cloves garlic, minced

1 tablespoon chili powder

1 tablespoon ground cumin

1 (15-ounce) can pinto beans, drained and rinsed

1 (15-ounce) can black beans, drained and rinsed

1 (14.5-ounce) can diced tomatoes, drained

1 (14.5 ounce) can stewed tomatoes, drained

1 cup diced cherry tomatoes

Heat the oil in a large frying pan over medium heat. Add the onions, peppers, and celery and sauté for 5 minutes, until the vegetables are soft. Add the garlic and cook for 2 minutes. Add the chili powder and cumin and cook, stirring, for 2 minutes, or until fragrant. Transfer the mixture to a slow-cooker. Add the pinto beans, black beans, diced canned tomatoes, stewed tomatoes, and cherry tomatoes. Stir gently to mix well. Cover and cook on low for 6 to 8 hours.

Dinner from the Pantry

On very busy nights, try these fast meals, which will serve 4 to 6, and might provide leftovers for the next day's lunch. A couple of them use canned cream of mushroom soup—a food I avoided until I discovered organic brands, which are free of MSG and other artificial ingredients. Try to find an all-natural, MSG-free brand, such as Amy's.

Tuna-Noodle Casserole

Cook 1 pound of rotini or elbow pasta according to the package directions. Drain. Combine with 1 (10-ounce) can of organic mushroom soup (MSG-free), and 1 (6-ounce) can tuna, drained. Spoon into a 1-quart casserole dish and heat at 350°F for 20 minutes.

Quick Curry

Cook 1 cup of rice or couscous. Sauté 1 chopped onion and 2 unpeeled, chopped apples in 2 teaspoons of olive oil in a medium frying pan over medium heat for 5 minutes, until soft. Sprinkle in 1 tablespoon of curry powder and cook for 2 minutes. Add 1 (10-ounce) can of organic cream of mushroom soup (MSG-free), 1 (6-ounce) can of tuna, drained, and 1 cup of raisins. Serve hot, over rice or couscous.

Three-Pepper Shrimp and Pesto Pasta

Cook a 12-ounce package of penne according to the package directions. While the pasta is cooking, heat 1 tablespoon of olive oil in a large frying pan over medium heat. Add 1 (1-pound) package frozen red, green, and yellow pepper strips and 1/2 pound precooked, peeled frozen medium shrimp (about 2 cups). Cook and stir frequently for about 8 minutes, until both are heated through and soft. Drain any water from the skillet. Drain the pasta and toss with the peppers and shrimp. Add 1/2 cup of pesto, toss, and serve.

Pasta with Peas

Cook 1 pound of whole-wheat spaghetti, broken into 2-inch lengths. While the pasta is cooking, sauté an onion in 2 tablespoons of olive oil in a large frying pan over medium heat for about 4 minutes, until soft. Add 1 cup of frozen baby peas and cook for 1 minute longer, just until they are thawed. Beat 2 eggs with 1/4 cup grated Parmesan cheese in a small bowl. Drain the pasta and return it to the skillet. Pour the egg and cheese mixture on top of it, toss, and cook over medium heat for 3 or 4 minutes, until the mixture is heated through and the eggs are cooked. Add 1/2 cup diced ham if you wish. Serve hot.

Lambfree Shepherd's Pie Serves 6 to 8

In place of the traditional ground lamb and gravy filling, this spicy filling relies on a combination of vegetable flavors that come together nicely under the crust. With the beans it makes a complete meal, and a good choice for a winter weeknight supper. Heat leftovers in the microwave. Serve with a green salad and breadsticks.

1 pound Swiss chard

2 tablespoons olive oil

1 onion, diced

1 fennel bulb, trimmed and finely chopped

2 cups chopped mushrooms

1 tablespoon curry powder (optional)

1 (14-ounce) can cream of mushroom soup, preferably organic and MSG-free

1 (15-ounce) can Great Northern or cannellini beans, drained and rinsed

Salt and freshly ground black pepper

3 cups mashed potatoes

2 to 4 tablespoons milk (optional)

Preheat the oven to 375°F.

Remove the stems from the Swiss chard and coarsely chop the leaves. Bring a large saucepan of water to a boil over high heat, add the chard, and cook for 1 minute. Drain the chard and allow it to cool enough to handle. Using your hands, squeeze out the moisture, put the chard on a cutting board, and chop finely. Set aside.

Heat the oil in a large frying pan over medium heat. Add the onion and fennel and sauté for about 5 minutes, stirring frequently, until soft. Add the mushrooms and cook, stirring, for 3 minutes, or until they begin to give off some moisture. Add the curry powder and cook, stirring, for 2 minutes, or until fragrant. Remove from the heat. Add the Swiss chard, soup, and beans and gently stir together. Season with salt and pepper.

Spoon the mixture into a 10-inch pie pan. Cover the top with mashed potatoes, thinned with a little milk if necessary to make them easy to spread. Run a fork in both east-west and north-south directions across the top.

Bake for 30 minutes, or until the filling is bubbly. Let cool for 5 minutes before serving.

Sweet Potato Curry

This fragrant, meatless stew is packed with nutrients. One sweet potato alone contains three times more beta-carotene than $1/2$ cup of cooked carrots and is a good source of vitamins C and E, folate, and potassium. Serve the curry over rice, bulgur, couscous, or barley. And don't mention the sweet potato to a suspicious boy. He will never know it is in there. Leftovers will keep for 3 days in the refrigerator, making this a good choice to prepare ahead when you know the week will be busy.

2 tablespoons olive oil

1 large onion, diced

4 cloves garlic, minced

1 red bell pepper, diced

2 carrots, diced

1 stalk celery, diced

2 teaspoons curry powder

1 teaspoon ground cardamom

$1/2$ teaspoon ground ginger

1 large sweet potato, peeled and diced

1 (14.5-ounce) can diced tomatoes, with juice

$1/2$ cup coconut milk

$1/2$ cup roasted unsalted peanuts

$1/2$ cup raisins

Heat the oil in a large, heavy saucepan over medium heat. Add the onion and garlic and sauté for 5 minutes, or until both are soft but not brown. Add the bell pepper, carrots, and celery, stir, and cook for 5 minutes, or until the vegetables are soft. Add the curry powder, cardamom, and ginger, and gently stir until well mixed with the vegetables. Cook for 3 minutes. Add the sweet potato, tomatoes with juice, and coconut milk, stir, and cook for 2 minutes. Cover the pot, turn the heat down to medium-low, and simmer for 15 to 20 minutes, until the sweet potato is fork-tender. Stir in the peanuts and raisins, remove from the heat, and let sit, covered, for 5 minutes. Serve hot.

Soba with Broccoli and Marinated Tofu   Serves 6 to 8

If you rinse them after they're cooked, soba, or buckwheat noodles, don't stick together as they cool, making them a good food to serve at room temperature or cold. Use them to make salads for picnics or potlucks and to have something in the refrigerator that a boy can eat for a snack without reheating. Soba is usually sold in packages of three bundles, each weighing about 3 to 4 ounces. Use two bundles for this recipe. Tofu improves in flavor when it is marinated, so allow 30 minutes for it to absorb the flavors of the marinade before cooking it.

> 1 tablespoon peanut oil
>
> 3 tablespoons soy sauce
>
> 3 tablespoons rice vinegar
>
> 16 ounces firm tofu, cut into small cubes
>
> 8 ounces soba noodles
>
> 2 cups chopped broccoli
>
> $1/2$ cup chopped fresh cilantro

Combine the oil, soy sauce, and vinegar in a small bowl and blend with a whisk until smooth. Reserve 2 tablespoons of the dressing. Pour the remaining dressing into a shallow bowl, add the tofu, and toss it gently to coat well. Let the mixture sit for 30 minutes.

Bring a large saucepan of water to a boil over high heat, add the soba, and cook for about 5 minutes, until the noodles are soft but still firm to the bite. Drain in a colander, rinse with cold water, and drain again. Transfer the noodles to a large bowl.

Cook the broccoli in a steamer set over boiling water for 2 minutes, or bring a large saucepan of water to a boil over high heat, add the broccoli, and cook for 2 minutes. Drain well and add to the noodles.

Heat a large frying pan over medium heat. Add the tofu and any unabsorbed marinade and heat for about 2 minutes on each side, using tongs to turn the cubes. Add the warm tofu to the broccoli and noodles. Add the reserved 2 tablespoons of dressing to the mixture, and toss gently. Add the cilantro and toss again. Serve warm or cold.

VARIATION: Omit the tofu and broccoli. Toss the cooked soba with 2 to 3 tablespoons of the dressing, 2 tablespoons of sesame seeds, and $1/2$ cup chopped parsley.

Quiche

Allow several hours to make a quiche, so there is time for the pastry to chill before you roll it out. Although Swiss and Gruyère are traditional, you can use any shredded cheeses, including packaged Mexican blends. Leftovers taste good cold for lunch, or as an after-school snack, and they also provide a quick breakfast.

PASTRY FOR CRUST

1 cup whole-wheat flour

$1/2$ cup all-purpose flour

$1/4$ teaspoon salt

$1/4$ cup cold butter, cut into small chunks

$1/4$ cup olive oil

$1/4$ cup cold water

FILLING

5 eggs

$1^1/2$ cups half-and-half

2 teaspoons dried tarragon

$1/2$ cup chopped cooked turkey bacon or diced ham (optional)

1 cup shredded cheese

To make the crust, combine the flour, salt, and butter in a food processor and pulse for a few seconds, until the mixture forms crumbs. Add the oil and pulse again. With the machine running, add the water and pulse just until the crumbs begin to clump together. If necessary, use a rubber spatula to scrape down the sides of the bowl and pulse again.

Lay a sheet of waxed paper out on the counter and dump the crumbs onto it. Form them into a ball, flatten slightly so the dough looks like a giant hamburger patty, wrap in the waxed paper, and chill for 1 hour.

Preheat the oven to 425°F.

Roll the dough out into a circle on a lightly floured surface and fit it into a 9-inch pie pan. Crimp the edges. Place an 8-inch cake pan inside the crust-lined pan and bake for 8 minutes. Remove the cake pan, use a fork to firm up any parts of the crust that have sagged, and bake for 2 minutes. Remove the crust from the oven.

Combine the eggs, half-and-half, and tarragon in a mixing bowl and beat with a whisk until smooth. Sprinkle the bacon, if using, on the bottom of the crust and sprinkle the cheese on top of the bacon. Pour the egg mixture over the bacon and cheese. Bake for 10 minutes. Turn the oven temperature down to 350°F and bake for 25 to 30 minutes longer, until the top is beginning to brown and a knife inserted in the center comes out clean.

VARIATIONS:

• Sauté 1 diced onion and $1/2$ cup diced bell pepper or diced mushrooms in 1 tablespoon olive oil in a small frying pan over medium heat for 5 minutes, until soft, and add to the egg mixture before pouring it into the crust.

• Scatter 1 cup chopped cooked broccoli or asparagus over the cheese before adding the egg mixture.

• Season the egg mixture with 1 tablespoon fresh chopped chives, basil, or thyme instead of the tarragon.

Friday Night Frittata   Serves 4

This is a great, easy recipe to teach your son to cook for himself. Leftovers cook tasty sandwiches: heat wedges in the microwave for 2 minutes and put one or two between two slices of whole-grain bread. (Ketchup is optional.) Serve with a green salad and a plate of sliced apples and oranges.

> **1 tablespoon olive oil**
>
> **1 green or red bell pepper, seeded and chopped**
>
> **3 to 4 scallions, white part only, sliced**
>
> **8 eggs**
>
> **$1/4$ cup milk**
>
> **1 cup grated cheddar cheese or a blend of cheddar and
> Monterey jack cheese**
>
> **Salt and freshly ground black pepper**

Preheat the oven to 400°F. Heat the oil in a 10-inch cast-iron or ovenproof frying pan over medium-low heat. Add the bell pepper and scallions and sauté for about 5 minutes, stirring occasionally, until the vegetables are soft. Beat the eggs and milk in a large bowl and stir in the cheese. Pour the egg mixture over the pepper and scallions. Bake for 20 minutes, or until the top is puffy and brown. Cut into wedges and serve warm.

- Sauté a chopped onion along with the pepper.

- Add 1 cup chopped cooked ham or turkey to the sautéed vegetables before adding the egg-cheese mixture.

Greek Pizza   Serves 4

It is a lot easier than you might think to make your own pizza dough and bake your own pizza in the kitchen. The dough needs to rise for 2 hours, so plan it as a weekend lunch or supper treat. Since you are putting it together, you can control how much cheese goes on top, and experiment with a selection of vegetables, too. Get your teenager involved in shaping the dough and adding the toppings.

> **Pizza Dough (recipe follows)**
>
> **2 tablespoons fine cornmeal**
>
> **1 cup Yogurt Cheese (page 108)**
>
> **1 cup crumbled feta cheese**
>
> **4 teaspoons dried oregano or Greek seasoning blend**
>
> **Salt and freshly ground black pepper**

Prepare the dough according to the recipe directions.

Preheat the oven to 500°F.

Punch down the dough, turn it out onto a clean work surface, and knead for 5 minutes. Divide it into fourths. Hand pull and shape into four 8- to 10-inch crusts. Layer two crusts between parchment paper and set aside.

Sprinkle a baking sheet with 1 tablespoon of the cornmeal and arrange the remaining two crusts on top. Spread $1/4$ cup of yogurt cheese evenly on each, scatter $1/4$ cup of feta on each, and sprinkle each with 1 teaspoon of the oregano. Season with salt and pepper. Bake for 10 to 12 minutes, or until lightly browned. Repeat with the remaining two crusts.

VARIATIONS:

- For a more traditional pizza, cover the top with about $1/4$ cup tomato sauce and sprinkle each pizza with $1/4$ cup shredded mozzarella or Monterey jack cheese.

- Top the tomato sauce with your favorite roasted vegetables (page 100) and sprinkle with Parmesan cheese.

• Sprinkle the pizza with Parmesan cheese, add overlapping very thin slices of fresh tomato and 1 tablespoon of chopped fresh basil.

Pizza Dough
Makes four 8- to 10-inch pizza crusts

1¹/₂ cups warm (110°F) water

1 package active dry yeast

2 teaspoons salt

¹/₂ teaspoon garlic powder

2 tablespoons olive oil

4 cups all-purpose flour

In a large bowl, whisk together the water and yeast. Let stand for 5 minutes. Whisk in the salt, garlic powder, and oil. Stir in about 3¹/₂ cups of the flour, enough to form a soft dough. Sprinkle a work surface with the remaining flour, turn out the dough, and knead for about 5 minutes, or until smooth.

Lightly oil a large bowl. Put in the dough, turn to coat with oil, and cover with a clean towel. Let the dough rise for about 2 hours, or until it is puffy and light. (It is okay if the dough isn't doubled.)

The dough is now ready to be shaped, topped, and baked.

VARIATION: Use 2 cups whole wheat flour and 2 cups all-purpose flour.

Spinach Calzones
Serves 4 to 8

Wonderfully portable and suitable for snacks as well as family meals, calzones can be made with a wide range of fillings. Here they're stuffed with a fresh spinach-ricotta mixture. (Just ¹/₄ cup of ricotta contains 10 grams of protein.) Allow 2 hours for the dough to rise and about 30 minutes to bake the calzones.

Pizza Dough (above)

1 cup ricotta cheese

1 tablespoon olive oil

1 medium onion, finely chopped

1 cup chopped fresh mushrooms

1 pound fresh spinach, tough stems removed, and chopped

1 cup freshly grated Parmesan cheese

2 tablespoons chopped fresh basil

Salt and freshly ground black pepper to taste

Make the pizza dough according to the recipe instructions.

Place the ricotta in a strainer over a bowl and let sit for 15 minutes to drain.

Heat the oil in a large frying pan over medium heat. Add the onion and sauté, stirring occasionally, for about 5 minutes, until it is soft. Add the mushrooms and sauté for 3 minutes longer, just until they begin to lose some moisture. Stir in the spinach, cover the pan, and cook for 4 minutes, until the spinach wilts. Stir in the drained ricotta, Parmesan, and basil and season with salt and pepper. Place the mixture in a colander and let drain while you shape the dough.

Preheat the oven to 350°F.

Pull the dough apart into four tennis ball–sized pieces. Let each piece rest for about 10 minutes. On a lightly floured surface, roll one piece out into a circle about 8 inches in diameter. Spoon about $2/3$ cup of the drained filling onto one-half of the dough, fold up, and seal, turning the edges under. Repeat with the other three pieces. Place the calzones on a lightly greased baking sheet.

Bake for 30 minutes, or until nicely browned.

Rice, Barley, and Tomato Stew Serves 4 to 6

Barley, often overlooked in favor of rice or pasta, is high in fiber and serves as a culinary workhorse in stews, where it holds onto its firm texture and nutty flavor. This dish makes a great meal on a cold night, served with a green salad and whole-wheat rolls. Give at least an hour to cook.

1 tablespoon olive oil

1 onion, finely chopped

1 carrot, finely chopped

1 stalk celery, finely chopped

3 cloves garlic, minced

4 cups chicken stock or broth

1 (14.5-ounce) can diced tomatoes, with juice

2 teaspoons dried thyme

$^1/_2$ cup brown rice

$^1/_2$ cup pearl barley

1 (15-ounce) can kidney beans, drained and rinsed

Freshly grated Parmesan cheese

Heat the oil in a Dutch oven over medium heat. Add the onion, carrot, and celery and sauté for about 8 minutes, stirring frequently, until the vegetables are very soft. Add the garlic and sauté for 2 minutes. Add the stock, tomatoes, thyme, rice, and barley. Stir, turn the heat up to high, and bring just to a boil. Turn the heat down to low, cover, and simmer for 40 minutes.

Add the beans and cook, covered, for 20 minutes longer, or until the rice and barley are cooked and the stew is thick. Serve hot, sprinkled with Parmesan cheese.

VARIATION: Add 2 cups sliced, cooked chicken sausages along with the beans.

Pasta with Fresh Tomatoes   Serves 6

It is worth waiting for ripe, garden fresh tomatoes before trying this recipe. As you take in the benefits of lycopene, you'll savor the flavor. Allow time for the ingredients to sit and get wonderfully juicy. This combination tastes especially great on a very hot day.

4 to 6 medium ripe tomatoes, chopped

2 cloves garlic, minced

3 tablespoons chopped fresh basil

1 teaspoon salt

$^1/_4$ cup olive oil

1 pound whole-wheat fettuccine

$^1/_2$ cup grated Parmesan cheese

Combine the tomatoes, garlic, and basil in a bowl. Sprinkle with salt. Add the olive oil and toss. Let the mixture sit at room temperature for 4 to 6 hours to let the tomatoes release a lot of their juice and to allow the flavors to sharpen.

Bring a large pot of water to a boil, add the pasta, and cook, stirring frequently, according to the package instructions, until the pasta is tender but still firm to the bite. Drain and return to the pot. Add the tomato mixture and toss. Serve in shallow bowls, sprinkled with cheese.

Cavatappi with Spinach and Beans

Serves 4 to 6

Adapted from a Leafy Greens Council recipe, this winning combination provides a complete meal in one bowl. It comes together quickly, so you need to have all the ingredients prepared and ready for last-minute combining. It will win over those who don't love spinach, and it makes great leftovers to reheat in the microwave or enjoy cold. Cavatappi is a corkscrew-shaped pasta. If you can't find it, use rotini or casserole elbows and cook according to the package directions.

   1 tablespoon salt

   8 ounces cavatappi

   2 tablespoons olive oil

   2 cloves garlic, minced

   1 (15-ounce) can cannellini or other white beans, drained and rinsed

   4 cups chopped baby spinach leaves

   1 cup (4 ounces) shredded Asiago cheese

   Salt and freshly ground black pepper

Bring a large pot of water to a boil. Add the salt, then the cavatappi, and stir for 2 minutes. Cook for about 6 minutes longer, until the pasta is tender but firm to the bite.

   While the pasta cooks, heat the oil in a large frying pan over medium heat. Add the garlic and sauté for 3 minutes, stirring frequently. Add the beans and cook, stirring occasionally, until the pasta is ready.

   Drain the pasta in a colander in the sink and immediately put the spinach in the bottom of the hot pasta pot. Pour the drained pasta on top, add the beans and garlic, and sprinkle with the cheese. Cover and let the mixture sit for 2 minutes. Turn out into a large serving bowl, season with salt and pepper, toss, and serve.

Real Mac and Cheese

Serves 6 to 8

Most of us have succumbed to the charms of packaged mac and cheese, which often saves the evening, since kids tend to love it. Here's an easy way to make something closer to the classic dish, which begins life with a thin white sauce. It is a great, old-fashioned lunch or dinner. Serve with sliced tomatoes.

   1 tablespoon salt

   1 pound cavatappi or casserole elbows

2 cups milk

2 tablespoons butter

2 tablespoons all-purpose flour

1 cup shredded cheddar or a mix of cheddar and Swiss cheese

$1/2$ cup grated Parmesan cheese

Salt and freshly ground black pepper

Bring a large pot of water to a boil. Add the salt and the pasta and stir for 2 minutes. Cook until tender but still firm to the bite, about 6 more minutes for the cavatappi and 4 more minutes for the elbows.

While the pasta cooks, heat the milk over low heat in a small saucepan (don't let it boil). Melt the butter over medium-low heat in a medium saucepan, add the flour, and stir with a whisk until smooth. Let the mixture bubble for 2 minutes, stirring frequently. Pour in the hot milk and cook, stirring constantly with the whisk for several minutes, until the sauce begins to thicken slightly. Add the cheese and cook for 2 minutes, or until the cheese is melted and the sauce is smooth. Season with salt and pepper. Turn the heat down to low and keep the sauce warm. Stir it occasionally. Drain the pasta and return it to the pot. Add the sauce and toss to mix. Serve hot.

NOTE: Keep a few boxes of packaged macaroni and cheese in the pantry and teach your son to make them. The best choices won't contain artificial ingredients. Teach him to omit the butter from the sauce ingredients (it isn't necessary) and to add 1 cup frozen peas and 1 cup frozen corn and cook over low heat until the mixture is heated through.

Dinner Salad   Serves 4

Here is a great way to get everyone in the family to eat more greens. The combination of warm meat, cold lettuce, crunchy vegetables, and fruit is a nice change from typical salads. If your son is suspicious about the colors and textures of mesclun mix, humor him with a plate full of iceberg or "white" lettuce from Romaine hearts, but add just a few leaves of baby spinach or red leaf lettuce here and there. Try to gradually get him accustomed to eating colored and dark lettuces, which contain more nutrients than very pale greens.

8 cups mesclun mix

1 tablespoon olive oil

1 pound stir-fry beef strips or top sirloin cut into thin strips

1 red bell pepper, cut into strips

1 cucumber, peeled and chopped

2 stalks celery, sliced

1 jicama, peeled and chopped

1 cup fresh raspberries, blueberries, or chopped apple

$^1/_2$ cup feta or blue cheese

Raspberry vinaigrette (bottled or homemade)

Arrange the mesclun mix on four large dinner plates.

Heat the oil in a large frying pan over medium-high heat. Add the beef and sauté, stirring frequently, for about 4 minutes, until the meat is cooked through. Scatter some of the cooked strips on top of each salad serving. Add some bell pepper, cucumber, celery, jicama, raspberries, and feta to each plate and drizzle each with about 2 tablespoons of dressing. Serve while the meat is still warm.

VARIATIONS:

• Instead of beef, use a pork tenderloin or cooked, frozen shrimp, reheated in boiling water for a few minutes.

• For a cold salad, use drained canned tuna or salmon, or leftover cooked chicken, turkey, or beef.

Fried Rice   Serves 4 to 6

This amazingly easy and versatile dish is a great way to use up any leftover cooked meat. You can also make it with cubes of tofu; it also tastes fine with just rice and vegetables. This kind of quick supper is another example of why it is helpful to have some cooked rice on hand.

1 tablespoon olive oil

1 onion, diced

1 red or yellow bell pepper, diced

1 cup frozen baby peas

3 to 4 cups chopped cooked chicken, turkey, beef, pork, or lamb

2 cups cooked brown basmati rice

2 eggs

1 tablespoon water

2 tablespoons soy sauce

Heat the oil in a large frying pan over medium heat. Add the onion and pepper and sauté, stirring occasionally, for 5 minutes, or until the vegetables are soft. Stir in the frozen peas and cook for 2 minutes. Add the chicken and cook for 2 minutes longer. Add the rice, about $1/4$ cup at a time, stirring gently with a spoon after each addition, to mix it in with the other ingredients. Cook for about 4 minutes to heat it through.

Beat the eggs with the water in a small bowl.

Increase the heat to medium-high. Form a well in the center of the pan, add the eggs, let them cook for about 1 minute, and then stir them gently into the rice mixture. Cook for about 2 minutes. Sprinkle with soy sauce and serve hot.

Heavenly Hash   Serves 4

This humble dish, which can be made from almost any leftovers, always seems to appeal to boys. Teach them to make it for themselves, and you'll be surprised at how inventive they become. One of the secrets is using a heavy pan, such as one made of cast iron, that heats evenly and gives the hash a nice brown crust.

2 tablespoons olive oil

1 onion, finely chopped

2 stalks celery, finely chopped

2 cups leftover cooked chopped chicken or beef

2 cups mashed or diced cooked potatoes

1 cup chicken or beef stock or broth

Salt and freshly ground black pepper

Heat the oil in a heavy 10-inch frying pan over medium heat. Add the onion and celery and sauté, stirring frequently, for 5 minutes, until both are very soft. Add the meat and potatoes and continue cooking for about 5 minutes, turning frequently with a spatula, until both are starting to brown. Add the stock and stir it into the hash. Season with salt and pepper. Turn the heat down to low and let the mixture cook for about 10 minutes, until a brown crust forms on the bottom. Loosen the hash around the edges with the spatula and invert the pan over a large round platter. Serve hot.

Continued on page 192

Leftover Specials

When you have bits and pieces of leftovers in the refrigerator but you haven't planned anything for a meal, create a dinner platter supper, a smorgasbord on a plate. Teenagers love to eat this way. Set out a large oval platter, about 20 inches long, and fill it up with a variety of foods, keeping in mind those 4 or 5 recommended daily servings of vegetables and fruit. Think about the famous Cobb salads with their rows of ingredients as you put it together, but don't labor over it. Make it fun. This meal really does start with the plate, which provides an opportunity to be playful. (Our household favorites include a plain white turkey-shaped platter and a dark green flounder platter with eyes on the sides.) Once you see how much your son enjoys this kind of dinner, and how easy it is, you may well find yourself shopping for things to include: several different salads or side dishes from the deli along with a bit of sushi and some sliced, cooked fish, chicken, or beef.

1. Arrange any of the following ingredients on the platter, making rows and keeping each ingredient separate, rather than tossing them all together. Drizzle any salad items with dressing after they're assembled.

Shredded lettuce	Canned tuna or salmon, drained
Cherry tomatoes	
Baby carrots	Cubes of cheese
Chopped celery	Crumbled turkey bacon
Sliced cucumbers	Hard-cooked eggs
Sliced avocado	Steamed vegetables
Sliced fennel	Sliced apples, pears, melon, or banana
Sliced cold chicken or steak	
2 or 3 slices of rolled up deli turkey or ham	

2. Add a small dish (custard cup or doubled cupcake wrappers) of nuts, raisins or other dried fruit, or applesauce.

3. Add a roll, a breadstick, a rice cake, a few corn chips, or crackers.

4. Reheat leftovers in the microwave and spoon them onto the platter.

VARIATIONS:

- Use 2 cups flaked cooked seafood or cooked vegetables instead of chicken or beef.

- Substitute 2 cups cooked, mashed winter squash or sweet potatoes for the mashed potatoes.

- Add $1/4$ cup chopped toasted nuts during the last 10 minutes of cooking.

- After Thanksgiving dinner, add 1 cup stuffing and 1 cup cooked winter squash or chopped green beans, and use 1 cup gravy instead of stock.

CHAPTER 7

Sweet and Sensible Desserts and Drinks

As you think about ways to wake boys up to tastes that don't depend on sugar and fat, desserts can become problematic. Don't let them be. Instead, figure that desserts and special drinks are where boys who eat a balanced diet can safely enjoy 100 to 300 discretionary sugar calories a day. It is fine for them to have a few cookies or a piece of cake now and then. It isn't fine for them to eat a dozen cookies or half a chocolate fudge cake every day, or build a foot-high hot fudge sundae after snacking on candy and cookies along with a few soft drinks.

One of the most important things to teach your son is portion control—how to eat a modest dessert, not a quarter of a cake. To help get this message across, invest in some *small* bowls ($^1/_2$- to 1-cup capacity) and *small* plates (6- to 8-inch) for serving dessert. Don't use cereal or soup bowls, or dinner plates, which make smaller portions look skimpy. Whenever possible postpone dessert until at least 30 minutes after dinner, so it feels a bit more special. Dietitian Inger Hustrulid suggests that families stay home for a healthy dinner, but go out for dessert as a treat now and then, rather than eating fast-food meals. She also recommends bringing home a few cookies or the right number of cupcakes from a bakery instead of making several dozen cookies or a whole cake for just three or four people. If you do find time to bake, make half a recipe for cookies, or half a cake recipe and produce cupcakes instead of a two-layer cake. Look for ways to reduce the fat in recipes and work in nutritious ingredients such as granola, honey, whole-wheat flour, oatmeal, canned pumpkin, and nuts.

Highlight the sweetness of fruit as a treat by serving it as a dessert. You only need a few pieces to create an inviting selection. For example, combine raspberries, kiwis, and orange slices, or sliced strawberries, watermelon, and blueberries and serve topped with a dollop of yogurt and a small sprinkling of nuts. Keep a supply of unsweetened frozen fruit, as well as fresh fruit, on hand and encourage your son to make a low-fat smoothie for dessert, as a homework break, or as a snack before bed.

Keep a constant supply of 1 percent or skim milk and water in the refrigerator. Don't encourage boys to drink gallons of fruit juice when they're thirsty. While a glass of orange, apple, or blueberry juice is fine for an evening snack, fruit juices raise blood glucose levels quickly and don't provide the benefit of fiber found in fruit. (Real fruit along with a glass of water is always a better choice than juice.) Pay attention to labels when you shop. Supermarkets sell a lot of juice look-alikes. Avoid buying anything that uses the words "drink," "beverage," "cocktail," or "ade" in its name. Any beverage that contains as little as 5 percent fruit juice and lots of sugar is only masquerading as juice.

Strawberries with Yogurt and Brown Sugar   Serves 4

Just what the name promises, this is one of the easiest desserts to assemble. It will disappear in seconds. Strawberries are nutritious: just eight contain more vitamin C than an orange. The trick to keeping it healthy is using a small amount of brown sugar. Buy fresh berries at the height of their local season and leave the stems and caps on. Experiment with different flavors of yogurt, too.

1 quart fresh strawberries

1/2 cup plain or flavored yogurt

2 tablespoons light or dark brown sugar

Put the berries in a bowl. Put three $^1/_2$-cup ramekins in the center of a large platter. Put the yogurt in one, the brown sugar in one, and leave one empty for holding the caps and stems after the berries are eaten. Arrange the berries around the ramekins and invite your family to dip the berries first into the yogurt, then into the brown sugar.

Berries and "Cream"   Serves 4

Use fresh strawberries, blueberries, blackberries, or raspberries and dress them up a bit by making a batch of this low-fat alternative to whipped cream as a delicious topping. It is even suitable as a special touch at breakfast. It will keep, refrigerated and tightly covered, for up to a week. Use any variety of jam, seedless or not as you prefer, sweetened with fruit juice rather than sugar, and any kind of nuts for special texture and to complement just about any fresh fruit.

> $^1/_2$ **cup sour cream**
>
> $^1/_2$ **cup plain yogurt**
>
> $^1/_4$ **cup fruit-sweetened seedless raspberry jam**
>
> **1 pint fresh strawberries, sliced, or blueberries,**
>   **blackberries, or raspberries**
>
> $^1/_2$ **cup chopped pecans**

Combine the sour cream, yogurt, and jam in a food processor and blend until smooth. Arrange the berries in four serving bowls, add a dollop of topping to each, and sprinkle each with pecans.

VARIATION: Use unsweetened frozen fruit; zap it in the microwave for about 30 seconds, just enough to thaw it but not enough to make it soggy.

One-Crust Blueberry Pie   Serves 6 to 8

Instead of using two crusts, make this pie with just one, which cuts the quantity of fat in half and results in a healthier dessert. If you can, let the pastry chill in the refrigerator for about 30 minutes before you roll it out. If you can't spare that time, dust it with flour to keep it from sticking to the rolling pin.

> **Pastry for Single Pie Crust (recipe follows)**
>
> **1 pint fresh blueberries, preferably wild**
>
> **Juice of $^1/_2$ lemon**

1 tablespoon all-purpose flour

$1/4$ cup firmly packed light brown sugar

Preheat the oven to 425°F.

Make the pie pastry and refrigerate.

Combine the blueberries, lemon juice, flour, and brown sugar in a bowl and toss gently.

Roll out the pie crust on a lightly floured work surface, forming a circle about 12 inches in diameter. Line a 9-inch pie pan with the pastry. Spoon the blueberry filling into the pastry-lined pan and gently bring the edges of the pastry up toward the center of the pie. Don't worry if some of the berries in the center of the pie are not covered with crust. The pie will look rustic.

Bake for 10 minutes. Reduce the oven temperature to 350°F and bake for 30 minutes longer, or until the crust is lightly browned and the filling is bubbling. Cool on a rack for 30 minutes before serving.

VARIATION: Use 4 to 5 medium, peeled sliced apples instead of the blueberries.

Single Pie Crust

1 cup all-purpose flour

$1/2$ cup whole-wheat pastry flour

1 teaspoon sugar

$1/4$ teaspoon salt

$1/4$ cup cold butter, cut into chunks

$1/4$ cup olive oil

$1/4$ cup cold water

Combine the flours, sugar, and salt in a food processor and pulse to blend. Add the butter and oil and pulse again until damp crumbs form. With the motor running, add the water and blend just until the mixture starts to clump together. Turn the dough out onto a sheet of waxed paper, form it into a disk, and refrigerate for 30 minutes. The pastry is now ready for rolling out according to the recipe instructions.

Makes crust for one 9-inch pie.

Blueberry Crisp

Traditional recipes for fruit crisps contain a stick or more of butter and are loaded with so much sugar it often obscures the taste of the fruit. Here is a lighter version that lets the berries shine. Fresh, wild blueberries taste divine, but cultivated berries will work, too, and so will frozen. Serve topped with vanilla yogurt.

FILLING

1 quart fresh blueberries

2 tablespoons light brown sugar

Juice of 1 lemon

TOPPING

1 cup old-fashioned rolled oats

$1/4$ cup firmly packed light brown sugar

$1/2$ cup whole-wheat flour

3 tablespoons olive oil

$1/2$ cup finely chopped walnuts or pecans

Preheat the oven to 375°F. Lightly grease a 7 by 11-inch or 8 by 10-inch baking dish.

To make the filling, combine the berries, brown sugar, and lemon juice in a mixing bowl and toss very gently with a rubber spatula. Transfer the berries to the prepared baking dish.

To make the topping, combine the oats, brown sugar, and flour in a food processor and pulse for several seconds. Add the olive oil and pulse just until the mixture looks like damp crumbs. Transfer the mixture to the mixing bowl and stir in the nuts. Sprinkle the topping over the fruit.

Bake for 30 minutes, or until the top is lightly browned and the fruit is bubbling. Remove from the oven and let sit for at least 15 minutes. Serve warm or cold.

VARIATION: Use sliced, unpeeled peaches or apples in place of the blueberries.

One-Crust Cranberry-Apple-Walnut Pie

Serves 6 to 8

This is a colorful pie to make at Thanksgiving time, or when fresh summer fruits aren't available. Cranberries are a good source of vitamin C, and they turn the apples a lovely pink. Leftovers tend to disappear at breakfast time.

Pastry for Single Pie Crust (page 196)

2 cups whole cranberries

1^1/$_2$ cups cider

^{1}/$_2$ cup honey

1 cup raisins

3 apples, peeled and chopped

1 cup chopped walnuts or pecans

Make the pie pastry and refrigerate.

Combine the cranberries, cider, and honey in a large saucepan, bring just to a boil over medium-high heat, turn the heat down to medium-low, and simmer for 5 minutes, until the cranberries begin to pop. Add the raisins and apples and cook for 5 minutes. Remove the pan from the heat and let sit for 30 minutes to cool and to let the fruits absorb the cider. Stir in the walnuts.

Preheat the oven to 425°F.

Roll out the pie pastry on a lightly floured work surface, forming a circle about 12 inches in diameter, and fit it into a 9-inch pie pan. Using a slotted spoon, transfer the filling into the crust, leaving any juice behind. (Use the juice as a sauce for yogurt, or discard.) Gently bring the edges of the pastry up toward the center of the pie, leaving some of the filling uncovered in the center.

Bake for 10 minutes. Reduce the oven temperature to 350°F and bake for 30 minutes, or until the crust is lightly browned and the filling is bubbling. Cool on a rack for 30 minutes before serving.

Mom's Apple Pie

Serves 6 to 8

Few things are as reassuring as a homemade pie sitting on the counter. This one is an indulgence, made with butter in the crust. On the night you serve it, keep dinner light—a stir-fry or vegetarian chili—to balance the meal. And cut small slices. It tastes great warm or cold and is always good the next day. If you can find them, use Northern Spy apples, an old-fashioned, thin-skinned variety with hauntingly sweet yellow-white flesh that stays firm when baked. Or combine at least two varieties such as Cortland, McIntosh, Pippin, or Granny Smith.

Pastry for a Double-Crust Pie (recipe follows)

$1/3$ cup finely ground pecans

4 or 5 whole apples, peeled and sliced

2 tablespoons all-purpose flour

$1/8$ teaspoon salt

$1/2$ cup firmly packed light brown sugar

1 tablespoon freshly squeezed lemon juice

$3/4$ teaspoon ground cinnamon

Make the pastry and refrigerate.

Preheat the oven to 400°F.

Roll out one crust on a lightly floured work surface, forming a circle about 11 inches in diameter. Line a 9-inch pie pan with the crust. Sprinkle the pecans over the bottom.

Put the apples in a bowl. Combine the flour, salt, and brown sugar in a small bowl, whisk to blend, and add to the apples along with the lemon juice and cinnamon. Toss gently to coat the apples, and spoon them into the pastry-lined pan.

Roll out the top crust to the same size, fit it over the filling, crimp the edges, and cut vents with a knife or fork.

Bake for 1 hour, or until the top is golden brown. Cool on a wire rack for at least 20 minutes. Serve warm or at room temperature.

Pastry for a Double-Crust Pie

3 cups all-purpose flour

1 teaspoon salt

2 tablespoons sugar

1 cup cold unsalted butter, cut into bits

$1/2$ cup cold water

Combine $1^1/2$ cups of the flour, $1/2$ teaspoon of the salt, and 1 tablespoon of the sugar in a food processor and pulse to blend. Add half the butter and pulse again. With the motor running, add $1/4$ cup of the water and blend just until the mixture starts to clump together. Turn the dough out onto a sheet of wax paper and form it into a disk. Repeat with the remaining ingredients. Refrigerate for 30 minutes.

Baked Apples Serves 6

This old-fashioned dessert uses whole-wheat bread, a good source of fiber, but no one will know it is in there. If you leave the apples unpeeled you'll get the nutritional advantage of the skins but they may separate a bit from the slices. For a very smooth texture, peel the apples. Serve topped with yogurt.

6 slices whole-wheat bread

$1/2$ cup fruit-sweetened apricot jam

5 medium apples, thinly sliced

Preheat the oven to 300°F. Lightly grease a 1-quart round baking dish.

Cut the crusts from the bread. Leave two pieces whole. Cut two pieces in half diagonally, forming two triangles. Spread the apricot jam thickly on the bread. Arrange two slices in the baking dish, and fit two of the triangles in at the sides, so the bottom of the dish is almost covered with bread. Scatter apple slices on top of the bread, almost covering it. Add the remaining bread and cover with all the remaining apples, so you can't see the bread. Cover.

Bake for 1 hour. Turn off the oven, but leave the dish in the oven for 15 minutes longer, to let the bread absorb most of the juice. Serve hot, warm, or cold.

Ambrosia Parfait Serves 4

Turn this old favorite into a healthier dessert by substituting yogurt for the traditional sour cream and forgetting about the marshmallows. Look for fruit packed in juice rather than sugary syrup. Leftovers will keep for up to 3 days in the refrigerator.

1 cup vanilla yogurt

1 cup cottage cheese

1 (8-ounce) can sliced peaches, drained

1 (11-ounce) can mandarin orange sections, drained

1 (8-ounce) can crushed pineapple, drained

$1/2$ cup shredded unsweetened coconut

Set out four 1-cup parfait glasses or dessert bowls. Combine the yogurt and cottage cheese in a food processor and blend until smooth. Put several peach slices in the bottom of each glass. Top each with $1/3$ of the yogurt mixture.

Spoon several orange sections on top of the yogurt mixture layer in each glass. Top this layer with half of the remaining yogurt mixture. Spoon a layer of pineapple on top of the yogurt in each glass. Add the remaining yogurt mixture and sprinkle each dessert with coconut. Cover each glass tightly with plastic wrap and chill for about 4 hours before serving.

VARIATIONS:

- Add a sprinkling of slivered almonds or chopped walnuts or toasted wheat germ along with the coconut.

- Use fresh fruit instead of canned, but don't plan to keep it in the refrigerator for more than 4 hours. It will get watery otherwise.

Sizzling Pineapple   Serves 4

Something wonderful happens to pineapple when it is grilled. Try this easy dessert at your next cookout, and put your son in charge of cooking it. Or, use your oven broiler for a very close approximation. Buy dead ripe pineapples, which will smell sweet and give just slightly when you press on them with your thumbs.

Keeping some of the leaves attached to each piece makes this a beautiful and very exciting dessert to attack. Cut any leftovers into chunks and serve with vanilla yogurt and chopped pecans.

> **1 ripe pineapple**
>
> **2 tablespoons freshly squeezed lemon juice**
>
> **2 tablespoons light brown sugar**

Preheat the grill to medium and oil the grill grate, or preheat the oven broiler. Using a large knife, slice the pineapple in half, keeping the leaves on and cutting straight through the middle of them. Slice each half again lengthwise. You will have four wedges, each with leaves attached.

In a small bowl combine the lemon juice and brown sugar, and stir with a spoon until the sugar dissolves. Using a pastry brush or the back of a spoon, smooth the sugar mixture along the cut sides of each wedge. Grill the wedges, cut side down for about 5 minutes. Turn and grill the other cut side for about 5 minutes more, until the glaze begins to sizzle. Serve hot, with forks and knives, on oval platters.

Zit Tip

It is normal for your son's skin to break out as he becomes a teenager. Don't assume that what he eats necessarily has a connection. "That old thing about too much chocolate or greasy food affecting your skin is a myth," says Erie, Pennsylvania, dermatologist Scott Lim. "There are no hard and fast rules about avoiding certain foods to cure acne. Stress, rather than food, usually aggravates problems with the skin." Lim explains that balanced meals and common sense are important for healthy looking skin. "Don't eat too much of any one thing. If you think you see a correlation between a certain food and a skin problem, avoid that food for a while and see what happens."

Lim also warns against vigorously scrubbing the face, which can make the inflammation worse. And he says kids create more blemishes by squeezing the ones they have.

Chocolate Pudding   Serves 6

Packaged pudding and mixes from the supermarket contain high-fructose corn syrup and trans fats, plus long lists of artificial ingredients. This ultimate comfort food has much more flavor and character when you make it from scratch. Boys will devour it. This version is adapted from a recipe created by Amanda Hesser, via Dorie Greenspan, for *The New York Times.*

> 5 ounces bittersweet chocolate
>
> 2 tablespoons unsweetened cocoa powder
>
> 2 tablespoons cornstarch
>
> $1/4$ teaspoon salt
>
> 2 cups milk
>
> 4 tablespoons sugar
>
> 1 egg
>
> 1 teaspoon vanilla extract

Melt the chocolate in a double boiler over simmering water and set aside to cool.

Combine the cocoa, cornstarch, and salt in a small bowl and blend with a whisk until smooth. Set aside.

Combine the milk and 2 tablespoons of the sugar in a medium saucepan and cook over medium heat, stirring once or twice, for several minutes, until it just comes to a boil.

While the milk is heating, combine the egg and remaining 2 tablespoons of sugar in a food processor and pulse until smooth. Add the cocoa mixture and pulse until smooth. When the milk is hot, slowly add the egg and cocoa mixture to the pan, stirring constantly with a wooden spoon and keeping the heat at medium for about 3 or 4 minutes, until the pudding thickens. Don't let it boil and watch that it doesn't stick on the bottom of the pan.

Return the pudding to the food processor, add the cooled, melted chocolate and vanilla, and pulse just until smooth. Pour the pudding into six $^1/_2$-cup ramekins. Let cool for 15 minutes.

Cover each with plastic wrap to prevent a thick skin from forming. Chill for at least 6 hours before serving.

Chocolate Mousse
Serves 8

Unlike the traditional French dessert, which uses eggs, this lighter version relies on gelatin for its texture. It takes only a few minutes to prepare, but it will make dessert feel like a special occasion. Since it contains cream, monitor portion size by using $^1/_2$-cup ramekins and balance your meal by serving a light dinner, such as fish or a dinner salad. Make it several hours ahead to provide time for the mousse to set. Serve garnished with sliced strawberries or fresh raspberries.

1 cup semisweet chocolate chips

$^1/_4$ cup hot water

1 envelope (2 teaspoons) unflavored gelatin

1 tablespoon instant espresso powder

1 pint whipping cream

Put the chocolate in a small bowl and heat in the microwave for 1 to $1^1/_2$ minutes, just until most of the chocolate is melted. Stir with a spoon until smooth.

Pour the hot water into a small bowl, add the gelatin and espresso powder, and stir until dissolved. Add the mixture to the melted chocolate and stir until smooth.

Beat the whipping cream until peaks just begin to form. Add the chocolate mixture and continue beating until well blended and very stiff peaks form. Spoon the mousse into eight $1/2$-cup ramekins or dessert dishes.

Chill for at least 1 hour before serving.

Chocolate Bread Pudding Serves 6 to 8

Adapted from a 1943 Fannie Farmer recipe, this oven-baked dessert provides a great way to use up leftover whole-wheat bread. If your son likes things with a nutty, seedy texture, make the crumbs from a wholesome seven-grain bread. If he doesn't like bits in things, use a plain whole-wheat bread with no added seeds. Serve in bowls, topped with yogurt.

4 ounces unsweetened baking chocolate

3 cups milk

2 cups fresh whole-wheat bread crumbs

$1/4$ cup honey

2 eggs

1 teaspoon vanilla extract

Preheat the oven to 325°F. Lightly butter a 2-quart baking dish.

Combine the chocolate and milk in a heavy saucepan and cook, over medium heat, stirring frequently, until the chocolate melts, about 5 minutes. Add the crumbs, and take the pan off the heat. Let the mixture sit for 10 minutes.

Add the honey, eggs, and vanilla and beat with a whisk until smooth. Pour the mixture into the prepared baking dish.

Bake for 1 hour, or until the top is firm. (You may still see some liquid around the edges. That's okay.) Remove the pudding from the oven and let it cool.

Cover with plastic wrap and chill overnight before serving.

Frying-Pan Fruit Puff Serves 6

Based on a French favorite known as clafoutis, this quick and easy dessert is a favorite with boys, especially if you don't go on about how many eggs it contains. It is also low in sugar and provides a good way to help your family enjoy dessert that isn't all about sweetness. Use fresh, pitted cherries if you can find them. Put a trivet on the table and bring the dessert in hot from the oven so everyone can admire it before you cut it into slices.

1 teaspoon butter

4 eggs

2 tablespoons sugar

$1/4$ teaspoon salt

2 teaspoons vanilla extract

1 cup milk

$2/3$ cup all-purpose flour

2 cups pitted fresh or frozen, thawed dark sweet cherries (14 ounces)

Confectioners' sugar

Preheat the oven to 425°F. Grease a 10-inch cast-iron frying pan or shallow ovenproof baking dish with the butter.

Combine the eggs, sugar, salt, vanilla, and milk in a blender and blend well. Add the flour and blend until smooth. Let sit for about 30 seconds and blend once more. Pour the batter into the prepared frying pan. Arrange the cherries on the top (they will sink).

Bake for 20 to 30 minutes, until the batter puffs up and the top is slightly brown. Dust the top with confectioners' sugar and serve at once.

VARIATION: Substitute thinly sliced, unpeeled apples or peaches for the cherries.

Twenty-Five-Minute Cupcakes

Instead of making an entire cake, which is easy to overeat, turn to cupcakes, which are portion-appropriate and easily portable. They appeal to all ages. Keep a stack of muffin-pan liners in the drawer. Here are two recipes that each make six cupcakes. The yellow cupcakes will remind you of birthday cakes you had as a child; the chocolate cupcakes are made with whole-wheat flour and don't require a mixer. If you need to make a dozen, combine them in one 12-cup muffin pan and bake as one batch.

Continued on next page

Yellow Cupcakes with Caramel-Pecan Frosting

Makes 6 cupcakes

CUPCAKES

1 cup all-purpose flour

1 teaspoon baking powder

$1/4$ teaspoon salt

$1/2$ cup granulated sugar

$1/4$ cup butter, softened

2 eggs

$1/2$ teaspoon vanilla extract

$1/4$ cup milk

CARAMEL-PECAN FROSTING

2 tablespoons butter

$1/4$ cup firmly packed light or dark brown sugar

1 cup confectioners' sugar

1 tablespoon sour cream

$1/2$ cup chopped pecans

Preheat the oven to 375°F. Line a 6-cup muffin pan with paper liners. Combine the flour, baking powder, and salt in a bowl and stir with a whisk. Set aside.

Combine the sugar and butter in a mixing bowl and beat with an electric mixer on medium speed for about 1 minute, until well mixed. Add the eggs and vanilla and beat until smooth. Add the dry ingredients alternately with the milk, stopping the mixer and scraping the bottom of the bowl once, to form a smooth batter. Spoon the batter evenly into the six liners.

Bake for 20 minutes, or until the tops feel firm to the touch and the edges are just starting to brown. Cool on a rack for 10 minutes. Remove from the pan and frost.

To make the frosting, combine the butter and brown sugar in a small saucepan and cook over medium heat, stirring, until the butter and sugar melt and are smooth. Transfer the mixture to a mixing bowl. Add the confectioners' sugar and sour cream and beat for 1 minute at medium speed, or until smooth and thick. Using a flat-bladed knife, spread the frosting on the cupcakes. Sprinkle on the pecans and gently press them into the frosting.

One-Bowl Chocolate Cupcakes with Chocolate Frosting

Makes 6 cupcakes

CUPCAKES

1 cup whole-wheat flour

$1/2$ cup firmly packed light brown sugar

2 tablespoons unsweetened cocoa powder

$1/4$ teaspoon salt

$1/4$ teaspoon baking soda

$1/2$ cup buttermilk

2 tablespoons canola oil

$1/2$ teaspoon vanilla extract

2 tablespoons cold water

CHOCOLATE FROSTING

2 tablespoons butter

1 tablespoon cocoa powder

$1/2$ teaspoon vanilla extract

2 tablespoons milk

$1^1/2$ cups confectioners' sugar

$1/4$ cup semisweet chocolate chips

Preheat the oven to 350°F. Line a 6-cup muffin pan with paper liners.

Combine the flour, brown sugar, cocoa powder, salt, and baking soda in a bowl and blend with a whisk. Add the remaining ingredients and stir to form a smooth batter. Spoon the batter evenly into the six liners.

Bake for 20 minutes, or until the tops feel firm to the touch. Cool on a rack for 10 minutes. Remove from the pan and frost.

To make the frosting, melt the butter in a small saucepan and remove from the heat. Add the cocoa powder and whisk until smooth. Pour the mixture into a mixing bowl and add the vanilla, milk, and confectioners' sugar. Beat for 1 minute at medium speed, or until smooth and fluffy. Using a flat-bladed knife, spread the frosting on the cupcakes. Gently press a few chocolate chips into the top of each one.

Yellow Cake with Chocolate-Walnut Frosting

Perfect for a birthday, to celebrate the end of exam week, or to perk up the family during a prolonged spell of dull, gray weather, this cake proves it is easy to make one from scratch. Covered, it keeps for up to 1 week.

CAKE

2 cups all-purpose flour

2 teaspoons baking powder

$^1/_4$ teaspoon salt

$^1/_2$ cup butter, at room temperature

$^3/_4$ cup sugar

1 egg

3 egg yolks

1 teaspoon vanilla extract

$^1/_4$ cup plain yogurt

$^3/_4$ cup milk

CHOCOLATE-WALNUT FROSTING

4 squares (4 ounces) unsweetened baking chocolate

2 tablespoons butter

$2^1/_2$ cups confectioners' sugar

$^1/_4$ cup plain yogurt

$^1/_4$ cup milk, plus more as needed

1 cup chopped walnuts

Preheat the oven to 350°F. Grease and flour two 8- or 9-inch cake pans. Combine the flour, baking powder, and salt in a bowl and blend with a whisk. Set aside. Combine the butter and sugar in a mixing bowl and beat until well blended. Add the egg and egg yolks and beat until smooth. Scrape the bottom of the bowl and beat again. Add the vanilla and yogurt and beat until smooth. Add the dry ingredients alternately with the milk, beating after each addition, until the batter is smooth. Divide the batter between the two pans and lightly smooth the tops.

Bake for 20 to 25 minutes, until the tops are lightly browned and spring back when you gently touch the center, or when a toothpick inserted in the center comes out clean. Let the cakes cool on a rack for 10 minutes. Remove from the pans and let cool completely before frosting.

To make the frosting, combine the chocolate and butter in the top of a double boiler set over simmering water and heat until melted. Transfer the mixture to a mixing bowl. Beat in 1 cup of the confectioners' sugar. Add the yogurt and beat in 1 more cup of the confectioners' sugar, along with 2 tablespoons of the milk, until the frosting is smooth. Add the remaining $1/2$ cup confectioners' sugar and the remaining 2 tablespoons milk and beat until the frosting is very smooth. Using a wide-bladed knife, immediately frost the top of one of the cakes, add the second cake, and cover the top and sides of both with the remaining frosting. If the frosting starts to harden, add $1/2$ teaspoon of milk to the bowl and beat again until smooth. Sprinkle the walnuts on the top of the cake and gently press them into the frosting with a spatula.

VARIATION: Add $1/4$ cup shredded unsweetened coconut and $1/4$ cup chopped pecans to the filling. Cover the top of the frosted cake with $1/2$ cup chopped pecans and $1/2$ cup flaked shredded unsweetened coconut.

Polenta Cake

Serves 10 to 12

Inspired by a recipe from Marcella Hazan's *More Classic Italian Cooking,* this wholesome cake can be made with a number of dried fruits. Give it plenty of time to cool. It will keep for at least a week, tightly covered, in the refrigerator.

2 cups water

1 cup coarse cornmeal

$1/2$ teaspoon salt

$1^1/2$ tablespoons olive oil

$1/4$ cup firmly packed light brown sugar

$1/3$ cup chopped pecans or walnuts

$1/2$ cup dried blueberries

$1/2$ cup dried cherries

1 egg

1 cup all-purpose flour

2 tablespoons milk, half-and-half, or light cream

6 ounces dark chocolate, coarsely chopped

Preheat the oven to 400°F. Grease a 9-inch round cake pan.

Bring the water to a rolling boil in a large saucepan. Trickle in the cornmeal and cook, stirring constantly, for about 2 minutes. Add the salt and oil, turn the heat down to medium, and continue cooking and stirring until the cornmeal thickens and begins to pull away from the sides of the pan, about 5 minutes longer. (The cornmeal will look like mush.) Remove it from the heat.

Add the brown sugar, pecans, blueberries, and cherries and stir until smooth. Add the egg and beat until blended. Add the flour and stir until it disappears into the batter. Scrape the batter into the prepared pan.

Bake for 40 to 45 minutes, until the top is firm and just starting to brown. Cool on a rack for 1 hour. Place a cake plate on top of the cake and invert it.

Heat the milk in a small saucepan over low heat. Add the chocolate and heat, stirring several times, just until it melts. Spread the melted chocolate over the top of the cake and let sit for 30 minutes, or until the chocolate hardens. (Refrigerate it on a hot day.) Cut into small wedges and serve.

Upland Pumpkin Cake

Serves 6 to 8

Boys who like pumpkin pie will love this easy cake, which starts its life almost as a pie, but isn't. (It is a good recipe for cooks who are insecure about pie crust.) Plan to make this cake when you'll be in or near the kitchen for about 1 hour, since it has several steps. Serve topped with vanilla yogurt or whipped cream.

CAKE BASE

$1/2$ cup whole-wheat flour

1 cup old-fashioned rolled oats

$1/4$ cup firmly packed light brown sugar

$1/4$ cup butter, cut into chunks

2 tablespoons canola or olive oil

PUMPKIN FILLING

1 (15-ounce) can pumpkin

1 (12-ounce) can evaporated milk

2 eggs

$1/3$ cup firmly packed light brown sugar

1 teaspoon ground cinnamon

$1/2$ teaspoon ground ginger

¹/₄ teaspoon ground cloves

¹/₄ teaspoon freshly grated nutmeg

NUT TOPPING

¹/₂ cup chopped pecans

¹/₄ cup firmly packed light brown sugar

Preheat the oven to 350°F.

To make the base, combine the flour, oats, and sugar in a food processor and pulse to blend. Add the butter and oil and pulse again, just until the mixture forms damp crumbs. Transfer the mixture to an 8 by 8-inch cake pan and press it down with your fingers to form a smooth layer. Bake for 15 minutes, or until lightly browned.

While the base is baking, make the filling. Combine the pumpkin, evaporated milk, eggs, brown sugar, cinnamon, ginger, cloves, and nutmeg in a mixing bowl and blend with a whisk until smooth.

When the base is baked, pour the filling mixture on top and bake for 30 minutes. While the filling bakes, make the topping. Combine the pecans and brown sugar in the food processor and pulse until blended. Remove the cake from the oven (the filling will not be completely set) and sprinkle on the topping. Bake for 10 minutes longer, or until a knife inserted in the center comes out clean. Let cool for 15 minutes before serving.

Coconut-Carrot Cake   Serves 10 to 12

This recipe is adapted from one created by Redwood Hill Farm in California. The yogurt gives the cake a tender texture that improves as it sits. It will taste best if you can bake it one day before serving. Make it in minutes in just one bowl, using muscle power and a whisk. Omit the frosting if you wish, and dust the top lightly with confectioners' sugar.

CAKE

6 tablespoons canola oil

³/₄ cup firmly packed light brown sugar

3 large eggs

1 tablespoon baking soda

2 cups whole-wheat flour

1 teaspoon ground cinnamon

1 cup plain yogurt

2 cups grated carrots

1 cup chopped walnuts

1 cup shredded unsweetened coconut

MAPLE YOGURT FROSTING

$^1/_2$ cup Yogurt Cheese (page 108)

$^1/_2$ cup cream cheese

1 tablespoon maple syrup

Preheat the oven to 350°F. Grease a 9 x 13-inch pan.

To make the cake, combine the oil, brown sugar, and eggs in a large mixing bowl and blend with a whisk until smooth. Whisk in the baking soda. Add the flour, cinnamon, and yogurt, and blend with the whisk until smooth. Fold in the carrots, walnuts, and coconut and stir until smooth. Spread the mixture into the prepared pan.

Bake for 25 to 30 minutes, until the top is lightly browned and firm. Cool the cake on a rack. Frost, if desired, when the cake is completely cool.

To make the frosting, combine the yogurt cheese, cream cheese, and maple syrup in a food processor and pulse until smooth. Using a flat-bladed knife, spread the frosting on the cake.

Maple-Pecan Apple Cake with Almond-Yogurt Topping

Serves 6 to 8

With full flavor and an appealing texture, this cake is a good example of how whole-wheat flour and just 2 tablespoons of oil can produce a dessert your family will enjoy. It travels well, making it a good choice for picnics or a tailgate lunch before a football game. Serve it with the yogurt cheese topping, a healthy substitute for whipped cream. Top a leftover slice with peanut butter.

CAKE

$1^1/_2$ cups whole-wheat flour or whole-wheat pastry flour

1 teaspoon baking powder

$^1/_2$ teaspoon baking soda

$^1/_2$ teaspoon salt

$^1/_4$ teaspoon freshly grated nutmeg

$^{2}/_{3}$ cup Yogurt Cheese (page 108)

1 egg

2 tablespoons canola or walnut oil

$^{1}/_{3}$ cup plus 2 tablespoons maple syrup

2 medium apples

$^{1}/_{3}$ cup chopped pecans

TOPPING

1 cup Yogurt Cheese (page 108)

1 tablespoon maple syrup

1 teaspoon almond extract

Preheat the oven to 350°F. Lightly grease an 8-inch-square or 9-inch round baking pan.

To make the cake, combine the flour, baking powder, baking soda, salt, and nutmeg in a bowl and mix with a whisk. Set aside.

Combine the yogurt cheese, egg, oil, and $^{1}/_{3}$ cup of the maple syrup in a bowl and beat until smooth. Shred the apples, unpeeled, on a box grater or in a food processor. If the apples are very juicy, put them in a colander and squeeze to remove excess moisture. (You should have $1^{1}/_{2}$ cups.) Stir the apples into the batter. Add the dry ingredients and stir gently until no dry spots remain. Using a rubber spatula, scrape the batter into the prepared pan, spreading it evenly. Sprinkle the pecans over the top. Drizzle evenly with the remaining 2 tablespoons of maple syrup.

Bake for 40 to 45 minutes, or until the cake is firm to the touch and a toothpick inserted in the center comes out clean. Cool on a rack for 5 minutes.

To make the topping, combine the yogurt cheese, maple syrup, and almond extract in a bowl and beat with a whisk until creamy.

Serve the cake with a dollop of topping.

Instant Raspberry Angel Food Cake

Serves 8 to 10

When you need a special dessert in a hurry, buy three ingredients at the supermarket and pull it all together in less than 5 minutes. In the unlikely event that any is left over, store it in the refrigerator with a mixing bowl as a cover; the cake will keep reasonably well for 2 days.

1 (8-inch) round plain or chocolate angel food cake

1 pint whipping cream

2 tablespoons seedless raspberry jam

Set a cake plate out on the counter. Cut the cake in half horizontally. Pour the whipping cream into a mixing bowl, add the jam, and beat until stiff peaks form. With a sandwich spreader or a butter knife, cover one of the cut surfaces with a thick layer of whipped cream. Put the second half of the cake on top of the first and slather the cake with the remaining whipped cream. Serve immediately.

Yogurt Cheesecake   Serves 6 to 8

Here is a low-fat dessert that tastes surprisingly rich. Allow time to make yogurt cheese, a low-fat alternative to cream cheese and sour cream, for this creamy cheesecake. Use any flavor of yogurt you prefer for the filling, and top the cake if you wish with fresh fruit to complement the yogurt flavor.

CRUST

10 whole cinnamon graham crackers

2 tablespoons butter, melted

3 to 4 tablespoons canola oil

FILLING

1 (8-ounce) package reduced-fat cream cheese

1 cup Yogurt Cheese (page 108)

$1/4$ cup firmly packed light brown sugar

1 cup (8 ounces) strawberry yogurt

2 eggs, beaten

Preheat the oven to 325°F.

To make the crust, put the graham crackers in a heavy-duty plastic bag and crush with a rolling pin. Combine the graham crackers, melted butter, and 3 tablespoons of canola oil in a mixing bowl. Blend with a fork until the crumbs are evenly moistened. Add the remaining tablespoon of canola oil if they seem dry. Press the mixture into a 9-inch pie pan. Bake for 8 minutes.

While the crust is baking, make the filling. Put the cream cheese in a mixing bowl and beat with an electric mixer at medium speed until very smooth and creamy. Add the yogurt cheese and brown sugar and beat until smooth, stopping the mixer once to scrape the cream cheese from the bottom of the bowl with a rubber spatula. Add the yogurt and eggs and beat again until smooth. Pour the mixture into the prepared crust.

Bake for 1 hour, or until the center is set and doesn't jiggle when you gently shake the pan. Let the cheesecake cool to room temperature.

Cover with foil and chill for at least 4 hours before serving.

Blueberry Hermits

Makes 36

A perfect picnic treat, these old-fashioned cookies travel well. Tightly covered, they'll keep for at least 5 days. Since one batch makes three dozen, they are a good choice for a team dinner or a bus trip to an away game. Hermits are traditionally made with raisins, but this version uses tasty dried blueberries, which are rich in vitamin C and potassium.

> 2 cups all-purpose flour
>
> 1 teaspoon baking soda
>
> 1 teaspoon ground cinnamon
>
> 1 teaspoon ground cloves
>
> 1 teaspoon ground ginger
>
> $1/2$ teaspoon salt
>
> $1/2$ cup canola oil
>
> $1/2$ cup unsweetened applesauce
>
> $1/2$ cup firmly packed light brown sugar
>
> $1/2$ cup dark molasses
>
> 2 eggs
>
> 1 cup (8 ounces) dried blueberries

Preheat the oven to 350°F. Lightly grease a 12 by 18-inch baking sheet with 1-inch sides.

Combine the flour, baking soda, cinnamon, cloves, ginger, and salt in a bowl and blend with a whisk. Set aside.

Combine the oil, applesauce, brown sugar, and molasses in a mixing bowl and beat with an electric mixer at medium speed until smooth. Use a spatula to scrape the bottom of the bowl and beat again. Add the eggs and beat until well mixed. Gradually beat in the dry ingredients until the batter is smooth.

Stir in the blueberries by hand. Spoon the mixture onto the prepared baking sheet, smoothing it into the corners. (It will be very thick.)

Bake for 20 minutes, or until the top is springy to the touch and the edges are just starting to brown. Cool on a wire rack. Cut into bars.

VARIATION: Substitute raisins, dried currants, dried cherries, or dried cranberries for the blueberries.

Molasses Crinkle Cookies

Makes 18

Among its many virtues, ginger is said to have a calming effect on the stomach, making it an antidote for motion sickness and seasickness. In these cookies it seems to relieve stress from too much homework or an impending AP exam. Tightly covered, they will keep for a week.

$1/2$ **cup raisins**

$1/2$ **cup very hot water**

2 tablespoons sugar

2 cups all-purpose flour

2 teaspoons ground cinnamon

2 teaspoons ground ginger

1 teaspoon baking soda

$1/4$ **teaspoon salt**

$3/4$ **cup firmly packed dark brown sugar**

$1/4$ **cup canola oil**

$1/4$ **cup dark molasses**

1 egg

Put the raisins in a small bowl and pour the hot water over them. Set aside for 10 minutes. Put the 2 tablespoons of sugar into a flat dish and set aside.

Preheat the oven to 350°F. Grease a large baking sheet or line with parchment paper.

Combine the flour, cinnamon, ginger, baking soda, and salt in a mixing bowl and blend with a whisk.

Transfer the raisins and any liquid in the bowl to a food processor and pulse. Add the brown sugar, oil, molasses, and egg and pulse for several seconds, until the mixture is well blended. Pour into the bowl with the dry ingredients and stir with a spoon to mix well. The dough will be quite stiff.

Using a teaspoon and your hands, shape the dough into 2-inch balls, roll them in the sugar in the dish, and arrange about 2 inches apart on the prepared baking sheet. Press each cookie gently with your hand to flatten it.

Bake for 10 to 12 minutes, until the tops of the cookies have developed little cracks and the edges are firm. Transfer to a rack to cool.

VARIATION: Use $1/2$ cup diced dried apricots or prunes instead of the raisins.

Oatmeal-Chocolate Chip Cookies   Makes 18 to 20

Make these cookies when your son isn't home, and he will be thrilled to discover them later. The oatmeal gives them a wonderful texture. They'll keep for a week, tightly covered.

   $1^1/2$ cups all-purpose flour

   1 teaspoon baking soda

   $1/2$ teaspoon salt

   $1/2$ cup butter, at room temperature

   $1/2$ cup white sugar

   $1/2$ cup firmly packed dark brown sugar

   2 eggs

   1 teaspoon vanilla extract

2 cups old-fashioned rolled oats

1 cup chopped walnuts or pecans

1 cup semisweet chocolate chips

Preheat the oven to 350°F. Line a baking sheet with parchment paper. Combine the flour, baking soda, and salt in a mixing bowl and blend with a whisk until smooth. Set aside.

Combine the butter, white sugar, brown sugar, eggs, and vanilla in a mixing bowl and beat for about 30 seconds at medium speed, until smooth. Add the dry ingredients and beat just until blended. Add the oats, nuts, and chocolate chips and very slowly beat just until mixed. Using a tablespoon, drop the dough onto the prepared baking sheet, leaving about 2 inches between cookies.

Bake for 10 to 12 minutes, until the cookies are lightly browned and firm. Remove from the oven and let sit for 5 minutes. Transfer the cookies to a rack to cool completely.

VARIATIONS:

• Substitute $1/2$ cup olive oil for the butter and bake for 15 minutes.

• Replace 1 cup of the oatmeal with 1 cup toasted wheat germ or oat bran.

Chocolate-Coconut Cookies   Makes 20

Adhere to the baking time. These cookies will seem too soft when you take them out of the oven, but they become firm as they cool. They're a good treat to take on a road trip since they improve with age and always taste better the second day or even third day—if they're around that long.

$3/4$ cup whole-wheat flour

$1/4$ cup unsweetened cocoa powder

$1/2$ teaspoon baking soda

$1/4$ cup butter, at room temperature

$1/4$ cup olive oil

$1/2$ cup white sugar

$1/2$ cup firmly packed light brown sugar

1 egg

1 teaspoon vanilla extract

1¹/₂ cups old-fashioned rolled oats

1 cup semisweet chocolate chips

¹/₂ cup shredded unsweetened coconut

¹/₂ cup chopped walnuts or pecans

Preheat the oven to 325°F. Line a baking sheet with parchment paper. Combine the flour, cocoa, and baking soda in a small bowl and blend with a whisk or fork. Set aside.

Combine the butter, oil, and sugars in a mixing bowl and beat until smooth. Add the egg and vanilla and beat for 30 seconds. Add the flour mixture and mix until blended. Add the oats, chocolate chips, coconut, and nuts and beat slowly just until blended. Using a tablespoon, drop the dough onto the prepared baking sheet, leaving about 2 inches between cookies.

Bake for 12 to 15 minutes, until the cookies have spread out and are set. Don't worry if they look slightly wet. Remove from the oven and let sit for 5 minutes. Transfer the cookies to a rack to cool completely.

Iced Tea   Serves 4

You can find jugs, cans, and bottles of sweetened iced tea at the supermarket. Do you know they contain an average of 26 grams of sugar per cup—as much sugar as soft drinks? A better choice is to make your own iced decaffeinated tea, which actually will quench a boy's thirst. Keep a pitcher of it in the refrigerator and help your son get used to drinking something that isn't loaded with sugar.

4 cups water

6 decaffeinated black or herbal tea bags

1 tablespoon honey

Juice of 1 lemon

Bring the water to a boil in a saucepan, remove from the heat, add the tea bags, cover, and steep for several minutes. Discard the tea bags. Add the honey and stir with a whisk until it dissolves. Stir in the lemon juice. Pour the tea into a large pitcher. Let cool, then chill for at least 2 hours before serving over ice.

Think About Drinks

Teenage boys seem to always be thirsty. Do whatever you can to discourage them from guzzling soft drinks. A 12-ounce can contain 40.5 grams or 10 teaspoons (!) of sugar, cleverly brewed to have a pleasant, rather than sickly sweet, taste. Many brands of soft drinks also contain 20 to 40 milligrams of caffeine. (A cup of regular coffee averages about 80 milligrams of caffeine.) Discourage your boy from drinking energy drinks, which are also high in sugar and caffeine. Marketed to students, some deliver as much as a heart-racing 182 milligrams of caffeine per bottle.

Avoid diet soft drinks sweetened with aspartame and other artificial ingredients. Researchers at Purdue University's Department of Psychological Sciences suggest that artificial sweeteners may alter the body's natural ability to register calories based on a food's sweetness, leading to an inability to regulate food intake and body weight. Better choices are spritzers, blends of sparkling water and fruit juice concentrates which come in a wide range of flavors, and seltzer, also available in various flavors.

Install a filter on your tap water or arrange to have a dispenser and plenty of good drinking water easily available in your household. Buy 24-packs of bottled water and put them in your son's bedroom, so he gets into the habit of quenching his thirst with water while he's studying or relaxing.

Ginger-Pomegranate Tea   Serves 6

A century ago, farm boys working at the dusty job of haying fields were given jugs of water mixed with ginger and lemon to quench their thirst. Today, this beautiful red beverage satisfies teenagers who come home thirsty after sports.

> 4 cups water
>
> 4 ginger tea bags
>
> 1/4 cup honey
>
> 2 cups pomegranate juice
>
> Juice of 1/2 lemon

Bring the water to a boil in a saucepan, remove from the heat, add the tea bags, cover, and steep for 10 minutes. Discard the tea bags. Add the honey and blend with a whisk until it dissolves. Stir in the pomegranate and lemon juices. Pour the tea into a large pitcher. Let cool. Chill for at least 2 hours before serving over ice.

SHOPPING TIP: Look for pomegranate juice in health food stores and wherever Middle Eastern foods are sold. If you can't find it, substitute unsweetened cranberry juice.

Raspberry-Apple Iced Tea
Serves 4

A combination of herbal tea and fruit juice makes a great thirst quencher and is a much better choice than a soft drink since it doesn't deliver a blast of sugar. Experiment with different flavors. Make it in the morning or at night and allow plenty of time for it to chill.

> **4 cups water**
>
> **4 raspberry tea bags**
>
> **1 cup apple juice**
>
> **2 tablespoons freshly squeezed lemon juice**

Bring the water to a boil in a saucepan. Remove from the heat, add the tea bags, cover, and steep for 10 minutes. Discard the tea bags. Add the apple juice and lemon juice. Pour into a large pitcher. Let cool. Chill for at least 2 hours before serving over ice.

VARIATIONS: Use ginger tea with cranberry or pear juice or mint tea with blueberry juice.

Watermelon Cooler
Serves 2

Watermelon is the least-expensive fruit per pound, and it is a good source of vitamins A and C, plus the carotenoid antioxidant lycopene, also found in tomatoes. It is a good fruit to buy often, especially in the summer when watermelons are at their sweetest and cheapest. When you cut into a watermelon that looks perfect on the outside, but turns out to be grainy or a bit mushy on the inside, turn to this thirst-quenching solution. It is perfect on a hot summer day.

> **3 cups watermelon chunks**
>
> **1 cup water**

Combine both the watermelon and water in a blender and whir until smooth. Set a fine strainer over a pitcher or bowl, pour in the mixture, and let it drain for about 10 minutes. Discard the solids in the strainer. Serve the juice over ice.

VARIATIONS:

• Add other fruits, such as strawberries or blueberries, to the mixture for a variety of flavors.

• Pour the watermelon juice into ice cube trays and freeze. Use the cubes to flavor ice tea or to heighten the taste of a watermelon cooler. (Freezing the juice is also a good way to keep a quantity on hand.)

Icy Fruit H₂O

Serves 4

Water flavored with fruit juice may be the next big wave of commercially bottled drinks. Stay ahead of the game and save money by making your own blends at home. Buy juices and juice blends that don't contain any added sugars or sweeteners. There are dozens to choose from, including cranberry, blueberry, pear, and apple. Getting your family in the habit of using juice as a flavoring agent for water is a good idea. The combination delivers more taste than water but fewer calories and sugar than straight juice. By adding ice and mixing it in the blender, it becomes especially appealing and thirst-quenching.

1 cup unsweetened fruit juice

3 cups water

4 ice cubes

Combine all the ingredients in a blender and whir until smooth.

VARIATION: Forego the blender. Combine the fruit juice and water in a pitcher with a cover or in a clear, rinsed-out juice bottle and store in the refrigerator.

Homemade "Soda"

Serves 1

Instead of filling up your refrigerator with soft drinks, which are loaded with ingredients that could be harmful to your health (way too much sugar and high-fructose corn syrup in regular soda or aspartame in diet soda), buy plain or fruit-flavored seltzer in cans, and show your son how to use flavoring to make his own fizzy drinks. Fruit syrups are sold in grocery stores and on line. Look for brands that are relatively low in sugar and artificial ingredients. Experiment to find your family's favorites.

2 to 3 teaspoons fruit syrup

1 (12-ounce) can seltzer

Ice cubes

Spoon the syrup into a tall (16-ounce) glass. Pour in the seltzer, stir until blended, and drop in some ice cubes.

Hot Mulled Cider Serves 10

Allow about 1 hour to make this fall and winter favorite on the stovetop, or put it together and keep it warm in a slow-cooker. It is a welcoming drink for football game afternoons or holiday parties. For the best flavor, use cider from freshly squeezed apples, without added water or preservatives.

10 cups apple cider

Juice of 1 lemon

4 cinnamon sticks, each about 3 inches long

8 whole cloves

Combine all the ingredients in a large, stainless steel saucepan. Heat over medium-low heat for 30 minutes, stirring occasionally. Turn the heat down to low and simmer the cider for 30 minutes longer, until it is very fragrant and spicy. Or, combine all ingredients in a large slow-cooker. Cover and heat on the high setting for 60 minutes or until the cider is hot. Turn the heat down to low. Ladle into mugs.

Hot Chocolate Serves 1

Steer away from packaged hot-chocolate mixes that use water. They are very high in sugar and contain hydrogenated oils and artificial ingredients. If you depend upon a mix, use just 1 teaspoon per cup of milk, not the more commonly recommended 3 tablespoons. The best choice is to combine your own blend of cocoa and sweetener.

1 cup milk

1 teaspoon unsweetened cocoa powder

1 teaspoon honey or sugar

Heat the milk in a small saucepan over medium heat for about 2 minutes, until it is hot but not bubbling. Add the cocoa powder and honey and blend with a whisk until smooth. Pour into a mug and serve hot.

Pick Me Ups

There are lots of reasons why a teenage boy may need some special TLC now and then: not making a team, playing football or soccer in a cold rain, not getting a part in the play, doing poorly on a test or paper, worrying about college acceptances, catching a cold. Make him a cup of tea or hot chai sweetened with honey and lightened with milk. Or, try these three quick, hot drinks that can help. Serve in a mug.

Restoration Toddy

Bring 1 cup of chicken stock or broth just to a boil in a small saucepan. Beat an egg in a small bowl, add it to the stock, turn the heat down to medium, and cook for 5 minutes, stirring occasionally. Add 2 tablespoons of grated Parmesan cheese and cook for 1 minute longer. Serve very hot, topped with a bit of chopped parsley.

Hot Cider

Fill a mug with cider and heat in the microwave.

Hot Veggie Juice

Fill a mug with tomato juice or vegetable juice. Add 1 teaspoon of Worcestershire sauce and stir. Heat in the microwave.

Wake-Up Smoothie   Serves 1

If your son claims to hate mangoes, don't mention that there's a mango in this mixture. Just pour it into a tall glass, add a straw, and give it to a boy who's still mostly asleep.

1 ripe mango, peeled and diced

1 cup vanilla yogurt

$^1/_2$ cup orange juice

Combine all the ingredients in a blender and mix until smooth. Pour into a tall glass and serve.

Making Smoothies

Keep the blender out on the counter, not tucked away in a closet or cabinet, and get into the habit of making smoothies. They're a great breakfast treat and a filling after-school snack. Encourage your son to make his own. Teenagers enjoy playing with the machine and may surprise you with their willingness to try new combinations of ingredients.

Keep bananas on hand for smoothies. Before they get too ripe, peel them, cut in half, and freeze in a plastic container with a tight-fitting lid so they're easy to toss in. Adding ice helps to stretch the ingredients and makes smoothies deliciously cold and thick.

Stock the freezer with bags of unsweetened, frozen fruit which usually contain more vitamins and other nutrients than fresh fruit that sits around in the grocery store or in your kitchen. Choices abound, from strawberries, raspberries, blackberries, and both wild and tame blueberries, to tropical fruits including pineapple, mango, and papaya. Look for blends of fruit, too. Buy several 8 or 12-ounce glasses for serving smoothies, and keep some straws handy.

Berry Smoothie   Serves 2

Put this drink together and sample a spoonful before giving it to your son. If it seems too tart, sweeten it with honey.

2 cups fresh or frozen unsweetened strawberries, blueberries, or raspberries (or a mixture)

1 cup milk or soy milk

$^1/_2$ cup silken tofu or yogurt

$^1/_2$ cup apple juice

$^1/_2$ frozen banana

1 to 2 tablespoons honey (optional)

Combine the berries, milk, tofu, apple juice, and banana in a blender and blend for 1 minute. Let the mixture sit for a minute or two and mix again. Taste and add honey, if needed. Pour into tall glasses and serve.

Blackberry Smoothie

Serves 1

Just 1 cup of blackberries provides 7 grams of fiber, making this lovely purple nondairy drink a great way to get an important component into a boy's diet. And while he might object to the seeds when eating blackberries, they go right up a straw, unnoticed.

1 cup frozen blackberries

1 cup vanilla soy milk or rice milk

4 ice cubes

Combine all the ingredients in a blender and mix until smooth. Pour into a tall glass and serve.

Opening-Night Pineapple Smoothie

Serves 1

When your son is getting ready for a stage appearance that involves singing or delivering lines, make him this refreshing drink. Pineapple juice has long been a favorite of opera singers, and it can't hurt a changing voice.

1 cup pineapple juice

1/2 cup silken tofu or lemon yogurt

4 ice cubes

Combine all the ingredients in a blender and mix until smooth. Pour into a tall glass and serve.

Sports Booster

Serves 1

During games and practices, water in moderate amounts is the best drink; fruit juice or soft drinks can zap a boy's energy and cause cramps if he's working very hard. Here's a "day-of" drink to have several hours before exercise, for stamina. The banana delivers a good bit of potassium, which helps muscles contract. It also helps maintain a normal heartbeat. Peanut butter may sound like an odd addition to a drink, but it adds protein, texture, and flavor, and blends right in with the other ingredients. If possible, grind your own peanut butter in the store from fresh peanuts.

1 banana

1/4 cup smooth unsweetened peanut butter

2 cups milk or soy milk

Combine all the ingredients in a blender and mix until smooth. Pour into a tall glass and serve.

VARIATION: Use 1 cup milk and 1 cup vanilla yogurt.

Piña Nolada
Serves 1

Since the 1950s, piña coladas, which blend rum, coconut, and pineapple, have been a signature cocktail at Caribbean resorts. This nonalcoholic version, made with coconut milk instead of the classic (and heavier) cream of coconut, is a delicious cold drink on a hot day. Pour leftover coconut milk into ice cube trays and freeze it; store the cubes in a zippered plastic bag. Two cubes from an average-sized tray equal $1/4$ cup. Experiment with other fruits, such as strawberries or bananas. Making this drink for a teenager can also provide a good opportunity to talk with him about alcohol, and show him that a "cocktail" doesn't have to contain liquor to taste great.

> **1 cup diced fresh pineapple**
>
> **$1/4$ cup coconut milk**
>
> **4 ice cubes (or more to taste)**

Combine all the ingredients in a blender and mix until smooth. Pour into a tall glass and serve.

Lassi
Serves 2

Indian restaurants serve this cooling drink, which helps cut the heat from very spicy foods. It goes well with fresh fruit and is wonderfully refreshing on a very hot day.

> **1 cup plain yogurt**
>
> **2 cups milk**
>
> **2 tablespoons honey**
>
> **$1/2$ teaspoon ground cinnamon**
>
> **6 ice cubes**

Combine all the ingredients in a blender and mix until smooth. Pour into tall glasses and serve.

VARIATIONS:

• Use almond milk, rice milk, or soy milk.

• Add 1 chopped mango.

Limeade

A nice change from lemonade, this refreshing drink is a great reward for mowing the lawn on a hot day. The fresh lime juice sharpens the flavor.

¹/₄ cup fresh lime juice

2 tablespoons frozen limeade concentrate

4 ice cubes

Combine all the ingredients in a blender and mix until smooth. Pour into a tall glass and serve.

Index